OUTLAWS OF MEDIEVAL SCOTLAND

OUTLAWS OF MEDIEVAL SCOTLAND:

CHALLENGES TO
THE CANMORE KINGS, 1058–1266

R. Andrew McDonald

TUCKWELL PRESS

First published in Great Britain in 2003 by
Tuckwell Press Ltd
The Mill House
Phantassie
East Linton
EH40 3DG
Scotland

ISBN 1 86232 236 8

A catalogue record is available
on request from the British Library

Typeset by Hewer Text Ltd, Edinburgh
Printed and bound by Bell and Bain Ltd

FOR JACQUELINE

CONTENTS

PREFACE

When the Scottish king William the Lion sent his armies northward in 1211 and 1212 in a bid to vanquish a dynastic rival named Guthred MacWilliam, he was engaging in a grim business that had also occupied many of his predecessors as kings of Scots. In fact, the various chronicles, annals, sagas, poems, charters, and other materials from which the history of medieval Scotland must be constructed contain scattered, laconic, and sometimes cryptic references to challenges, insurrections and uprisings led by a variety of native warlords and discontented dynasts against Malcolm III and the Scottish kings descended from him and his second wife, Margaret, in the period between about 1058 and 1266. Although there are some ambiguous signs of resistance in the reign of Malcolm himself, the frequency of the challenges intensified under his sons, Alexander I and David I, building to a crescendo in the time of William the Lion, between 1180 and 1215. There were sporadic instances of opposition from the 1220s to the 1260s, but the last really serious insurrection took place in 1234–35. Its leader subsequently endured sixty years of captivity, so that when he was finally released in 1296 the line of kings descended from Malcolm III and Margaret was extinct: outlived, ironically, by one of their last opponents. Pathetic old Thomas of Galloway nevertheless offers up a potent reminder that opposition forms an important, though much neglected, theme running through the entire history of the so-called 'Canmore dynasty'; moreover, these kings, regarded as the makers of the medieval kingdom, did not always have things their own way, and were forced to take up arms against a formidable array of rivals with surprising frequency.

This book concerns itself with the challenges to the Scottish kings between the mid-eleventh and late thirteenth centuries. It explores the nature of opposition and the motivations of the main rivals of the kings in an attempt to better understand the political culture of the era, and in order to restore balance to the historical writing on the period, which seems to the author to be heavily slanted toward the Scottish kings at the expense of their opponents. It is argued that, when viewed from the perspective of the challenges faced by the Scottish kings, the twelfth and thirteenth centuries appear somewhat less peaceful, stable and prosperous, and the dynasty descended from Malcolm III and Margaret rather less secure, than conventional wisdom has dictated for the last half-century or so. Indeed, the road to success for the Canmore kings was littered with the bodies of rivals.

The challenges to the Scottish kings and the intriguing, if often elusive, individuals who spearheaded them have captivated me from the time I undertook my doctoral dissertation under the supervision of Ted Cowan and Elizabeth Ewan at the University of Guelph between 1989 and 1993. The thesis considered, among other things, many of the twelfth- and thirteenth-century insurrections, and one of the more formidable of the king's enemies, Somerled MacGillabrigte of Argyll, figured prominently in my 1997 book, *The Kingdom of the Isles: Scotland's Western Seaboard c.1100–c.1336* (Tuckwell Press), which nevertheless could not and did not offer a systematic investigation of all the challenges faced by the Scottish kings in the period. Following the completion of that study, I decided to undertake an examination of the kings of Scots descended from Malcolm III and Margaret (the so-called 'Canmore kings'), but still everywhere I turned I was confronted by more of the king's enemies, and the themes of resistance and political violence in twelfth- and thirteenth-century Scotland loomed larger and larger in my consciousness. When I realised that what was intended to be a concluding chapter in that project dealing with the rivals of the Canmore kings had suddenly reached an unmanageable eighty pages in length, the idea of this book was born. The publication of several shorter pieces on the theme in 1999 and 2002, along with some encouragement from Benjamin T. Hudson, convinced me that there was enough material, not to mention, as I increasingly perceived, a dire need, for a monograph on the subject.

This book is the result, and I hope that it needs no justification. Historians have been little interested in the enemies of the Scottish kings in the twelfth and thirteenth centuries, and even less so in the challenges that they led: a few sentences here and there in general works on medieval Scotland constitute pretty much all that scholars have had to say about these events until the 1980s and 1990s. Although the recent groundswell of interest in the rugged outer zones of the Scottish kingdom (regions that sheltered many of the king's enemies), as in Scottish history generally, has certainly contributed to our knowledge of the medieval kingdom as a whole, and has cast valuable light upon several of the challenges and the figures that led them, there remains no comprehensive study that assesses all of the various uprisings, their impact on the medieval Scottish realm, their overall significance in Scottish history or their place in historical writing. My aim, then, is to highlight the centrality of challenges to the kings and political violence in general in Scottish history between about 1100 and the late thirteenth century, and this book argues that such opposition needs to become recognised for what it is: a central theme in the history of Scottish political culture and centre-periphery interactions in the period. Careful consideration of these challenges means that some orthodox views of Scottish society in the period under consideration may need to be re-evaluated.

A word about the title, *Outlaws of Medieval Scotland.* I should make clear that this book does not use the term 'outlaw' in the strict legal sense of one who is deprived of the protection and benefit of the law as the result of being placed under the sentence of outlawry, although the monumental Scottish legal text *Regiam Majestatem* makes it clear that outlawry was known in Scotland during the period under consideration.[1] Nor do I employ the term in the – perhaps romantic – sense of bands of robbers living marginally and preying upon travellers (or robbing the rich to aid the poor).[2] Rather, 'outlaws' is utilised as a loose description of individuals who were involved in political unrest and found themselves at odds with the Scottish kings without necessarily incurring the penalty of outlawry. Having said this, however, it must be noted that at least one individual (Adam the son of Donald, seized at Coupar Angus abbey in 1186) could be described in a contemporary source as 'the king's outlaw' (*uthlagis regis*) – suggesting that some, at least, of the figures with whom this study is concerned might have been outlaws in the legal sense as well. For most, however, there is no such specific, legalistic evidence of outlawry, and accordingly I use the term in a loose and non-legal fashion.

I have endeavoured to write with the informed and interested but not necessarily specialist reader in mind. References have been provided to permit readers to follow up on the sources of information and ideas presented here, but the notes are not, for the most part, discursive in nature and have been kept as brief as possible. On the matter of source materials, two principles have guided my writing. First, wherever possible the primary sources – the contemporary raw materials from the period under discussion – have been allowed to speak directly, and, accordingly, the reader will find significant excerpts from medieval texts and documents. Second, as a general rule those sources have been quoted in translation (although reference is normally provided to the original as well); only when it seems important to the argument at hand have I provided the original in the text. The student of medieval Scotland is fortunate to have ready access to a wide range of documents in translation, and these have been cited throughout; when necessary, my own summaries or translations are given. In adhering to these principles my conviction is that the topic can be

1 *Regiam Majestatem* has two entries on outlawry; both refer to the circumstances under which people are pronounced outlaws, i.e. after non-appearance at court. The first reference draws heavily on the English legal text of Glanvill and is very early, and both suggest that Scottish legal procedure drew heavily here on English models. Neither of the entries suggests that the crown could pronounce a man outlawed on its own authority, i.e. by 'notoriety' as was the case in England. *Regiam Majestatem and Quoniam Attachiamenta*, ed. Lord Cooper (Edinburgh, 1947), 166–7, 359–60. I am grateful to Dr. Cynthia Neville for advice on this matter.

2 On outlawry and outlaws, see generally J. Bellamy, *Crime and Public Order in England in the Later Middle Ages* (London and Toronto, 1973), as well as M. Keen, *The Outlaws of Medieval Legend* (London and New York, revised ed. 1977, reprinted New York, 1989).

better understood if the records that underpin it remain firmly in the foreground and are allowed to speak for themselves; indeed, the relationship of the sources to the challenges they described forms one of the more important sub-themes of the study.

The topic is by no means free of difficulties. Two of the most serious relate to the nature of the surviving source material and its interpretation. Not only are texts and documents sparse to begin with, but those that do survive are almost universally sympathetic to the Scottish kings and tend to characterise their rivals as rebels, traitors, outlaws, and brigands who disturbed the peace of the kingdom; their challenges are usually described in terms of 'rebellions' and 'revolts'. Such language is common in the medieval sources and has been adopted, perhaps rather uncritically, by most modern writers on the subject (including, it should be noted, myself), to the point that it has become commonplace to read of a host of 'rebellions' and 'revolts' in the twelfth and thirteenth centuries. The use of such terms may unintentionally obfuscate as much as it clarifies, however, and in adopting them we may also unintentionally be adopting the perspectives of the surviving texts, themselves often pro-royal in outlook. For this reason I have attempted to avoid terms like 'revolt' and 'rebellion' in this study, although it is difficult consistently to provide useful alternatives. Another problem arising from the sympathies of the documents is simply their brevity where the king's enemies and their activities are concerned; they are often extremely laconic, if not downright cryptic (as in the famous entry in the Holyrood Chronicle which relates how, in 1163, 'King Malcolm moved the men of Moray'). Inevitably, therefore, there are major gaps in our knowledge; gaps that must be filled by inference, informed speculation, analogies, and by utilising whatever scraps of material are available, however tenuous, problematic, or seemingly insignificant. At the end of the day, however, it is not possible to provide an account free from all speculation and without lingering doubts. Many problems will inevitably remain open to debate, and I hope that this book will provide a stimulus for further investigation and discussion of what I believe has been a largely neglected theme in historical writing on medieval Scotland.

Professor A. A. M. Duncan's *The Kingship of the Scots, 842–1292: Succession and Independence* (Edinburgh 2002) appeared too late to be utilised in the writing of this work, but contains much of value on the present subject; readers will find some points of interpretation on which we differ.

R.A.McD.
St Catharines, Ontario
September 2002

ACKNOWLEDGEMENTS

This book has benefited from the generous assistance and advice of many people. I would like to thank Benjamin T. Hudson for first suggesting that I write a full-length monograph on this subject, and for his assistance throughout the endeavour. I am also indebted to those who have offered criticism on all or part of the manuscript: Ted Cowan, Archie Duncan, Seán Duffy, Elizabeth Ewan, David Mullan, Cynthia Neville, and Alex Woolf. As is customary at this juncture, it must be emphasised that the author bears sole responsibility for errors of fact or interpretation in the work.

Many of the ideas in the book first took shape as papers presented at the International Medieval Congress in Leeds between 1999 and 2002, and I am grateful to the participants who attended those sessions and made constructive criticisms, especially Judith Green, Simon Taylor, and Alex Woolf. I also thank Pauline and Donald Hood for their warm hospitality on the occasion of those conferences. Special thanks are directed to my friend and colleague Graham Reynolds for his infectious enthusiasm and constant interest in the research represented by this book, and to Konrad Kinzl for fifteen years' worth of guidance and encouragement. Finally, without the congeniality of outstanding colleagues at the University College of Cape Breton (where it was begun) and Brock University (where it was completed) the book may have taken longer to finish.

A major research grant from the Social Sciences and Humanities Research Council of Canada (SSHRC) is gratefully acknowledged, as are smaller awards from the University College of Cape Breton and Brock University.

It is a pleasure to thank Robin Gillis and Kimberley Fraser for assisting with the compilation of the bibliography and the notes; Rob Falconer for providing materials from the world-class Scottish collection at the University of Guelph; Barry Gabriel for producing the maps; Mary Campbell for her unparalleled ability to track down rare and obscure volumes; and the editors of the *Canadian Journal of History* for permission to adapt and utilise parts of my paper on "Treachery in the Remotest Territories of Scotland:' Northern Resistance to the Canmore Dynasty, 1130–1230,' *CJH* 33 (August 1999), pp. 161–92. A word of thanks is also due to the Institute for Historical Research in London, where the final research was carried out in the summer of 2002.

John and Val Tuckwell have, as always, proven a pleasure to work with, and I am grateful for the opportunity to collaborate with them again on this present volume.

The biggest debts, however, lie closer to home. My mother and father have my deepest gratitude for their steadfast support of my career choice. I must again thank my feline companion of many years, Erin, for not only taking a less active role at the keyboard this time around, but also for continuing to remind me when it is time to return my thoughts to the present. But the most heartfelt thanks of all go to my wife, Jacqueline, who has lived with this book for the last three years and who has been my editor of first and last resort. The dedication does not begin to repay the tremendous debt that she is owed.

TIMELINE OF CHALLENGES
TO THE SCOTTISH KINGS

1057	Macbeth slain by Malcolm III
1058	Lulach, Macbeth's stepson, slain by Malcolm III
1078	campaign against Máelsnechtai, son of Lulach, by Malcolm III
1085	Donald son of Malcolm perishes 'unhappily'; death of Máelsnechtai
1116	Lodmund son of Donald killed by the men of Moray
c. 1116	Alexander I ambushed at Invergowrie by men of Moray; royal forces defeat Moravians at 'Stokfurd'
1124	David I challenged by Angus of Moray and Malcolm
1130	battle of Stracathro; Angus of Moray slain
1134	campaign(s) against Malcolm; he is captured and incarcerated at Roxburgh
1140s	Wimund, bishop of the Isles, active against David I
1153	death of David I; uprising of Somerled of Argyll and sons of Malcolm
1154	Arthur, who intended to betray King Malcolm, slain in judicial combat
1156	Donald son of Malcolm captured at Whithorn and incarcerated at Roxburgh
1157	Malcolm IV reconciled with Malcolm 'MacHeth'
1160	'revolt of the earls' at Perth; Scottish campaigns in Galloway; retirement of Fergus of Galloway to Holyrood abbey; treaty between Somerled and the king
1161	Fergus of Galloway dies; possible insurrection in Moray
1163	'King Malcolm moved the men of Moray'
1164	invasion of Clyde valley by Somerled and his death at battle of Renfrew
1168	Malcolm 'MacHeth' dies
1175	reign of terror in Galloway by Uhtred and Gilbert, sons of Fergus; Uhtred killed by Gilbert
1175–84	Scottish campaigns in Galloway
1175–85	Roland of Galloway engaged in vengeance for murder of his father, Uhtred
1179	King William campaigns in Ross and constructs castles at Redcastle and Dunskeath
1181	Donald MacWilliam ravages Moray and Ross and possibly wrests these areas from Scottish royal control

1185	Roland of Galloway fights two battles in Galloway; royal campaigns against Roland; peace between Roland and English and Scottish kings
1186	Adam son of Donald seized at Coupar Angus abbey; his followers burned alive
1187	royal expedition against Donald MacWilliam; Donald slain at Mam Garvia by Roland of Galloway
1196/97–	
1202	royal expeditions against Earl Harald Maddadsson of Orkney/Caithness
1206	death of Earl Harald Maddadsson
1211–12	Guthred MacWilliam ravages Ross; royal campaigns in Ross; Guthred executed
1214	King William in Moray; treaty with earl of Orkney/Caithness
1215	incursion by Donald Bàn MacWilliam and his defeat by Ferchar Maccintsacairt
1221	the king and a royal army at Inverness, against Donald MacNeil
1221–22	Royal expedition(s) against Argyll and the Isles
1222	Burning of Bishop Adam of Caithness at Halkirk
1223	Possible MacWilliam insurrection
1228	Thomas de Thirlestane killed, part of Inverness burnt, and some of the king's lands plundered by Gillescop, possibly a MacWilliam
1229	Gillescop and his sons perish
1230	execution of MacWilliam infant at Forfar
1234	death of Alan of Galloway without legitimate male heir; Gallovidian insurrections
1235	Thomas of Galloway, illegitimate son of Alan, rises, is defeated, and incarcerated
1247	insurrection in Galloway
1249	King Alexander II dies at head of expedition to subdue chieftains of Hebrides
1262	Scottish royal expedition ravages Skye
1263	'Battle of Largs': Norwegian attempt to assert sovereignty in Western Isles fails
1264	Dugald MacRuairi fights Scottish army in Caithness
1266	Treaty of Perth cedes Western Isles to Scotland from Norway
1286	King Alexander III's council considers release of Thomas of Galloway
1296	Thomas of Galloway briefly released from captivity by Edward I

TABLE I

KINGS OF SCOTLAND AND ENGLAND, 1057–1286

SCOTLAND		ENGLAND	
Macbeth	1040–57	Edward the Confessor	1042–66
Lulach	1057–58	Harold II	1066
Malcolm III	1058–93	William I the Conqueror	1066–87
Donald Bàn	1093–94	William II Rufus	1087–1100
Duncan II	1094	Henry I	1100–35
Donald Bàn	1094–97	Stephen	1135–54
Edgar	1097–1107	Henry II	1154–89
Alexander I	1107–24	Richard I	1189–99
David I	1124–53	John	1199–1216
Malcolm IV	1153–65	Henry III	1216–72
William I	1165–1214	Edward I	1272–1307
Alexander II	1214–49		
Alexander III	1249–86		

TABLE 2

ROYAL KINDREDS AND DYNASTIC RIVALRIES

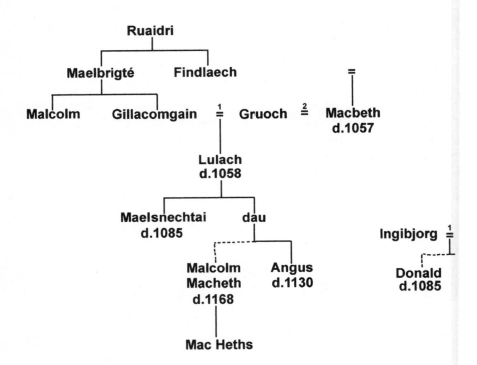

Note: dotted lines indicate uncertain relationship

IN 11TH–12TH CENTURY SCOTLAND

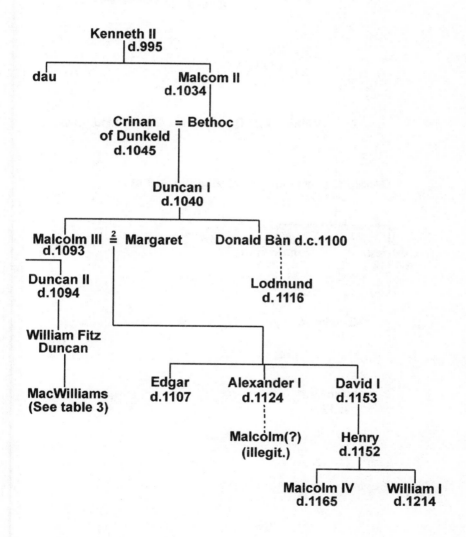

Cenél Gabrain

Kenneth II
d.995

dau   Malcom II
d.1034

Crinan = Bethoc
of Dunkeld
d.1045

Duncan I
d.1040

Malcolm III $\overset{2}{=}$ Margaret   Donald Bàn d.c.1100
d.1093

Duncan II
d.1094   Lodmund
d.1116

William Fitz
Duncan

MacWilliams   Edgar   Alexander I   David I
(See table 3)   d.1107   d.1124   d.1153

Malcolm(?)   Henry
(illegit.)   d.1152

Malcolm IV   William I
d.1165   d.1214

TABLE 3

THE MACWILLIAMS

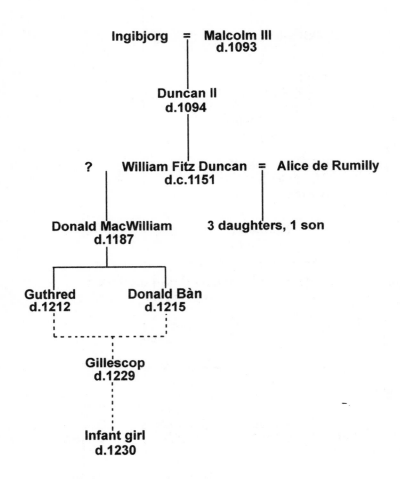

Note: dotted lines indicate uncertain relationship

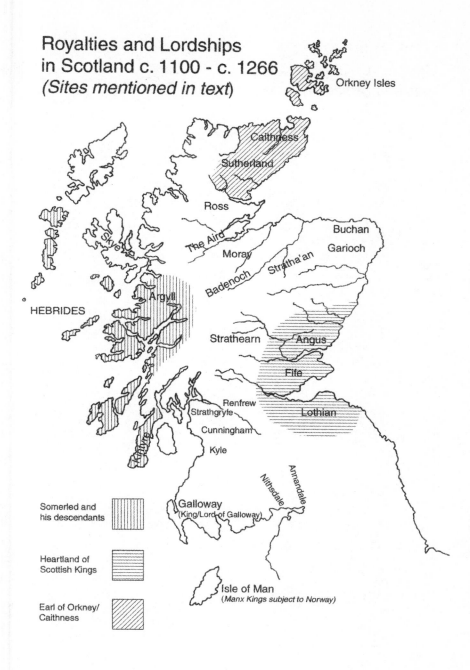

Royalties and Lordships
in Scotland c. 1100 - c. 1266
(*Sites mentioned in text*)

Orkney Isles

Caithness

Sutherland

Ross

Skye

The Aird

Buchan

Moray

Garioch

Stratha'an

Badenoch

Argyll

HEBRIDES

Strathearn

Angus

Fife

Renfrew
Strathgryfe

Cunningham

Lothian

Kyle

Nithsdale

Annandale

Somerled and
his descendants

Heartland of
Scottish Kings

Earl of Orkney/
Caithness

Galloway
(King/Lord of Galloway)

Isle of Man
(*Manx Kings subject to Norway*)

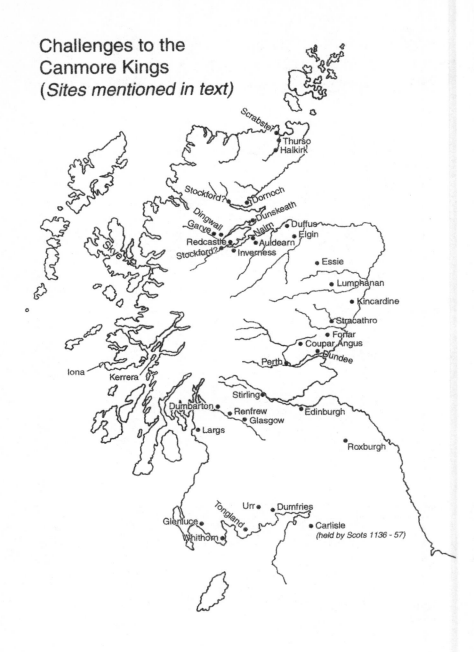

Challenges to the
Canmore Kings
(*Sites mentioned in text*)

Scrabster

Thurso
Halkirk

Stockford?
Dornoch
Dunskeath

Dingwall
Garve
Nairn
Duffus
Elgin

Redcastle
Auldearn

Stockford?
Inverness

Essie

Lumphanan

Kincardine

Skye

Stracathro

Forfar
Coupar Angus
Dundee

Perth

Iona
Kerrera

Stirling

Dumbarton
Renfrew
Glasgow
Edinburgh

Largs

Roxburgh

Urr
Dumfries

Tongland

Glenluce
Carlisle
(*held by Scots 1136 - 57*)

Whithorn

THE CANMORE KINGS,
THEIR ENEMIES AND THE HISTORIANS

In 1211 William king of Scotland sent a huge army together with all the nobles of the kingdom into Ross against Guthred MacWilliam. The king himself followed when he was able to come . . . On the way he built two castles, laid waste pretty well all of Ross, and took or killed as many of the said Guthred's supporters as he could find. But Guthred himself always avoided the king's army, meanwhile laying ambushes for it whenever he could by night or day, and driving off booty from the lord king's land.

For fifty years, from the first appearance of Guthred's father Donald in northern Scotland in about 1180, through Guthred's invasion of 1211–12, and down to the death of an infant girl, the last of the line, at Forfar in 1230, the MacWilliam kindred challenged the Scottish kings with invasions, insurrections, plundering, and guerrilla-style warfare like that described above by the fifteenth-century chronicler Walter Bower in his *Scotichronicon*.[1] Remarkable as the annals of MacWilliam opposition to the Scottish kings are, however, this kindred did not stand alone in its enmity toward the royal house. To the ranks of Guthred and his kinsmen may be added a long list of further rivals that spans the formative era of the eleventh to thirteenth centuries and includes mysterious individuals like Angus of Moray, Malcolm 'MacHeth', and Wimund, bishop of the Isles, not to mention better-known figures like Somerled MacGillabrigte, king of the Hebrides and Kintyre, Fergus, lord of Galloway, and Harald Maddadsson, earl of Orkney/Caithness, as well as many of their descendants.

Although there are ambiguous signs of opposition from the time of Malcolm III, it was not until midway through the reign of his son Alexander I that the stakes were raised and there unfolded the first in a long series of clashes between the successors of Malcolm and a wide variety of discontented dynasts and native warlords with axes to grind. Indeed, it is a startling but seldom-acknowledged fact of twelfth- and thirteenth-century Scottish history that, from the 1110s onward, no decade for over a century was free of conflicts of one kind or another. The challenges reached a crescendo in the MacWilliam insurrections between 1180 and 1215, but the embers of resistance continued to

---

1 Walter Bower, *Scotichronicon*, gen. ed. D.E.R. Watt (9 vols. Aberdeen, 1987–97) iv, 464–5; Bower here relies on a contemporary source: see note 45 below.

smoulder in the remoter territories of Scotland through the 1220s and 1230s, and even as late as 1264 one of Somerled's descendants is said to have battled a Scottish army in Caithness.[2] Apart from the chronological framework, the geographical setting is also significant, since the challenges were not restricted to one particular locality: Walter Bower, describing Guthred MacWilliam's impact, remarked that he 'plagued many parts of the kingdom of Scotland'.[3] This comment on the far-reaching nature of the insurrections is, if somewhat exaggerated, still broadly applicable. Malcolm III and his successors weathered challenges from Galloway in the southwest, Argyll and the Isles in the west, and in the far north from Moray, Ross, Caithness and Orkney. Nor was the unrest confined, as one chronicler put it when describing an insurrection of 1230, to the 'remotest territories of Scotland'.[4] On several occasions various opponents carried the struggle into the heartland of the Scottish monarchy. Alexander I was attacked at Invergowrie near Dundee in about 1116; the constable of David I fought off an invasion at Stracathro in Angus in 1130; Malcolm IV was besieged at Perth in 1160; and Adam son of Donald, described as the 'king's outlaw', was seized and his warband slain at Coupar Angus abbey in 1186.

Although individual challenges and isolated threads of resistance have received occasional and sporadic treatment by historians, twenty-five years of intensive scholarship on medieval Scotland has failed to yield a methodical study of the subject, which thus remains a much-neglected theme of twelfth- and thirteenth-century history. This book, which is intended to fill an obvious lacuna in Scottish historiography, explores the causes, courses, and consequences of opposition to the Scottish kings from Malcolm III to Alexander III, between about 1058 and 1266, concentrating on the most intense period of resistance between 1124 and 1235. The first chapter provides a narrative overview of the conflicts between the Canmore kings and their rivals, drawing together in one place a detailed discussion of all known instances of opposition; this is something that has never, to the best of the author's knowledge, been undertaken before. Chapter 2 offers an examination of the leaders around whom opposition crystallised and the motives behind their uprisings, while the third chapter assesses military aspects of the insurrections, evaluates their overall impact upon the kingdom of Scots, and considers why they were ultimately unsuccessful.

---

2 *Icelandic Sagas and other historical documents relating to the settlements and descents of the Northmen on the British Isles*, ed. G. Vigfusson and trans. G.W. Dasent (4 vols., Rolls Series, London, 1887–94): Volume 4: *The Saga of Hakon and a fragment of Magnus Saga*, trans. G.W. Dasent (London, 1894), 377. The Saga is translated in, and subsequent references to it utilise, *Early Sources of Scottish History AD 500 to 1286*, trans. A.O. Anderson [*ES*] (2 vols. Edinburgh, 1922; repr. Stamford, 1990) ii, 648–9.

3 Bower, *Scotichronicon*, iv, 466–7.

4 'in extremis finibus Scotiae': *Chronicon de Lanercost*, ed. J. Stevenson [*Chron Lanercost*] (Edinburgh, 1839), 40–1.

Political violence is a prominent theme in the history of medieval Scotland, as in medieval Europe as a whole, but the period from the eleventh to the thirteenth centuries is generally regarded as more peaceful and stable than both the preceding and following eras; it is not without some justification that the reign of Alexander III, and perhaps by extension much of the thirteenth century, is often regarded as a 'Golden Age'.[5] This is due in large measure to the fact that from 1097 until 1286 the descendants of King Malcolm III and his second wife, Margaret, ruled Scotland without interruption – the so-called 'Canmore dynasty' after the by-name of *Ceann Mór* (Great Chief) by which Malcolm became known.[6] After a brief civil war following the deaths of Malcolm and Margaret in 1093, their son Edgar succeeded to the kingship. His brothers Alexander I and David I followed him in the royal office, and David (whose son, Earl Henry, predeceased him) was in turn succeeded by his grandsons Malcolm IV and William I (the Lion). William was followed by his son, Alexander II, and grandson Alexander III, whose death effectively marked the end of the dynasty.

The early Canmore kings inaugurated, and their successors consolidated, a thoroughgoing transformation of Scottish society, characterised by a process of 'Europeanisation' or modernisation of the kingdom.[7] David's reign was the turning point; by his death in 1153 the process, though hardly complete, was well advanced, and its defining characteristics present. Colonists from England and the Continent (conveniently described as 'Anglo-Normans') settled in Scotland alongside the native aristocracy; lands (mostly south of the Forth) were granted in return for military service; knights and castles made their first appearance.[8] The growth of towns (burghs) and the introduction of coinage signalled

---

5 See N.H. Reid, 'Alexander III: The Historiography of a Myth', in *Scotland in the Reign of Alexander III, 1249–86*, ed. N.H. Reid (Edinburgh, 1990), 181–213.

6 It is difficult to know how to designate the descendants of Malcolm III and Margaret: though commonly known as the Canmore dynasty (see, e.g., R. Oram, *The Canmores: Kings & Queens of the Scots 1040–1290* (Stroud, 2002)), the by-name is not attested in sources contemporary with Malcolm III. Some historians have preferred to use the term 'MacMalcolm' dynasty (e.g. M. Lynch, *Scotland: A New History* (London, revised ed. 1992), Ch. 6), and Gordon Donaldson has even utilised the rather unsatisfactory (because suggestive of matrilineal succession, as well as an undue Scandinavian influence) 'Margaretsons': *Scottish Kings* (London, 1967, repr. New York, 1992), 14. For the purposes of this study, the term 'Canmore dynasty' will be retained, while its limitations are acknowledged.

7 See R. Bartlett, *The Making of Europe: Conquest, Colonization and Cultural Change 950– 1350* (London and Princeton, 1993), for the term 'Europeanization' and its broader application.

8 Whether or not Scotland was feudalised in the twelfth century depends largely upon where one stands in the debate over the value of the term 'feudalism' to the historian's vocabulary. Some scholars advocate expunging it entirely, /cont'd over

economic transformation, while the foundation of territorial bishoprics and the patronage of new religious orders by kings and nobles alike marked ecclesiastical change and renewal.[9] Largely because this transformation was undertaken at the initiative of the Scottish kings and was overseen by them, rather than by foreign conquerors, the introduction of new ideas, settlers and institutions has been regarded as a relatively, if not entirely, peaceful process: a 'peaceful Norman conquest' as one scholar rather famously, if paradoxically, summed it up, while another, in a memorable phrase, described David as a 'royal emigration agent'.[10] The twelfth-century kingdom of the Scots has thus been regarded as a balance of old and new in which native Scottish and contemporary European elements were successfully synthesised.[11] Yet despite the relative harmony that seems to have prevailed, there were disaffected elements, too – individuals who, for a variety of reasons, opposed the kings of Scots descended from Malcolm and Margaret, raised armies against them, and most often paid with their lives. This

while others regard it as 'an appropriate means of describing a particular form of social organisation which was found widely throughout western Europe and came increasingly into prominence in Scotland in the twelfth century': A.D.M. Barrell, *Medieval Scotland* (Cambridge, 2000),15. Important works dealing with the debate over 'feudalism' in a European context are S. Reynolds, *Fiefs and Vassals: The Medieval Evidence Reinterpreted* (Oxford, 1994), as well as E.A.R. Brown, 'The Tyranny of a Construct: Feudalism and Historians of Medieval Europe', *American Historical Review* lxxix (1974), 1063–88.

9 See the important works of R.L.G. Ritchie, *The Normans in Scotland* (Edinburgh, 1954); A.A.M. Duncan, *Scotland: The Making of the Kingdom* (Edinburgh, 1975); G.W.S. Barrow, *Kingship and Unity: Scotland 1000–1306* (London, 1981, repr. Edinburgh, 1989); and *idem*, *The Anglo-Norman Era in Scottish History* (Oxford 1980); D. Walker, *The Normans in Britain* (Oxford 1995) and R. Frame, *The Political Development of the British Isles 1100–1400* (Oxford, 1990). An excellent recent survey is that of Barrell, *Medieval Scotland*.

10 Ritchie, *Normans in Scotland*, xi, xiv; J. Coutts, *The Anglo-Norman Peaceful Invasion of Scotland 1057–1200. Origin of Great Scottish Families* (Edinburgh, 1922), vi; despite its main title, this work is essentially a gazetteer of Scottish families with origins in the Anglo-Norman period.

11 See G.W.S. Barrow, *David I of Scotland (1124–1153): The balance of new and old* (Reading, 1985), reprinted in *Scotland and Its Neighbours in the Middle Ages* (London, 1992); and A. Grant, 'Scotland's "Celtic Fringe" in the Late Middle Ages: The MacDonald Lords of the Isles and the Kingdom of Scotland,' in *The British Isles 1100–1500*, ed. R.R. Davies (Edinburgh, 1988), 119 (for the notion of a hybrid kingdom). There is much of value in C. Neville, 'A Celtic Enclave in Norman Scotland: Earl Gilbert and the Earldom of Strathearn, 1171–1223', in *Freedom and Authority. Historical and Historiographical Essays Presented to Grant G. Simpson*, ed. T. Brotherstone and D. Ditchburn (East Linton, 2000), 75–92; and see also R.A. McDonald, 'Old and New in the Far North: Ferchar Maccintsacairt and the early earls of Ross, c. 1200–1274', in *The exercise of power in Medieval Scotlamd, 1200–1500*, ed. S. Boardman and A. Ross (Dublin: forthcoming).

book offers an exploration of these challenges and the men who led them. It further argues that the paradigm of opposition to the Crown provides a significant and largely overlooked theme permeating the entire history of the Canmore dynasty from its origin to its twilight. As Bruce Webster has recently remarked, 'the history of Scottish kingship from the eleventh century to the thirteenth is a mixture of consolidation and internal challenges'.[12]

Despite the lack of any book-length study of the challenges to the Scottish kings in the twelfth and thirteenth centuries, there nevertheless remains a considerable amount of secondary literature to be taken into account. Among the pioneers of the study of medieval Celtic Scotland were William Forbes Skene (1809–92) and Eben William Robertson (1815–74). Skene, a career lawyer rather than a full-time historian who became Historiographer Royal for Scotland in 1881, wrote at some length on the subject of resistance to the Scottish kings in both his early study, *The Highlanders of Scotland* (1837), and in his later and vastly influential magnum opus, *Celtic Scotland: A History of Ancient Alban* (1876–80).[13] As the narrative of the latter reached the reign of David I in the early twelfth century, Skene's study became largely devoted to the various insurrections faced by the Scottish kings descended from Malcolm III and Margaret. As Skene himself put it, from the reign of David I it remained only to notice 'the fitful struggles of her Celtic subjects to resist the power which was gradually but surely working out this process of incorporation and the consolidation of the various districts which comprised it into one compact kingdom'.[14] Although Skene's work has come under fire from modern critics and has, accordingly, been either rejected or revised at nearly every juncture, *Celtic Scotland* retains of enduring significance for the many valuable suggestions and observations that its author made and remains noteworthy for his critical attitude toward the source materials.[15] As one

---

12 B. Webster, *Medieval Scotland: The Making of an Identity* (Basingstoke and London, 1997), 22.
13 *The Highlanders of Scotland: Their Origin, History, and Antiquities; with a Sketch of their Manners and Customs, and an account of the clans into which they were divided, and of the state of society which existed among them* (2 vols. London, 1837); *Celtic Scotland: A History of Ancient Alban* (3 vols. Edinburgh, 1876–80, 2nd edition 1886–90). Skene's other scholarly contributions included the standard edition of Fordun's chronicle (in the Historians of Scotland series (Edinburgh, 1871)) – which has yet to be superseded – as well as *Book of the Dean of Lismore: English and Gaelic Selections* (Edinburgh, 1862), *Chronicles of the Picts and Scots* (Edinburgh, 1867), an edition of early sources, and a critical edition of Welsh source materials, *The four ancient books of Wales, containing the Cymric poems attributed to the bards of the sixth century* (Edinburgh, 1868).
14 Skene, *Celtic Scotland*, i, 460.
15 Skene had been exposed to German schools of philology and history while in Germany in 1824: *Dictionary of National Biography*, ed. S. Lee [*DNB*] (63 vols. London, 1885–1900), lii, 338.

authority put it, '*Celtic Scotland* cannot be ignored by anyone investigating the first millennium and a half of Scottish history'.[16]

The stature of Skene's work has had the unfortunate side-effect of obscuring the researches of another pioneer in the field of medieval Scottish history, E.W. Robertson. His *Scotland Under Her Early Kings: A History of the Kingdom to the Close of the Thirteenth Century* (1862), though subsequently eclipsed by Skene's *Celtic Scotland*, was certainly no less important; Skene himself regarded Robertson's study as 'a work of great merit, [which] exhibits much accurate research and sound judgment'.[17] An Oxford-educated lawyer and, later, justice for Leicestershire whose premature death no doubt deprived the scholarly community of further significant insights, Robertson 'combined with the position of a country squire the habits of a thorough student and an ardent book collector'.[18] *Scotland Under Her Early Kings* showed tremendous originality and depth of research, and it can be argued that, since its publication predated that of Skene's *Celtic Scotland*, it was Robertson who placed the study of this period of Scottish history on a sound, critical basis. Like Skene, Robertson made careful and judicious use of the authorities, and he too devoted considerable attention to the insurrections of the twelfth and thirteenth centuries, so that this topic became a major theme in his work. There is, however, a certain irony in the fact that, although Skene's study went on to become much more famous than that of Robertson, Robertson deftly avoided several pitfalls into which Skene slipped.[19] As modern historians gradually rediscover many of Robertson's original ideas,[20] his

---

16 E.J. Cowan, 'The Invention of Celtic Scotland', in *Alba: Celtic Scotland in the Middle Ages*, ed. E.J. Cowan and R.A. McDonald (East Linton, 2000), 4.

17 Skene, *Celtic Scotland*, i, 19–20.

18 *DNB*, xlviii, 404–5. In addition to *Scotland Under Her Early Kings: A History of the Kingdom to the Close of the Thirteenth Century* (2 vols. Edinburgh, 1862), Robertson's only other study was *Historical Essays In Connexion With The Land, The Church, &cá* (Edinburgh, 1872). The first part of this book dealt with 'Standards of the Past in Weight and Currency', while other sections considered 'The Year and the Indiction', 'The Land', and 'Chapters of English History Before the Conquest'. The whole displays a remarkable breadth of learning spanning ancient and medieval history.

19 Skene identified Malcolm MacHeth with Wimund (*Celtic Scotland*, i, 463), an error dating back at least to the fourteenth century, which Robertson demolished (*Early Kings*, i, 219–22, and especially the note on 221–2). Skene was also (along with W. Reeves) responsible for propagating the notion that Ferchar Maccintsacairt was descended from the hereditary abbots of Applecross (*Celtic Scotland*, i, 483–4) – but Robertson argued that he was 'probably the *Cowarb* of the church lands in Ross, representing the head of the old family of the district' (*Early Kings*, ii, 4 n). Skene's hypothesis on Ferchar's origins, which has been repeated for the better part of a century, has only recently been rejected by scholars who are finally realising that Robertson was probably right after all: see A. Grant, 'The Province of Ross and the Kingdom of Alba', in *Alba*, especially 118–20 and note 145. This is an excellent example of how Skene's work completely eclipsed that of Robertson, but also of the merit of the latter's study, which deserves to be much better known.

20 See Grant, 'The Province of Ross', especially 118–20 and note 145.

reputation continues to be rehabilitated and his stature as a pioneer in the field, alongside Skene, is becoming more firmly established. Like Skene's *Celtic Scotland*, the Scottish medievalist can no longer ignore Robertson's study.

It is perhaps ironic that, from such promising beginnings in the second half of the nineteenth century, Scottish historical studies should have had to wait another hundred years for the insurrections of the twelfth and thirteenth centuries to re-enter the scholarly consciousness. Thus, although many general histories of the Highlands and Islands, as well as more specialised regional studies, have had something to say about the role of these regions in throwing up challenges to the Scottish kings,[21] the thread that had figured so prominently in the work of Skene and Robertson was left largely untouched until the 1980s and 1990s.[22] That this should be the case is the result of a shift of emphasis in the study of medieval Scotland. By the 1970s and 1980s, as Scottish studies entered what has been called a 'second Scottish Enlightenment',[23] scholarship became firmly fixed upon processes of state formation. This concentration is nowhere plainer than in the titles of two seminal studies in medieval Scottish historical writing that have profoundly influenced subsequent generations of scholars: Archibald Duncan's *Scotland: The Making of the Kingdom* (1975) and Geoffrey Barrow's *Kingship and Unity: Scotland 1000–1306* (1981). Both books were part of series designed to produce scholarly guides to the history of Scotland: Duncan's volume anchored the *Edinburgh History of Scotland*, while Barrow's was the second volume in the *New History of Scotland*. If Skene and Robertson placed the study of medieval Celtic Scotland on a sound scholarly basis, then Duncan and Barrow laid the foundations that carried it forward into the twenty-first century.[24] It is, of course, asking too much of a general survey to illuminate every aspect of a topic, but the emphasis of both works on state-formation and building – topics that are inextricably bound up with the development of a stable, unitary dynasty – meant that opponents of the Scottish kings

---

21 See for instance D. Mitchell, *A Popular History of the Highlands and Gaelic Scotland From the Earliest Times till the Close of the 'Forty-Five* (Paisley, 1900); Sir Herbert Maxwell, *History of Dumfries and Galloway* (Edinburgh and London, 1896); C. MacDonald, *History of Argyll* (Glasgow, 1950).

22 It is striking, for instance, that *The Moray Book*, ed. D. Omand (Edinburgh, 1976), has virtually nothing to say about the various challenges to the Scottish kings that were rooted in the northern territories of Moray and Ross. I.F. Grant and H. Cheape, *Periods in Highland History* (London, 1987), touches fleetingly on the subject. M. Newton, *A Handbook of the Scottish Gaelic World* (Dublin, 2000), devotes two brief paragraphs to the subject in a chapter entitled 'A Gaelic History of Scotland'.

23 *The Oxford Companion to Scottish History*, ed. M. Lynch (Oxford, 2001), vi. See also the entry on 'Historians', at 308–10.

24 Not surprisingly, both scholars have been taken to task by the critics for various perceived offences: see the review of Duncan's *Making of the Kingdom* by D.P. Kirby in *English Historical Review* xci (1976), 837–41, as well as the comments of R. Oram, 'Gold into Lead? The State of Early Medieval Scottish History', in *Freedom and Authority*, 32–43.

were, inevitably, accorded relatively little space in these books. To be fair, however, both works do acknowledge the various challenges faced by the Scottish kings, and Professor Duncan's lengthy study discusses nearly every instance of opposition within the broader context of its chronological and thematic development of the reigns of the twelfth- and thirteenth-century kings. Moreover, both scholars have contributed significantly to the topic in a variety of other influential publications.[25]

By the time the final volumes of the *New History of Scotland* were appearing in the mid-1980s, medieval Scottish historiography was blossoming as more specialised works appeared.[26] Thus, when Alexander Grant surveyed the achievements of Scottish historical writing in the mid-1990s he noted that, 'Over the last twenty or thirty years immense progress has been made in our understanding of virtually every aspect of medieval Scotland'.[27] Of particular relevance for the study of the opponents of the Scottish kings has been an intensification of interest in the rugged outer Atlantic zones of the Scottish kingdom – regions that were dominated by dynasties with autonomous or semi-autonomous standing, and that were closely linked with challenges and insurrection throughout the period in question. Indeed, the relationship and interactions between centre and periphery are now firmly established on the historiographical map of Scotland (as in historical studies generally) as a topic of considerable importance.[28]

25 See for instance the introductory chapters to Barrow's editions of *The Acts of Malcolm IV King of Scots 1153–65* (*Regesta Regum Scottorum* Volume I. Edinburgh, 1960) and *The Acts of William I King of Scots 1165–1214* (*Regesta Regum Scottorum* Volume II. Edinburgh, 1971), which contain a good deal of information on various insurrections; the same author's 'Macbeth and Other Mormaers of Moray', in *The Hub of the Highlands: The Book of Inverness and District*, ed. L. MacLean (Inverness, 1975), 109–22, also has much to say on the MacHeths and MacWilliams, as does his study of 'Some Problems in Twelfth- and Thirteenth-Century Scottish History – A Genealogical Approach', *Scottish Genealogist* xxv (1978), 97–112. A seminal article dealing with Argyll and the Hebrides in the twelfth and thirteenth centuries is A.A.M. Duncan and A.L. Brown, 'Argyll and the Isles in the earlier Middle Ages', *Proceedings of the Society of Antiquaries of Scotland* xc (1956–57), 192–220.

26 See R.A. McDonald, 'Introduction: Medieval Scotland and the New Millennium', in *History, Literature, and Music in Scotland 700–1560*, ed. R.A. McDonald (Toronto, 2002), 3–28, especially 3–8.

27 A. Grant, 'To the Medieval Foundations', *Scottish Historical Review* [*SHR*] lxxiii [Special Issue: Whither Scottish History? Proceedings of the 1993 Strathclyde Conference] (1994), 4.

28 On Scotland see, for instance, Barrell, *Medieval Scotland*, Ch. 4; the theme is addressed directly in J. Barrett *et al*, 'What Was the Viking Age and When did it Happen? A View From Orkney,' *Norwegian Archaeological Review* xxxiii (2000), 1–39. For the theme in a British context, see Frame, *Political Development of the British Isles*; R.R. Davies, *The First English Empire: Power and Identities in the British Isles 1093–1343* (Oxford, 2000); and M. Hechter, *Internal Colonialism. The Celtic Fringe in British National Development 1536–1966* (London, 1975). In a European context an important work is Bartlett, *The Making of Europe*, and for a different perspective entirely, see *Aspects of Arctic and Sub-Arctic History*, ed. I. Sigurðsson and J. Skaptason (Reykjavik, 2000), especially Main Theme 1: Centre and Periphery.

Among the peripheral regions of medieval Scotland, Galloway under its native lords, the descendants of Fergus, is perhaps the best served with recent specialised works. Daphne Brooke, Richard Oram, and Keith Stringer have made the field very much their own in a series of groundbreaking essays and monographs that cover fully the period of the native lordship from the 1140s to the 1230s and beyond.[29] Not surprisingly, much attention has been devoted to the first and last lords, Fergus and his great-grandson, Alan, and a pervasive theme of these studies has been the relations and interactions between the Scottish kingdom and Galloway, including colonisation and cultural interchanges. One result of this is that a good deal of ink has now been expended on the subject of the challenges that the Scottish kings faced from Galloway as well as the attitudes of the Scottish kings toward the region, and all three scholars have also succeeded in integrating Gallovidian politics of the period into the broader Irish Sea framework, thereby highlighting connections with Argyll, the Isles, Man and Ireland. The result of these studies is a fully developed view of the medieval lords of Galloway and their relations with the Scottish kings, and the debt of what follows to these scholars is immense.

Another area that has received considerable attention from scholars since the 1980s is Argyll and the Isles, a region that was, like Galloway, dominated by a powerful dynasty through the twelfth and thirteenth centuries: Somerled and his descendants, collectively known as the MacSorleys. Despite chapters on the period in earlier studies, as well as an important essay by A.A.M. Duncan and A.L. Brown (1956/7), no book- length study of the period in question existed until my own work dealing with the western seaboard between 1100 and 1336 was published in 1997.[30] This explored at some length the relations of

29 K.J. Stringer, 'Periphery and Core in Thirteenth-Century Scotland: Alan son of Roland, Lord of Galloway and Constable of Scotland', in *Medieval Scotland: Crown, Lordship and Community*, ed. A. Grant and K.J. Stringer (Edinburgh, 1993), 82–113, and *idem*, 'Acts of Lordship: The Records of the Lords of Galloway to 1234', in *Freedom and Authority*, 203–34; R. Oram, *The Lordship of Galloway* (Edinburgh, 2000); *idem*, 'Fergus, Galloway and the Scots', in *Galloway: Land and Lordship*, ed. R.D. Oram and G. Stell (Edinburgh, 1991), 117–30; *idem*, 'A Family Business? Colonisation and settlement in twelfth- and thirteenth-century Galloway', *SHR* lxxii (1993), 111–45; D. Brooke, *Wild Men and Holy Places: St Ninian, Whithorn and the Medieval Realm of Galloway* (Edinburgh, 1994); *idem*, *Fergus the King* (The Medieval Lords of Galloway 1. Whithorn, 1991).

30 Representative earlier works include: D. Gregory, *History of the Western Highlands and Isles of Scotland* 2nd ed. (Edinburgh 1881, repr 1975) and MacDonald, *History of Argyll* . See note 25 above for Duncan and Brown's essay. My own study is R.A. McDonald, *The Kingdom of the Isles: Scotland's Western Seaboard c.1100–c.1336* (East Linton, 1997, repr. 1998, 2002); some themes are pursued further in *idem*, 'Coming in from the margins: the descendants of Somerled and cultural accommodation in the Hebrides, 1164–1317', in *Britain and Ireland 900–1300: Insular Responses to Medieval European Change*, ed. B. Smith (Cambridge, 1999), 179–98.

Somerled and his descendants with the Scottish and Norwegian kings, and in the process had much to say of Fergus and Wimund as well as the MacHeths and MacWilliams. David Sellar's examination of the descendants of Somerled (2000) encompassed their relations with the Scottish kings, while Edward J. Cowan's essay (1990) on the acquisition of the western Isles by Scotland in the 1260s must now be considered essential reading on the topic.[31] As with Galloway, then, our knowledge of Argyll and the Isles in the twelfth and thirteenth century broadened considerably through the 1990s.

Central to the story of opposition to the Scottish kings are the northern territories of Moray and Ross, regions that, at times throughout the twelfth and thirteenth centuries, resembled battlegrounds between the kings and their enemies. To date these territories lack full-length studies of the medieval period, but the compensation for this is a wealth of outstanding essays. Following the path blazed by Geoffrey Barrow,[32] Edward J. Cowan's 1993 study of the historical MacBeth is much more wide-ranging than the title might suggest and is full of insights into not only one of Moray's most famous sons but also the enduring connection of this region with the MacHeths and MacWilliams as well as the theme of resistance to the Scottish kings in general. It was in this paper that Professor Cowan coined a term of some significance for the study of insurrection in twelfth- and thirteenth-century Scotland, by making reference to the existence of an 'anti-feudal faction' that stood opposed to the kings of Scots. In 1999 an important essay by Richard Oram examined the Scottish conquest and colonisation of Moray under David I, while in the same year another of my own studies took as its subject the MacHeth and MacWilliam kindreds, their opposition to the Scottish kings, and their connections with Moray and Ross. Meanwhile, a paper by Alexander Grant on the province of Ross (2000) further elucidated many aspects of opposition to the Scottish kings, at the same time highlighting how regional building blocks were incorporated into the medieval kingdom of Alba between the eleventh and thirteenth centuries.[33]

In the far north, the heavily Scandinavianised regions of Orkney and Caithness, like Moray and Ross, lack full-length studies of the medieval period,

---

31 W.D.H. Sellar, 'Hebridean Sea Kings: The Successors of Somerled', in *Alba*, 187–218; E.J. Cowan, 'Norwegian Sunset – Scottish Dawn: Hakon IV and Alexander III', in *Scotland in the Reign of Alexander III*, 103–31.

32 See note 25 above.

33 E.J. Cowan, 'The Historical MacBeth', in *Moray: Province and People*, ed. W.D.H. Sellar (Edinburgh, 1993), 117–41; R.A. McDonald, "Treachery in the Remotest Territories of Scotland:' Northern Resistance to the Canmore Dynasty 1130–1230', *Canadian Journal of History* xxxiii (1999), 161–92; R. Oram, 'David I and the Scottish Conquest and Colonisation of Moray', *Northern Scotland* xix (1999), 1–19; Grant, 'The Province of Ross', 88–126.

though general histories, especially of Orkney, and studies of the Viking Age proper, abound.[34] Barbara Crawford more than any other scholar since the 1980s has made the field very much her own, in a series of important articles dealing not only with the relations between the earls of Orkney/Caithness and the Scottish Crown but also with ecclesiastical themes in the far north.[35] To Crawford's articles may be added an excellent paper (1983) concerning Earl Harald Maddadson by Patrick Topping which provides important insight into his dealings with the Scottish kings, as well as an essay (1982) on Caithness in the sagas by Edward J. Cowan which also contains much of value.[36]

Taken altogether, then, much has been written since the 1980s on the peripheral regions of the Scottish kingdom that were so closely and intricately bound up with opposition to the Scottish kings. But if our knowledge of these regions and their rulers has been tremendously improved over the past twenty-five years, the picture, as far as the challenges to the Scottish kings and the individuals that orchestrated them is concerned, is still largely incomplete. It therefore remains to pick up the various threads of insurrection and weave them together into a complete tapestry.[37]

Trends in scholarship apart, there is one very good reason why the challenges to the Scottish kings of the twelfth and thirteenth centuries have remained in the background of historical writing: the nature of the sources. It has been remarked of the source material for the western seaboard of Scotland in the twelfth and thirteenth centuries that:

> Our knowledge ... must be gleaned from a diverse, patchy, and often confusing array of chronicles, annals, sagas, charters, poems, genealogies, and clan histories of Scottish, Irish, Norse, Manx, and English provenance, written in Latin, Gaelic, Scots, and Norse languages. Not all are contem-

---

34 See for instance W.P.L. Thomson, *History of Orkney* (Edinburgh, 1987), and B. Crawford's seminal study, *Scandinavian Scotland* (Leicester, 1987).

35 B. Crawford, 'The Earldom of Caithness and the Kingdom of Scotland, 1150–1266', in *Essays on the Nobility of Medieval Scotland*, ed. K.J. Stringer (Edinburgh, 1985), 25–43; 'Norse Earls and Scottish Bishops in Caithness: A Clash of Cultures', in *The Viking Age in Orkney, Caithness and the North Atlantic*, ed. C. Batey, J.Jesch and C. Morris (Edinburgh, 1995), 129–47.

36 P. Topping, 'Harald Maddadson, Earl of Orkney and Caithness, 1139–1206', *SHR* lxii (1983), 105–20; E.J. Cowan, 'Caithness in the Sagas', in *Caithness: A Cultural Crossroads*, ed. J. Baldwin (Edinburgh, 1982), 25–44.

37 Works such as those of J.L. Roberts, *Lost Kingdoms: Celtic Scotland and the Middle Ages* (Edinburgh, 1997), and Webster, *Medieval Scotland*, have gone a considerable distance toward remedying the drought on the topic of opposition, but neither is concerned exclusively with the subject.

porary with the events that they purport to describe, nor are they of equal authority . . .[38]

This same caveat holds true for the topic under consideration in this book, and although this is not the place for an extended discussion of the provenance of the various sources utilised in this study,[39] a few cautionary notes must be sounded at the outset. First and foremost, strictly contemporary and eyewitness accounts – the most desirable kind, of course – are few and far between. Neither of the two twelfth-century 'Scottish' chronicles of Holyrood and Melrose was written specifically as a history of Scotland, although they do, of course, contain, much of value for the historian of medieval Scotland; moreover, they were composed at monasteries located within the heartland of the kingdom, by largely alien elements in Scottish society, namely, the newly introduced reformed religious orders. The mid-thirteenth-century *Chronicle of Man*, composed, it is thought, at Rushen, traces the history of the Manx kings and their relations with the rulers of Scotland, England and Norway from circa 1066 to 1266 and in doing so illuminates various aspects of Scottish history. It is, however, often very confused and therefore remains of uneven value, particularly in its chronology.[40] The Irish Annals are another source largely contemporary with the period under consideration. Composed within a Gaelic cultural orbit, they often show considerable interest where Moray is concerned up to the early twelfth century, and frequently provide our sole source of contemporary information for instances of opposition related to the rulers of that region.[41] In addition to these sources a handful of Anglo-Norman and English chronicles also shed light on the rivals of the Scottish kings. These include the *Ecclesiastical History* of Orderic Vitalis, composed at St. Evroul in

38 McDonald, *Kingdom of the Isles*, 4–5. On the sources for the Highlands generally, see G.W.S. Barrow, 'The Sources for the History of the Highlands in the Middle Ages', in *The Middle Ages in the Highlands*, ed. L. MacLean (Inverness, 1981), 11–22.

39 In addition to the specific works cited below, see the important studies by B. Webster, *Scotland from the Eleventh Century to 1603* (Ithaca, N.Y. and London, 1975); A. Gransden, *Historical Writing in England, c.550 to c. 1307* (London, 1974); and K. Hughes, *Early Christian Ireland: Introduction to the Sources* (Ithaca, New York, 1972). There is also much of value on the early sources in B.T. Hudson, 'Historical Literature of Early Scotland', *Studies in Scottish Literature* xxvi (1991), 141–55.

40 *Chronicle of the Kings of Mann*, trans. G. Broderick (Edinburgh, 1973), i-x. Other editions include: *The Chronicle of Man and the Sudreys*, ed. P.A. Munch and Rev. Dr. Goss (Douglas, 1874); *Cronica Regum Mannie & Insularum. Chronicles of the Kings of Man and the Isles BL Cotton Julius Avii*, transcribed, translated with an introduction by G. Broderick [*Chron Man*] (Douglas, 1991). Unless otherwise indicated, this last edition is utilised throughout.

41 S. Duffy, 'Ireland and Scotland 1014–1169: contacts and caveats', in *Seanchas. Studies in Early and Medieval Irish Archaeology, History and Literature in Honour of Francis J. Byrne*, ed. A.P. Smyth (Dublin, 2000), 348–56.

Normandy between about 1114 and 1141 – which is uneven at best on Scottish material – as well as the chronicles of William of Newburgh (died c.1200) and Roger of Howden (died c.1202). Both Newburgh and Howden possessed first-hand information on several key topics: Newburgh, for instance, claims to have spoken personally with Wimund, the bishop of the Isles who harassed King David I toward the end of his reign, while Roger of Howden was well-informed on affairs in both Galloway and the far north from the 1170s to the 1190s.[42] Of course, like the Irish annals, the focus of these sources is not primarily Scottish, and they are, moreover, often unsympathetic to the rivals of the Scottish kings, in part, at least, because they generally regarded the inhabitants of the peripheral regions of Scotland as backward and barbaric. Of the Norse sources the two most important are unquestionably the *Orkneyinga Saga*, composed about 1200 as a history of the Orkney jarls, and Sturla Thordarsson's *Hakon's Saga* of the later thirteenth century, which is central to our understanding of events on the western seaboard in that turbulent era. Both sagas are based on oral traditions and present numerous problems of interpretation and under-standing for historians – but, on the other hand, without their unique per-spective much valuable information would undoubtedly be wanting.[43]

Moving beyond the strictly contemporary (i.e. twelfth- and thirteenth-century) material, there remain the later medieval chronicles of John of Fordun (c. 1380), Andrew of Wyntoun, prior of Loch Leven (c. 1415), and Walter Bower, abbot of Inchcolm (c. 1445). Appended to Fordun's fourteenth-century chronicle are *Gesta Annalia* or 'Yearly Deeds', entries hitherto regarded as

---

42 On these historians see, in addition to the work of Gransden cited in note 39 above, M. Chibnall, *The World of Orderic Vitalis* (Oxford, 1984) – which is thin on his Scottish content and connections; N. Partner, *Serious Entertainments: The Writing of History in Twelfth-Century England* (Chicago and London, 1977), with its fine discussion of William of Newburgh; and, of many studies on Roger of Howden, the relevant papers by John Gillingham, 'The Travels of Roger of Howden and his views of the Irish, Scots and Welsh', *Anglo-Norman Studies* xx (1997), 151–69 (reprinted in *The English in the Twelfth Century: Imperialism, National Identity, and Political Values* (Woodbridge, 2000)); and D. Corner, 'The *Gesta Regis Henrici Secundi* and *Chronica* of Roger, Parson of Howden', *Bulletin of the Institute for Historical Research* lvi (1983), 126–44.

43 On the sagas in general and their value to Scottish historical studies, see R. Power, 'Scotland and the Norse Sagas', in *Scotland and Scandinavia 800–1800*, ed. G.G. Simpson (Edinburgh, 1990), 13–24, where the observation is made (p. 14) that: 'their [the sagas'] authenticity as historical documents must always be in question, but, generally speaking, the nearer their authors were to the period in which the events they describe took place, the more they can be trusted historically'. On *Orkneyinga Saga*, see P. Foote, 'Observations on *Orkneyinga Saga*', in *St Magnus Cathedral and Orkney's Twelfth-Century Renaissance*, ed. B. Crawford (Aberdeen, 1988), 192–207, and on *Hakon's Saga* the apposite comments of Cowan, 'Hakon IV and Alexander III', 103–10.

Fordun's unfinished work but now known to have been derived from several independent sources of circa 1285, one of which was a Scottish history charting important events in the kingship from the reign of Malcolm III down to the time of Alexander III and patently not authored by Fordun. This gives *Gesta Annalia* much greater credibility than has previously been assumed.[44] The value of Bower's *Scotichronicon*, which may not be immediately apparent given its fifteenth-century date of composition, is evident in the passage cited at the head of this chapter dealing with Guthred MacWilliam: this is based upon an otherwise unknown but clearly contemporary source believed to resemble a detailed itinerary, and demonstrates how later medieval chronicles may preserve valuable nuggets of historical ore.[45] To this potpourri of texts spanning the eleventh to fifteenth centuries can be added various types of contemporary documentary material, including a voluminous body of charter and legal evidence, as well as tantalising inventories and summaries of records that are now frustratingly lost but that nevertheless provide important clues.[46] In short, the nature of the evidence is such that no titbit, however seemingly insignificant or irrelevant, can be overlooked.

It is not difficult to see why modern scholars have had to labour so hard in order to rescue the MacWilliams and the other rivals of the Scottish kings from the brink of the abyss of historical obscurity. Not only are the sources widely scattered and of greatly varying value, but most, if not all, are generally sympathetic, for one reason or another, to the Scottish kings and unsympathetic to their rivals. In contrast to post-conquest England, where the works of English writers like Eadmer and John of Worcester or half-English authors like William of Malmesbury and Orderic Vitalis provide at least some indication of English attitudes about the Norman conquest and settlement,[47] or even contemporary Wales and Ireland where native annals register sentiment about the Anglo-Norman penetration,[48] the historian searches in vain for narrative sources

44 See D. Broun, 'A New Look at *Gesta Annalia* Attributed to John of Fordun', in *Church, Chronicle and Learning in Medieval and Early Renaissance Scotland*, ed. B. Crawford (Edinburgh, 1999), 9–30.

45 Bower, *Scotichronicon*, iv, 616–7, 631; see also ix, Chaps. 14–25.

46 J.M. Thomson, *The Public Records of Scotland* (Glasgow, 1922), provides a good discussion of the fate of Scotland's early records from the period under consideration in this book.

47 See A. Williams, *The English and the Norman Conquest* (Woodbridge, 1995), 165–76. With its concentration upon the conquered rather than the conquerors in England after 1066, this important study has provided many insights and a good deal of inspiration for my own work. Similar themes are pursued in *Worsted in the Game: Losers in Irish History*, ed. C. Brady (Dublin, 1989).

48 R.R. Davies, *Domination and Conquest: The experience of Ireland, Scotland and Wales 1100–1300* (Cambridge, 1990), 27; see also the observations on the Welsh sources in R. Turvey, *The Welsh Princes 1063–1283* (London and New York, 2002), 7–12.

reflecting unambiguously the perspective of the enemies of the Scottish kings. There is no Moray, Galloway, or Argyll chronicle to set alongside the pro-royal Scottish sources (although *Orkneyinga Saga* perhaps comes closest to remedying this deficiency with its concentration on the Orkney jarls, and *Hakon's Saga* displays sympathy for the Hebridean chieftains caught between the dual millstones of Scottish and Norwegian royal authority), and if there ever existed a text that might retell the 'Secret History of the MacWilliams', for example, then it has either subsequently vanished or lies as yet undiscovered. If the victors are responsible for writing history, and if the winners in late-eleventh- to thirteenth-century Scottish history were Malcolm III and his successors, then it is a further tribute to the scale of their triumph that their rivals have been all but forgotten. As Professor Rees Davies has remarked in a contemporary Welsh context, 'A rather exclusive concentration on the 'winners,' on those dynasties which came to dominate native Wales from the mid-twelfth century onwards, may distort our perspective',[49] a comment that loses none of its validity when applied to the Scottish scene.

This becomes evident if we compare the remarks of the English chronicler Ailred of Rievaulx on the death of David I with those of Roger of Howden on the demise of David's distant kinsman, Donald MacWilliam (Guthred's father), who harassed King William the Lion from the 1170s until his death in 1187. Ailred writes:

> Although he [David] has found a place worthy of his soul, yet his death demands our mourning. For who, apart from a man who grudges peace and progress to human affairs, would not mourn for a man so much needed in the world, when he has been removed from human affairs. Youths and girls, old men and young, put on sackcloth, and sprinkle yourselves with ash. Let your cry be heard on high, and your mourning in the celestial regions.[50]

Then there is Roger of Howden, moralising over the defeat and death of Donald MacWilliam in 1187:

> And because of the evils he had wrought neither grief nor lamentation, neither even any sorrow was caused by his death. And no wonder: 'For the praise of the wicked is short, and the joy of the hypocrite as for a moment; if his pride ascend to the sky, and his head touch the clouds, like a dung heap he shall perish in the end.'[51]

---

49 R.R. Davies, *The Age of Conquest: Wales 1063–1415* (Oxford, 1987), 56.

50 Bower, *Scotichronicon*, iii, 142–3.

51 *Gesta Regis Henrici Secundi Benedicti Abbatis*, ed. W. Stubbs [*Gesta Henrici Secundi*] (2 vols., Rolls Series, London, 1867), ii, 7–9; trans. in *Scottish Annals from English Chroniclers AD 500–1286* [*SAEC*], trans. A.O. Anderson (London, 1908), 295. For discussion of the authorship of this work, see Chapter 1, note 66.

The contrasting celestial and scatological imagery of these passages neatly encapsulates the fates of the Scottish kings and their opponents at the hands of the medieval chroniclers and annalists; if it would be unfair to the likes of W.F. Skene and E.W. Robertson (not to mention many other historians of medieval Scotland) to suggest that Donald and his ilk have continued to languish in such an obscure and unpleasant place, it can hardly be said that they have received their due, either. Every archaeologist, however, is well aware that rubbish-heaps provide the richest sources of information about human activities of the past. Closer investigation of this particular dungheap serves to illuminate one of the more significant chapters in Scotland's hidden history, restoring a more balanced perspective to this crucial period in the development of the medieval kingdom.

ONE

'LONG HOSTILITY AGAINST THE MODERN KINGS':
The Scottish Kings and their Rivals,
1057 to 1266: A Narrative Overview

Donnchad rex Scotiae in autumno occiditur a duce suo Macbethad mac
Finnloech, cui successit in regnum annis 17.

Duncan, the king of Scotland, was killed in autumn by his *dux*, Macbeth,
Findláech's son, who succeeded to the kingship [and reigned for] seventeen
years.

These words, written on the Continent by an expatriate Irish monk named
Marianus Scotus, record one of the most famous instances of political violence
and dynastic strife in Scotland, when Macbeth MacFindláech slew his rival
Duncan I and seized the Scottish kingship in 1040. Appropriately enough,
Macbeth met his own end at the hands of Duncan's son, Malcolm, seventeen
years later, either at or as a direct result of the battle of Lumphanan in August
1057.[1]

Political violence and dynastic strife were facts of early medieval political
life, in tenth- and eleventh-century Scotland as elsewhere in Europe.[2] The
history of Scottish kingship is dominated by competition for the royal office
between rival but related segments of the royal kindred, and is littered with acts
of political violence similar to that perpetrated by Macbeth in 1040, or Malcolm
in 1057. More notable instances occurred in 966, when a battle was fought
between Dub the son of Malcolm and Cuilén the son of Indulf at Duncrub near
Perth, or in 1005 when Irish annals record 'a battle between the men of Alba
themselves, in which fell the king of Alba, i.e. Cinaed son of Dub'.[3] More famous
still is the internecine strife within the Cenél Loairn kindred of Moray, which
can be traced in the Irish annals of the 1020s and early 1030s. In 1020,
'Findláech, Ruadri's son, mormaer of Moray was slain by the sons of his

---

1 Marianus Scotus, *Mariani Scotti Chronicon*, ed. G. Waitz, in *Monumenta Germaniae
   Historica, Scriptores* V (Hanover, 1844), 557. Primary sources for Macbeth, including
   Marianus, are conveniently collected in *ES,* i, 579, 600–2.
2 *Violence and Society in the Early Medieval West*, ed. G. Halsall (Woodbridge, 1998),
   passim.
3 *ES,* i, 472–3, 521–2; *The Annals of Ulster (to AD 1131)*, ed. S. MacAirt and G.
   MacNiocaill [*AU* (MacAirt)] (Dublin, 1983), 435.

brother Máelbrigte'. In 1029 the death of Malcolm, the son of Máelbrigte, is recorded (although he is usually assumed to have been slaughtered, the annals do not actually say so, and a recent treatment has suggested that he died peacefully); and then in 1032 'Gillacomgain, Máelbrigte's son, the mormaer of Moray, was burned along with fifty of his men'. Again the sources are silent as to the perpetrator of this act, but suspicion has been cast on none other than Macbeth, who thereby avenged his father's killing twelve years earlier.[4]

On the surface, at any event, the long reign of Malcolm MacDuncan (Malcolm III, 1058–93), which occupies most of the second half of the eleventh century, seems to have brought an end to this dynastic strife. Not only did Malcolm take care to eliminate his rival Macbeth in 1057 as well as Macbeth's stepson and successor Lulach in early 1058, but Malcolm's reign was long, and he is regarded as the founder of an important dynasty that would rule Scotland without interruption from 1097 until the death of Alexander III in 1286. Taken together, these facts have contributed to the view that challenges to the Scottish kings were, if not eliminated entirely from the reign of Malcolm III, then at least relegated to the sidelines of political culture and almost predestined to failure.

In fact, the various chronicles, annals, sagas, charters and other documents from which our knowledge of the twelfth- and thirteenth-century kingdom of the Scots is gleaned contain many references to challenges to the Scottish kings descended from Malcolm III and his second wife, Margaret; a 'recurrent note of hostility' is, therefore, to be found in these reigns.[5] On this view, the reign of Malcolm III represents not so much an end as a beginning. One historian of the early Scottish kings has remarked that, 'The slaying of Lulach by Máel Coluim III [Malcolm III] marked the end of the old order among the Scots'.[6] In one sense this is certainly true: never again would the Cenél Loairn hold the kingship of the Scots, and there can be little doubt that the fortunes of this dynasty reached their zenith with Macbeth and Lulach. Moreover, the descendants of Malcolm III and Margaret would successfully monopolise the kingship for two centuries. But in another sense, the slaying of Lulach by Malcolm III was only the beginning. Malcolm III and his successors strove not only to eliminate anyone even remotely related to Macbeth or Lulach, but also found themselves opposed from other quarters as well: from dynasts descended from Malcolm III and his first wife, Ingibjorg of Orkney, and their supporters and allies, and from other powerful figures on the periphery of the Scottish

4 The sources are collected in *ES*, i, 551, 571; *AU* (MacAirt), 457, 467, 471. For further discussion of these events, see Cowan, 'Historical MacBeth,' in *Moray*, 119–122; N. Aitchison, *MacBeth: Man and Myth* (Stroud, 1999), *passim*, and B.T. Hudson, *Kings of Celtic Scotland* (Westport, Conn., and London, 1994), *passim*.

5 Ritchie, *Normans in Scotland*, 91; Mitchell, *History of the Highlands*, 202, made a similar observation in 1900.

6 Hudson, *Kings of Celtic Scotland*, 146; cf. Robertson, *Early Kings*, i, 124.

kingdom, some of whom claimed regnal status. The struggle against these figures endured almost as long as the dynasty that Malcolm inaugurated, and is arguably one of its defining characteristics. Viewed from this perspective, Lulach's death at the hands of Malcolm III stands, not at the conclusion, but rather at the head of what Professor E.J. Cowan has described as 'a chronicle of carnage',[7] and it was surely with some justification that a thirteenth-century English chronicler spoke of 'long hostility' against the Scottish kings from some quarters.[8]

A 'Chronicle of Carnage'?

The path of Malcolm III to the Scottish kingship was a bloody one. English and Irish accounts agree that a great battle was fought in 1054 in which Macbeth was put to flight and Malcolm appointed king; later tradition placed this battle at Dunsinan in Perthshire. Malcolm finished off his rival at Lumphanan near Aberdeen on 15 August 1057: a verse in the twelfth-century *Chronicle of Melrose* states that, 'in his reign there were productive seasons. But Duncan's son, named Malcolm, cut him off by a cruel death . . .' Seven months later, Macbeth's stepson, Lulach, who seems to have reigned briefly following the demise of his stepfather, was also slain by Malcolm: the verse chronicle records that, 'the unfortunate Lulach was king for three months [sic]: he fell by the arms of the same Malcolm. The man met his fate at Essie, in Strathbogie; thus, alas! through lack of caution, the hapless king perished'. A stone called Lulach's Stone marks the supposed site of the battle.[9] Such, at least, is the traditional interpretation of the events of 1054 to 1058, although another view, championed by Benjamin T. Hudson and based on a close reading of the enigmatic eleventh-century text known as the *Prophecy of Berchán* is gaining acceptance. On this view, it was Macbeth rather than Malcolm who was victorious at Lumphanan: Berchán claims that Macbeth was mortally wounded but died at Scone on the day after the battle. Hudson has also pointed to the fact that it was Lulach rather than Malcolm who succeeded Macbeth.[10]

Whichever view is taken, there is no doubt that Malcolm III dealt the Cenél Loairn a terrible blow with the slaying of Macbeth and Lulach – but it would appear that he was not entirely successful in exterminating either the dynasty or all of his potential rivals. The *Anglo-Saxon Chronicle* records that in 1078, 'King

7 Cowan, 'Historical MacBeth', 134.
8 *The Historical Collections of Walter of Coventry*, ed. W. Stubbs [Walter of Coventry] (2 vols. London, 1872–73), ii, 206; trans. *SAEC*, 330 n 1; the chronicler is referring to the challenges mounted by the MacWilliam kindred.
9 *ES*, i, 592–3, 600–4.
10 See Hudson, *Kings of Celtic Scotland*, 143–5, and *idem, The Prophecy of Berchán: Irish and Scottish High-Kings of the Early Middle Ages* (Westport, Conn., and London, 1996), 91 and 226.

Malcolm captured Máel-slaehta's [Máelsnechtai's] mother . . . and all his best
men, and all his treasures and his cattle, and he himself escaped with
difficulty'.[11] The individual in question, Máelsnechtai, was Lulach's son,
who was described in Irish Annals as 'king of Moray'. Although the circumstances that led up to this raid are unknown, it seems clear enough that Malcolm
III had been less than successful in eliminating all the members of Lulach's
kindred after the latter's demise in March of 1058. Indeed, Máelsnechtai himself
lived until 1085, when his *obit* appeared in Irish annals, where he is said to have
'happily ended his life' along with several other clerics.[12] These two brief
mentions of Máelsnechtai in contemporary chronicles raise many questions
about his position and status during Malcolm's reign. The reference to him as
'king of Moray' has inevitably led to the view that either the dynasty of Macbeth
and Lulach remained potent in the north some two decades after their
respective deaths, or else that Máelsnechtai acted as some sort of sub-king
in the region – perhaps, initially, he was permitted to act as *mormaer* under
Malcolm. On this view, it is possible that Máelsnechtai rose against Malcolm in
1078, and that Malcolm's expedition – the first of many that Scottish kings
would undertake in reaction to uprisings in the remoter regions of their realm –
represented an attempt to bring a recalcitrant *mormaer* and potential dynastic
rival to heel. On the other hand, it is far from clear why Malcolm would have
tolerated a potentially dangerous rival in this large, turbulent region, or why he
did not dispose of Máelsnechtai as he had disposed of Macbeth and Lulach –
although the events of 1078 suggest that he certainly tried, and that he was
successful, to a point, in subduing Máelsnechtai's supporters. In fact, it is even
possible that Malcolm did manage to tame Máelsnechtai: the inclusion of his *obit*
among those of clerics may be taken to indicate that Malcolm had forced him
into religious retirement.[13] Considering the extent of Malcolm's power by the
1070s and 1080s, it seems difficult to avoid the conclusion that, at the very least,
Máelsnechtai must have come to some agreement with the slayer of his father.[14]

11 *The Anglo-Saxon Chronicle*, ed. and trans. M. Swanton [*ASC*] (London, 1996), 213
(1078); *ES*, ii, 46.
12 *AU* (MacAirt), 519.
13 Máelsnechtai is mentioned as a donor to the Celtic monastery at Old Deer,
Aberdeenshire: see K. Jackson, *The Gaelic Notes in the Book of Deer* (Cambridge,
1972), 33–4, 42, 52–3.
14 See Grant, 'Province of Ross,' 102–3; A. Woolf, 'The 'Moray Question' and the
Kingship of Alba in the Tenth and Eleventh Centuries', *SHR* lxxix (2000), 145–64,
makes the novel and controversial suggestion that 'the kingdom of Muréb emerged
as Máel Coluim Cenn Mór's solution to the problem, since it legitimized the
dynasty's monopoly of the kingship of Alba whilst allowing Máel Snechta to retain
a royal title, albeit one which admitted more restricted ambitions' (p. 164). Other
scholars see the region as a distinct regnal entity from an earlier date: see, e.g.,
Duffy, 'Ireland and Scotland 1014–1169', 349–51.

Malcolm's campaign against Máelsnechtai in 1078 is not the only indication of internal dissent during his reign. It may be that the events of 1078 are somehow linked to another mysterious episode of 1085. In that year, according to Irish annals, 'Donald, Malcolm's son, king of Scotland . . . ended his life unhappily'.[15] Both the identity and the status of this individual are open to question. He may have been an otherwise unknown son of Malcolm III by his first wife, Ingibjorg of Orkney, and it has been suggested that he played some role in the government or administration of the north.[16] Similarly, the circumstances of his death are far from clear, but the wording of the annals – that he ended his life unhappily – suggests that his death occurred by mishap or else by violence.[17] It thus becomes tempting to connect the two events: could it be that the killing of Donald (whoever he was) represented vengeance for Malcolm's raid against Máelsnechtai in 1078?

Several medieval sources, including the twelfth-century Cistercian chronicler Ailred of Rievaulx and the fifteenth-century Scottish writer Walter Bower, preserve a story, ultimately derived, it seems, from an early and as yet unpublished version of Turgot's *Life of Margaret* that relates a conspiracy against Malcolm III by enemies unnamed. According to Bower, 'It was reported to him [Malcolm III] one day that a certain one of his chief nobles had arranged with his enemies to kill him'. The king, however, feigned ignorance of the plot, and, arranging during a hunt that he should be alone with the noble, shamed him into seeking forgiveness.[18] Is this episode somehow related to the other domestic disturbances hinted at in the 1070s and 1080s? Bower's editor thinks it at least possible that the unnamed enemies were members of the Moray dynasty or their supporters, which would square well with what little is known of the period and provide a potential link with the attack on Máelsnechtai in 1078 and the demise of Donald in 1085. Although no precise date is assigned to the event in Bower, its position in his chronicle would seem to suggest that it belongs to the early part of the reign – perhaps the first nine or ten years. If this dating is correct, it then becomes tempting to associate the unnamed enemies with the Moray dynasty, perhaps even Máelsnechtai himself.

So little is known of affairs in the north of Scotland in this period that no definitive answers are possible to the questions raised by these three enigmatic episodes from the reign of Malcolm III. But these tantalising references suggest that the political situation in the north was much more volatile than might otherwise be imagined, and hint at deep undercurrents of dissent beneath the surface of events during the long reign of Malcolm III. Although we need not

15 *AU* (MacAirt), 519.
16 See Robertson, *Early Kings*, i, 139 and n., and Grant, 'Province of Ross', 104–5.
17 See *ES*, ii, 47 n. 1.
18 *Scotichronicon*, iii, 30–35 and notes on 195.

necessarily agree with Skene that 'during a period of twenty-one years, Malcolm appears to have been engaged in constant attempts to reduce the northern districts',[19] ambiguous references like those in the *Anglo-Saxon Chronicle* and the *Irish Annals* emphasise the fact that the domestic affairs of Malcolm's reign remain largely neglected by historians in favour of the better-documented theme of Anglo-Scottish relations.

The death of Malcolm III and Edward, his eldest son by Margaret, in 1093 inaugurated a turbulent period characterised by struggles for the kingship that lasted until 1097. The contenders for the kingship were Malcolm's brother, Donald Bàn; Duncan, his eldest son by his first marriage to Ingibjorg; and Edgar, probably his eldest surviving son by Margaret. Donald succeeded in taking the kingship in 1093, only to be ousted in 1094 by Duncan, who was assisted in his bid for the royal office by the English king, William II (1087–1100). Duncan's reign lasted a mere six months, until he was slain and Donald, with help from Edgar's brother Edmund (described by an English chronicler as the only one of Margaret's sons who amounted to no good[20]) once again took the kingship.[21] Donald ruled until 1097 when Edgar, who, like Duncan, also had the backing of the English king, ousted him for good. Donald was captured, blinded, and imprisoned, and later chroniclers variously record his fate; one king-list states that Edgar killed him, while the near-contemporary William of Malmesbury says that Donald was killed by Edgar's younger brother David, with the aid of King William II of England.[22] The establishment of Edgar in the kingship in 1097 (most modern historians regard him as little more than a client-king of the English) marked the beginning of nearly 200 years of continuous rule by the descendants of Malcolm III and Margaret.[23]

For some twenty years after Edgar's succession nothing is heard of opposition to

---

19 Skene, *Highlanders*, i, 123–4.
20 William of Malmesbury, *Gesta Regum Anglorum. The History of the English Kings*, ed. and trans. R.A.B. Mynors, R.M. Thomson and M. Winterbottom (2 vols., *Oxford Medieval Texts*, Oxford, 1998), i, 727 [Book V, 400]: 'Edmund was the only son of Margaret who sank from this high standard [i.e. that of his brothers and sisters]: his uncle Donald's partner in crime, he cannot be held innocent of his brother's death, for he bargained that he should receive half the kingdom. Being taken, however, and imprisoned for life, he frankly repented, and on his deathbed gave instructions that his fetters should be buried with him, admitting that he was rightly punished for the crime of his brother's murder'.
21 *AU* (MacAirt), 529, state that Duncan 'was treacherously killed by his own brothers, i.e. by Domnall and Edmond' – for which read his uncle and his half-brother. The *Anglo-Saxon Chronicle* implicates Donald: *ASC*, 230 (1094).
22 William of Malmesbury, ed. Mynors *et al*, i, 727; see also *ES*, ii, 90 and n. 3, 100.
23 The sources for the events of 1093–97 are conveniently collected in *ES*, ii, 89–100; see also Duncan, *Scotland*, 121–6, and there is much of value for the period in W.E. Kapelle, *The Norman Conquest of the North: The Region and Its Transformation 1000–1135* (London, 1979).

the sons of Malcolm III. Since very little is known of the reign of Edgar (1097–1107), this may be due as much to the gaps in our knowledge as to a lack of opposition itself. It is not until midway through the reign of Edgar's brother and successor, Alexander I (1107–24), that the first hint of opposition occurs. In 1116 Irish annals state that 'Ladhmann son of Domnall, grandson of the king of Scotland, was killed by the men of Moray'.[24] It has been suggested that this Ladhmann (Lodmund) was the son of that Donald who perished in 1085, although this identification is not certain. Another suggestion would be that Lodmund was a son of Donald Bàn, Malcolm III's brother who had been deposed by Edgar in 1097.[25] This would accord not only with the description of him as the king of Scotland's grandson, but the Scandinavian origins of the name Lodmund also tie in nicely with Donald's links to the Western Isles,[26] a heavily Scandinavianised region. Alexander Grant has proposed that Donald may have been employed in the north during the reign of his brother, Malcolm III,[27] and if so then it is plausible that his son may have acted in a similar capacity during the reigns of Malcolm's successors. If nothing else, this brief entry shows that the situation in the north was far more complex than our sparse sources reveal, and that early twelfth-century Scotland was still home to disaffected and alienated elements.

Another instance of resistance, related only by the late medieval chroniclers Walter Bower and Andrew of Wyntoun, may be somehow related to the events of 1116. These sources give slightly differing accounts of what seems to be the same incident, in which King Alexander was attacked at Invergowrie near Dundee by what Bower calls 'ruffians of the Mearns and Moray'. In Bower's account, Alexander escapes, gathers a large army in southern Scotland, and then proceeds to campaign against his opponents. In Wyntoun's account Alexander chases his foes 'owre the Stokfurd into Ros' (perhaps the cattle ford of the Beauly river), where they are overtaken and slain. In both accounts the defeat of his opponents is used to explain the epithet of 'the Fers' (Fierce) accorded to Alexander, and Scone priory is said to have been founded in thanksgiving for the victory, but neither the precise date of the episode nor the names of the leaders of the 'ruffians' are supplied.[28] The

---

24 *AU* (MacAirt), 559.
25 Skene, *Highlanders*, i, 129–30.
26 John of Fordun, *Johannis de Fordun Chronica Gentis Scotorum*, ed. W.F. Skene [*Chron. Fordun*] (2 vols., Edinburgh, 1871–2) i, 188, where Donald is said to have fled to the Isles after the slaying of Duncan by Macbeth; the source is late, but Hudson, *Kings of Celtic Scotland*, 139, thinks this at least possible.
27 Grant, 'Province of Ross', 104.
28 Androw of Wyntoun, *Orygynale Cronykle of Scotland*, ed. D. Laing [*Orygynale Cronykle*] (3 vols., Edinburgh, 1872) iii, 174–5; Bower, *Scotichronicon*, iii, 104–7. See Roberts, *Lost Kingdoms*, 66, for the site of 'Stokfurd'; B.E. Crawford, *Earl & Mormaer: Norse-Pictis Relationships in Northern Scotland* (Rosemarkie, 1995), identifies two sites with this name in the north: map on p. 10.

reference to the foundation of Scone priory helps to pin down the chronology of the episode, however: though the exact date of its foundation is uncertain, historians generally place it between 1114 and 1120.[29] This in turn makes it very tempting to connect the events related by the Irish annals for 1116 with those described by Bower and Wyntoun, linked as they are by not only a coincidence of chronology but also by the apparent involvement of the men of Moray. On the other hand, exactly how the two accounts can be reconciled is difficult to know: the Irish annals make no mention of the Scottish king, while Bower and Wyntoun fail to name a Lodmund as having been involved in the events that they describe. If, as has been suggested, the Donald who was killed in 1085 was a regional governor of some sort in the north, then it might not be beyond the bounds of possibility to suggest that Lodmund held a similar position under Alexander I; perhaps he was slain in the ambush of Alexander at Invergowrie. Whether the killing of Lodmund in 1116 ought to be somehow connected to the attack upon King Alexander described by the later medieval chroniclers must remain an open question. Ultimately, the nature of opposition to Alexander's rule remains tantalisingly obscure; what is not in doubt is that the men of Moray had already emerged into the limelight as the inveterate opponents of the kings of Scots, a role they would frequently resume throughout the twelfth and early thirteenth centuries.

More tangible evidence of opposition to the sons of Malcolm and Margaret appears at the very outset of the long reign of Alexander's brother and successor, David I (1124–53). David was the youngest son of Malcolm and Margaret, already middle-aged when he succeeded to the kingship upon the death of his brother in 1124. Following the death of his parents in 1093, he (and his siblings) had been raised at the court of the Norman kings of England, William II and Henry I (1100–35). When David's sister, Matilda, married Henry I in 1100 his fortunes improved considerably; then, in 1113, King Henry married him to a wealthy English heiress, and David became an English earl. The English chronicler William of Malmesbury, in a famous passage, wrote of David that 'he had from boyhood been polished by familiar intercourse with the English, and rubbed off all the barbarian gaucherie of Scottish manners',[30] and David's long reign is noteworthy for the intensification of Anglo-Norman and European influences in Scotland.[31] Another characteristic of the reign, however, was the intensification of challenges – indeed, the first decade of David's reign, from 1124 until 1134, was marked by insurrections that required considerable

29 I.B. Cowan and D.E. Easson, *Medieval Religious Houses Scotland*, 2nd ed. (London, 1976), 97; G.W.S. Barrow, 'The Royal House and the Religious Orders,' in *The Kingdom of the Scots* (London, 1973), 171.

30 William of Malmesbury, ed. Mynors *et al*, i, 727 [Book v, 400].

31 See Barrow, *David I of Scotland, passim*. There is much of value on David I, particularly before he attained the kingship, in Kapelle, *Norman Conquest of the North*, 202–04, and in J. Green, 'David I and Henry I', *SHR* lxxv (1996), 1–19.

effort and resources to subdue. Arguably, it was not until the mid-1130s that David's position in the kingship was really secure, and even then he could still be challenged in the later years of his reign.

Shortly after the death of Alexander and the accession of David I in 1124, the Anglo-Norman chronicler Orderic Vitalis (whose reliability for Scottish affairs is uneven) recorded that 'Malcolm, a bastard son of Alexander, made a bid for his father's kingdom, and instigated two bitter wars against him'.[32] Orderic relates how David's forces defeated Malcolm and his supporters, but the timing of the insurrection, following as it did so closely upon David's succession to the kingship, is surely significant. Only six years later, David faced another uprising, this time from the combined forces of Angus, styled *comes Morafiae* or 'earl of Moray', and Malcolm, numbering five thousand men if Orderic's numbers can be trusted.[33] The king was absent in England and the task of meeting the invasion fell upon the shoulders of Edward, the son of Siward (probably the constable of Kings Alexander and David), who killed Angus and put his forces to flight. The fugitives were pursued into Moray, which was then conquered and its existence as an earldom suppressed.[34] Later tradition placed the battle at Stracathro in Angus.[35] The death of Angus and the defeat of the Moravians was noticed by Irish sources, with the *Annals of Ulster* recording, 'A battle between the men Scotland and the men of Moray in which four thousand of the men of Moray fell with their king . . . Aengus . . . a thousand, or a hundred, which is more accurate, of the men of Scotland fell'. The *Annals of Innisfallen* noted more laconically the 'slaughter of the men of Moray in Alba'.[36] The contemporary Cistercian chronicler Ailred of Rievaulx (an unashamed admirer) hailed David as 'a most invincible king, who had subdued to himself so many barbarous tribes, and who with little effort had triumphed over the men of Moray and of the Isles'.[37] The polarisation between Moray and Alba presented in these sources is noteworthy, and these entries make it clear that the defeat

32 *The Ecclesiastical History of Orderic Vitalis*, ed. and trans. M. Chibnall (6 vols., Oxford, 1968–80), iv, 276–7.

33 *Ecclesiastical History of Orderic Vitalis*, iv, 276.

34 *Ecclesiastical History of Orderic Vitalis*, iv, 276; Robert of Torigni, *Chronica Roberti de Torigneio*, in *Chronicles of the Reigns of Stephen, Henry II, and Richard I*, ed. R. Howlett [*Chron Stephen*] (4 vols., Rolls Series, London, 1884–89), iv, 118; trans. J. Stevenson, *Church Historians of England*, vol. iv pt. 2 (London, 1856), see 703 and n.1. On Edward 'son of Siward', see Sir A.C. Lawrie, *Early Scottish Charters prior to A.D. 1153* (Glasgow, 1905), nos. 36, 49, 91, 94, 105, 128, 134, 163, 230, 250, and p. 285; and Ritchie, *Normans in Scotland*, 161 and n. 2.

35 *Chron. Fordun*, i, 233; ii, 224.

36 *AU* (MacAirt), 579; *The Annals of Inisfallen (MS. Rawlinson B.503)*, ed. S. MacAirt [*AI*] (Dublin, 1951), 292–3.

37 Ailred's eulogy on David is preserved in Bower's *Scotichronicon*, iii, chapters 45–62, quotation at 154–55; see also *SAEC*, 230 n 1.

and slaughter of the Moray forces was an event of more than local importance, and impressed itself firmly upon the minds of contemporaries from Ireland to the Continent. In fact, the words of these annals foreshadow a recurrent theme in the history of Scotland in the twelfth century.

In 1134, the Scottish *Chronicle of Melrose* records, without providing any details, how Malcolm, who had been associated with Angus in the 1130 rising but had avoided the fate of his ally, was captured and imprisoned at Roxburgh.[38] Ailred of Rievaulx shed some further light on this event when he placed a speech in the mouth of Robert de Brus just before the battle of the Standard in 1138. In the course of his speech, de Brus reminds David I of the campaign against Malcolm and the assistance that Robert and his Anglo-Norman knights provided to the Scottish king:

> Remember when in a past year you demanded the aid of the English against Malcolm, the heir of his father's hatred and persecution, how joyful, how eager, how willing to help, how ready for the danger came Walter Espec and very many other nobles of the English to meet you at Carlisle; how many ships they prepared, how they made war, with what forces they made defence; how they terrified all your enemies, until they took Malcolm himself, surrendered to them; taken, they bound him; and delivered him over bound. So did fear of us while binding his limbs bind still more the courage of the Scots, and by quenching all hope of success, remove the presumption to rebel.[39]

Even making allowances for Ailred's (or Robert's) rhetoric, this sounds like a major military campaign, complete with a naval force, and it would probably be unwise to dismiss the threat that Malcolm posed to David in the early years of his reign. The removal of Malcolm from the scene seems to have ushered in a more stable time, and for the remainder of David's reign there is little mention of any opposition from this quarter. However, toward the end of his reign there occurred one of the more bizarre episodes in all of medieval Scottish history: the uprising of Bishop Wimund of the Isles.

Our most important source of information for Wimund and his activities is the *Historia Rerum Anglicarum* of the late twelfth-century English chronicler William of Newburgh. William was well informed on northern affairs, and, more importantly, he tells us that he was an eyewitness, having interviewed Bishop

---

38 *The Chronicle of Melrose from the Cottonian Manuscript, Faustina B. IX in the British Museum. A Complete and Full Size Facsimile in Collotype*, with an introduction by A.O. Anderson and M.O. Anderson and an index by W.C. Dickinson [*Chron. Melrose*] (London, 1936), 33 (1134); trans. *ES*, ii, 183; see also *Ecclesiastical History of Orderic Vitalis*, iv, 276.

39 Ailred of Rievaulx, *De Standardo*, in *Chron .Stephen*, iii, 193; trans. *SAEC*, 193–94 (translation revised by the author).

Wimund: 'Him indeed I have often seen afterwards at our Byland, and have learned his most insolent actions'.[40] What were these 'insolent actions'? According to William of Newburgh, Wimund was born in an obscure region of England. After training as a clerk and copyist, he became a monk at the abbey of Furness in Lancashire, and from there was sent to the Isle of Man, where he was chosen bishop because of his charismatic appeal. It was now that he 'feigned himself to be the son of the earl of Moray, and that he was deprived of the inheritance of his fathers by the king of Scotland'. Armed with his charisma and this story of disinheritance, Wimund soon acquired a substantial following with which he began to attack the territories of the Scottish king. William tells us that he boldly invaded Scotland, avoiding battle with the royal army but utilising guerilla tactics to harass his foe. Eventually the king of Scots was forced to come to terms with Wimund, and ceded to him territory around Furness in Cumbria. This agreement seems to have checked Wimund's raiding, but, Newburgh tells us, he became accustomed to living like a king and soon alienated some of his followers. His actions so enraged some of his people that they laid a trap for the warrior-bishop, seized and bound him, then proceeded to castrate him and put out his eyes, 'for the sake of the kingdom of Scotland, not for that of Heaven'. Following his mutilation, Wimund was sent to the Cistercian monastery of Byland in Yorkshire, where he lived until his death, and where he became known to William of Newburgh. But despite his mutilation and monastic retirement, William says that Wimund boasted that 'had he only the eye of a sparrow, his enemies should have little occasion to rejoice in what they had done to him'.

William of Newburgh's account, detailed as it is, still leaves many questions unanswered, and brief mentions of Wimund in other sources serve only to corroborate his existence without providing much more in the way of details about his career. William, for instance, does not provide any specific dates for Wimund's activities, but the positioning of these events in the chronicle suggests that they belong late in the reign of David I. This view is borne out by mentions of Wimund in other chroniclers and documents, and it can be deduced that he was active in the 1140s, being deposed around 1148.[41] The date of his death is unknown although he seems to have been dead by about 1180.[42]

---

40 William of Newburgh, *Historia Rerum Anglicarum*, in *Chron. Stephen*, i, 73–6; a good, recent translation is *The History of English Affairs*, trans. P.G. Walsh and M.J. Kennedy (Warminster, 1988), 103–7.

41 On Wimund, see R.A. McDonald, 'Monk, Bishop, Imposter, Pretender: The Place of Wimund in Twelfth-Century Scotland', *Transactions of the Gaelic Society of Inverness* lxviii (1992–94), 247–70.

42 A document of c. 1180 seems to indicate that Wimund was dead by that time: *Historical Manuscripts Commission: Tenth Report, Appendix, Part IV. The Manuscripts of the Earl of Westmorland, Captain Stewart, Lord Stafford, Lord Muncaster, and Others* (London, 1885), 323.

By the time King David died at Carlisle in 1153, his own son, Earl Henry, had predeceased him. The kingship thus passed to David's twelve-year-old grandson, Malcolm. Sandwiched between the long and memorable reigns of his grandfather David I and his brother, William I (the Lion), it is sometimes easy to overlook Malcolm IV's short reign (1153–65), but it was hardly uneventful. Although Malcolm is usually regarded as having made many concessions to his powerful Angevin neighbour, Henry II of England (1154–89), he was also responsible for consolidating many of his grandfather's innovations and for expanding royal authority. The most prominent characteristic of the reign, however, was without question domestic unrest, for the number of serious challenges that Malcolm faced was out of all proportion to his short tenure of the kingship.[43]

Within months of David's death and Malcolm's succession, Somerled MacGillabrigte, the ruler of Argyll and Kintyre, joined forces with the sons of the imprisoned Malcolm, and launched an insurrection against the new king. Perhaps fortunately for Malcolm IV, most of Somerled's attention over the next few years, from 1154 to 1156, was devoted to annexing the Isle of Man from his rivals, the Manx sea kings belonging to the dynasty of Godred Crovan (d. 1095) and establishing himself as king of the Isles. Even so, a Scottish chronicle lamented that this uprising 'perturbed and disquieted Scotland in great part'.[44] Then, in 1156, Donald, the son of Malcolm, was captured at Whithorn and imprisoned with his father at Roxburgh. His fate is not known, but from 1156 he disappears from the historical record. If the capture and imprisonment of Donald checked the uprising, there is no clear evidence of it until 1160, however, when a Scottish document refers to a treaty between Somerled and the Scottish king.[45] At this point Somerled, too, disappears from view and his activities for the next four years are unknown.

Perhaps related to these events of the 1150s, the *Chronicle of Holyrood* recorded an interesting episode in 1154, when 'Arthur, who intended to betray king Malcolm, perished in [single] combat [duello] on the third day before the Kalends of March [27 Feb]'; another set of annals adds the name of 'Ness of Calatria [Nesius de Kaletirio]' as another conspirator.[46] Precisely who these men were – Calatria, or Callendar, near Stirling, was the region between Carron and Avon[47] – has yet to be determined. One or both may have been native

---

43 The best account of Malcolm's reign remains the introduction to Barrow's edition of his acts: *Acts of Malcolm IV*, 3–26.

44 *Chron. Holyrood*, 124–5 (1153); *ES*, ii, 224.

45 *Acts of Malcolm IV*, no. 175.

46 *Chron. Holyrood* 125–26 (1154); *ES*, ii, 224; see also *Acts of Malcolm IV*, 8 and n. 2, 3. A 'Dufoter of Calateria' witnessed a grant to Glasgow cathedral in about 1136: *The Charters of David I: The Written Acts of David I King of Scots 1124–53 and of his son Henry Earl of Northumberland 1139–52*, ed. G.W.S. Barrow (Woodbridge, 1999), 81.

47 See Barrow, *Acts of Malcolm IV*, 8, and 40.

landholders in the region of Stirling who threw in their lot with Somerled and the sons of Malcolm in 1153: could it be that they intended to betray the king to Somerled and his allies?[48] On balance, more evidence is required before we may connect this reference with the uprising of 1153, but whoever these men were, and whatever the motivation behind their actions, this was evidently a case of treason tried by battle,[49] and, if nothing else, provides a tantalising hint of domestic disaffection in twelfth-century Scotland.

In 1157 there occured an episode that has often been regarded as somehow connected with the ongoing insurrection of 1153–60. The *Chronicle of Holyrood* tells how 'Malcolm MacHeth was reconciled with the king of Scots'. This Malcolm, whoever he was, was subsequently made earl of Ross, for King Malcolm addressed a document to him between 1160 and 1162, and when he died in 1168 he was accorded this title in his *obit*. Historians, who have long assumed that Malcolm MacHeth is identical with the Malcolm who is on the record as causing trouble for David I between 1124 and 1134, have been inclined to view his reconciliation with the king in the context of the capture of (as is supposed) his son Donald in 1156 and the collapse of the 1153 insurrection: I have argued elsewhere that, following the incarceration of Donald, Malcolm might have come to some sort of agreement with the king, whereby he was given the earldom of Ross in exchange for abandoning whatever claims underlay his animosity toward the kings of Scots.[50] It is, however, by no means certain that Malcolm MacHeth is the same individual as that Malcolm who was incarcerated in 1134, and so the exact meaning and significance of the events of 1157 remain cloudy; the problem of MacHeth and his identity is considered in greater detail in the next chapter.

In 1160, the same year as the treaty between Somerled and the king, and

---

48 It is interesting to note that a 'Master Arthur' witnessed two of Malcolm IV's charters in about 1160 and 1161 – *Acts of Malcolm IV*, no.131, 197. The name might be a Brittonic one, but it might just as easily have been brought to Scotland by Anglo-Normans familiar with Geoffrey of Monmouth's famous *History of the Kings of Britain*.

49 There is another reference to trial by battle in a Scottish context in a charter of King William which, in 1196 or 1197, freed the burgesses of Inverness from having to engage in trial by combat: Barrow, *Acts of William I*, no. 388. For the practice in a Scottish context see *Regiam Majestatem and Quoniam Attachiamenta*, ed. Lord Cooper (Edinburgh, 1947), 35–7 and 250–52; and in general, see R. Bartlett, *Trial by Fire and Water: The Medieval Judicial Ordeal* (Oxford, 1986), esp. chapter 6. Trial by battle was commonly used in cases of treason, and trial by ordeal in general seems to have been introduced to the Celtic regions of Britain by part of the wider process of Anglo-French penetration: Bartlett, *ibid*, 47–8. On this topic, see also D.M. Walker, *A Legal History of Scotland* (Edinburgh, 1988), i, 269–73, 283–94, who suggests that trial by battle was not very common in Scotland.

50 McDonald, 'Treachery in the Remotest Territories', 174–5.

perhaps somehow related to it, there occurred one of the most interesting and also most puzzling episodes in the history of opposition to the Scottish kings: the so-called 'Revolt of the Earls'. In 1159, the young Malcolm IV had accompanied King Henry II of England to Toulouse, in the hope of winning his spurs. Upon his return home, in 1160, he received a decidedly unfriendly reception from some of his native magnates when he was besieged at Perth. These events are known first and foremost from the two Scottish chronicles of Melrose and Holyrood. The *Chronicle of Melrose* relates that:

> In the year 1160, Malcolm, the king of Scots, came from the army at Toulouse. And when [Malcolm] had come to the city that is called Perth, Earl Ferteth and five other earls (being enraged against the king because he had gone to Toulouse) besieged the city, and wished to take the king prisoner; but their presumption did not at all prevail.

The chronicle goes on to relate how 'King Malcolm went three times with a great army into Galloway; and at last subdued them'.[51] The *Chronicle of Holyrood* also describes three campaigns against the Gallovidians, adding, immediately thereafter, that 'Fergus, the *princeps* [chief man] of Galloway, received the habit of a canon in the church of Holyrood at Edinburgh'.[52] The same source records the death of Fergus in 1161. There can be little doubt that Fergus was forced to abdicate as a result of the military campaigns of 1160 and that he ended his days as a canon of Holyrood, but whether or not there is a causal connection between the events at Perth and the military campaigns in Galloway is more problematic and is further examined in Chapter 2.

Not long after the revolt of the earls, the campaigns against Galloway, and the death of Fergus, the Moravians again appear in the record. The Holyrood chronicle cryptically recorded, under the year 1163, how 'King Malcolm moved the men of Moray' (*rex Malcolmus Murevienses transtulit*).[53] This statement was expanded upon by *Gesta Annalia* ('Yearly Deeds') appended to the chronicle of John of Fordun but not authored by him, which described how the 'rebel nation of the Moravienses . . . would, for neither prayers nor bribes, neither treaties nor oaths, leave off their disloyal ways, or their ravages among their fellow countrymen'; we are then told how King Malcolm raised an army and removed the inhabitants of Moray from that province, 'so that not even one native of that land abode there; and he installed therein his own peaceful people'.[54] This

---

51 *Chron. Melrose*, 36 (1160); *ES*, ii, 244–5.

52 *Chron. Holyrood*, 137 (1160).

53 *Chron. Holyrood*, 142 (1163).

54 *Chron. Fordun*, i, 256–7; ii, 251–2. *Gesta Annalia* is now known to represent two or possibly three Scottish histories that predate Fordun and that were appended to his chronicle at a late date; the earliest of these may have been composed by 1285: see Broun, 'A New Look at *Gesta Annalia*', 9–30.

enigmatic episode remains puzzling, and scholars have long sought the means to explain it. The fact that *Gesta Annalia* is now known to represent a source (actually several different sources) that predate Fordun means that this account may preserve an independent tradition, and should not be dismissed. The vagueness of the terminology also raises problems: the passage might refer to a transfer of the bishopric of Moray, a translation of martyrs' relics, or a relocation of the natives of the region.[55] Although it need not be agreed that this represents a twelfth-century highland clearance,[56] the statement in *Gesta Annalia* need not be dismissed out of hand, either. Indeed, the passage may well be related to the ongoing colonisation of Moray by King Malcolm IV, in which case an otherwise unknown insurrection remains a possibility. It may be no coincidence that the king gifted Innes and Nether Urquhart to Berowald, a Flemish colonist, around Christmas 1160, part of the long and drawn-out process by which royal authority was consolidated in the north, and it may well be significant that *Gesta Annalia* also mentioned an otherwise unrecorded ravaging of the land by the Moravians in 1161.[57] Whether these two events from 1160 and 1161 have any connection with the mysterious episode of 1163 cannot be determined with certainty, but taken altogether the indications are that Moray continued to be troubled into the second half of the twelfth century.

In 1164, Somerled, who disappears from the historical record following the events of 1160, reappears in dramatic style. Various contemporary chronicles and annals record how, having gathered a massive fleet of some 160 ships and filled them with warriors from the Hebrides, Kintyre, and Dublin, Somerled invaded the Scottish kingdom, landing on the shores of the Clyde near Renfrew. A clerk at the cathedral of Glasgow, who was an eyewitness to the invasion, composed, sometime not long afterwards, a Latin poem (the *Carmen de Morte Sumerledi*) that described the events of 1164:

> Gardens, fields and plough-lands were laid waste and destroyed;
> The gentle, menaced by barbarous hands, were overwhelmed.
> Wounded, Glasgow's people fled the blows of two-edged swords.[58]

Although later tradition asserted that Somerled was assassinated by one of his own men, the contemporary sources tell a different story. The *Carmen* recorded

---

55 *Chron. Holyrood*, 142–3 n. 2; Duncan, *Scotland*, 191.

56 R.L. MacKay, *The Clan Mackay* (Wolverhampton, 1977), 6.

57 *Acts of Malcolm IV*, no. 175; *Chron. Fordun*, i, 256; ii, 251. See also D.P. Kirby, 'Moray in the Twelfth Century', in P. McNeill and R. Nicholson, eds., *An Historical Atlas of Scotland c.400–c.1600* (St. Andrews, 1975), 49.

58 'Carmen de Morte Sumerledi', in Symeon of Durham, *Symeonis Monachi Opera Omnia*, ed. T. Arnold (2 vols., London, 1882–85), ii, 386–88; translated in *The Triumph Tree: Scotland's Earliest Poetry AD 550–1350*, ed. T.O. Clancy (Edinburgh, 1998), 212–4.

the demise of Somerled and his army at the hands of what appears to have been a hastily summoned local militia, aided, of course, by the supernatural powers of St Kentigern:

> The deadly leader, Somerled, died. In the first great clash of arms
> He fell, wounded by a spear and cut down by the sword.
> His son, too, the raging sea consumed
> And with him many thousands of wounded men in flight.[59]

Somerled's demise removed from the scene the man who must surely be counted as one of the king's most formidable opponents, as well as one who possessed strong connections to other rivals like Fergus of Galloway and Malcolm 'MacHeth'.

For his part, Malcolm IV was forced to contend with significant domestic opposition from the very beginning to the very conclusion of his reign. It began with the rising of Somerled and his nephews in 1153, and it was not long after Somerled's invasion of the Clyde valley in 1164 that Malcolm's physical condition began to deteriorate, leading to his premature death in 1165. Between these events there occurred the 'revolt of the earls' in 1160, several campaigns against the Gallovidians in 1160–61, and the retirement of Fergus, Lord of Galloway, not to mention whatever events underlay the cryptic remark of the Holyrood chronicle in 1163 about the transfer of the men of Moray. Malcolm has sometimes been regarded as a weak and perhaps pathetic king, yet it no doubt says much that he was able to weather these considerable challenges; indeed, even though he died at the premature age of twenty-five, he saw two of the most powerful and formidable rulers on the Scottish periphery – Fergus of Galloway and Somerled of Argyll – into their graves before his own death. It is fitting, then, that the Irish *Annals of Ulster*, recording the death of Malcolm, should describe him as 'Ceann Mór' (Great Chief), suggesting that contemporary estimations of his kingship may have been considerably more favourable than some modern ones.[60] Malcolm's evident mettle in the face of rivals like Fergus and Somerled may have been an important factor in the success of the dynasty that he represented.

The death of Malcolm IV without children (to later generations he was 'Malcolm the Maiden') brought his twenty-two-year-old brother, William, to the Scottish kingship. Historians divide William's long reign (1165–1214) into four unequal periods. The first, spanning the decade from 1165 to 1174, is

---

59 *Ibid.*

60 *The Annals of Ulster*, ed. and trans. W.M. Hennessy and B. McCarthy [*AU* (Hennessy & McCarthy)] (4 vols., Dublin, 1887–1901), ii, 148; *ES*, ii, 261; see the remarks of Skene, *Celtic Scotland*, i, 474.

marked by peace and stability. The second, from 1174 until 1189, marks the low-point of the reign, beginning with the humiliating capture of William at Alnwick in 1174 and the subsequent Treaty of Falaise in 1175 that subjected Scotland to fifteen years of English overlordship. The third period, from 1189 until 1209, is regarded as the zenith of the reign, with the king at the height of his power. From 1209 this gave way to a phase when the king was ageing and frequently ill, and when events were often beyond either his control or the control of his son and heir, Alexander, as yet relatively inexperienced.[61] Like his brother's reign, William's was also noteworthy for the number of challenges that it endured. From the time of the king's capture at Alnwick in 1174 right down to his death in 1214, not a decade passed that was free of challenges, which must, therefore, be considered a significant but neglected theme of his reign.

One of the first regions to command royal attention in William's reign was Galloway, where the situation remained explosive even after the death of Fergus in 1161. Following Fergus's retirement to Holyrood abbey, Galloway was divided between his two sons, Uhtred and Gilbert, perhaps in a deliberate move by Malcolm IV to weaken and defuse the threat from the south-west.[62] Although both men were sons of Fergus, it is generally accepted that they had different mothers: Uhtred is referred to as a relative of Henry II of England, while Gilbert is not. Sometime between 1161 and 1164 King Malcolm promulgated a charter notifying Uhtred and Gilbert and other local dignitaries that he had given his peace to men going to or lodging in Galloway.[63] It is difficult to see why such protection was necessary unless the region remained unsettled, and this document provides a good indication of continued instability in the south-west.

It is thought that relations between the two brothers were less than congenial even before 1160,[64] but the partition of Fergus's territory seems to have created further resentment between them. The English chronicler William of New-burgh relates that:

---

61 Barrow, *Acts of William I*, 4–21, is the best outline of the reign yet written. See also D.D.R. Owen, *William the Lion, 1143–1214: Kingship and Culture* (East Linton, 1997), *passim*.

62 *Acts of Malcolm IV*, 13.

63 *Acts of Malcolm IV*, no. 230.

64 Walter Daniel, the biographer of Ailred of Rievaulx, describes the political situation in Galloway in the late 1150s when he relates a visit of Ailred to Galloway. Daniel tells how Ailred 'found the petty king of that land incensed against his sons, and the sons raging against the father and each other . . . The king of Scotland could not subdue, nor the bishop pacify their mutual hatreds, rancour and tyranny'. W. Danielis, *Vita Aelredi Abbatis Rievall*, ed. and trans. F. Powicke [*Vita Aelredi*] (London, 1950), 45–6.

Gilbert, the elder, grieved that he had been defrauded of the entirety of his father's right, and ever hated his brother in his heart, although fear of the king restrained an outburst of the wrath he had conceived.[65]

Despite the apparent rivalry between the two heirs of Fergus, the capture of King William by the English at Alnwick in 1174 presented the Gallovidians with a golden opportunity. Apparently setting aside their differences, Gilbert and Uhtred united and unleashed what some modern historians have rightly described as a reign of terror upon the region. Roger of Howden, an English chronicler who had first-hand knowledge of the situation in Galloway in the 1170s, tells how the two brothers

> ... expelled from Galloway all the bailiffs and guards whom the king of Scotland had set over them; and all the English and French whom they could seize they slew; and all the defences and castles which the king of Scotland had established in their land they besieged, captured and destroyed, and slew all whom they took with them.[66]

According to Howden, they then approached Henry II of England and offered their allegiance. Envoys were dispatched (one of them Roger of Howden himself), but before any progress was made, Gilbert had his brother killed and approached Henry II again.[67] Roger of Howden recounts the treachery of Gilbert:

> And Malcolm, son of Gilbert, Fergus's son, came and besieged the island of Dee in which abode Uhtred, brother of his father . . . and captured him, and sent his butchers, commanding them to put out his eyes and to emasculate him and cut out his tongue; and so it was done. And they went away, leaving him half-dead; and shortly after he ended his life.[68]

It is rather difficult to square the rivalry of the two sons of Fergus in the late 1150s and the killing of Uhtred by Gilbert with the statement of Howden to the

65 William of Newburgh in *Chron. Stephen*, i, 186–87; trans. in *SAEC*, 257 n 1.
66 *Gesta Regis Henrici Secundi Benedicti Abbatis*, ed. W. Stubbs [*Gesta Henrici Secundi*] (2 vols., Rolls Series, London, 1867), i, 67–8; trans. in *SAEC*, 256. It is now generally accepted that Roger of Howden was the author of the *Gesta Regis Henrici Secundi*, previously attributed to 'Benedict of Peterborough', as well as the *Chronica* for which he has always been known. The current state of knowledge on the authorship of these works is usefully summarised in Gillingham, 'Travels of Roger of Howden', 151–69. See also Corner, '*Gesta Regis Henrici Secundi* and *Chronica* of Roger, Parson of Howden', 126–44.
67 *Gesta Henrici Secundi*, i, 79–80, 126; trans. in *SAEC*, 257, 268.
68 *Gesta Henrici Secundi*, i, 79–80; trans. in *SAEC*, 257. Where Anderson read 'insula de' as 'island of [blank]', Oram, *Lordship of Galloway*, 95, reads 'Island of Dee', probably Threave Island.

effect that they had set aside their differences in 1174, and it may be that Gilbert was the prime mover of events: this, at any rate, is what the author of *Gesta Annalia* appended to Fordun's chronicle thought.[69] Whatever the case may have been, there is little doubt that Galloway had exploded into violence. The English chronicler William of Newburgh, who lost no opportunity to disparage the inhabitants of the Celtic regions of the British Isles, described the conflicts in Galloway in a memorable phrase as 'barbarians raging against barbarians' (*barbaris in barbaros savientibus*), and summed up events with the remark that 'the whole kingdom of Scotland was disturbed'.[70]

Following the death of Uhtred, Gilbert offered the English king 2000 marks of silver, 500 cows, and 500 swine to receive him and release him from his 'subservience' to the Scottish king. But when Henry II, who was described as the cousin of Uhtred, heard of his murder, he 'refused to make any terms with these Galwegians'. Instead, once the Scottish king had performed homage and fealty to Henry at York in August 1175, he was given leave to take an army into western Galloway and subdue Gilbert. There is some evidence of both campaigns by the Scottish king and the construction of fortifications in this period: a charter of King William dated between 1175 and 1177 was given at Dumfries, while another charter, probably dating from 1179, refers to the 'old fortification' there, suggesting the existence of a new castle site as well.[71] It was no doubt as a result of the efforts of the Scottish king that Gilbert went to the court of Henry II in October 1176 and made his peace with Henry, giving his son, Duncan, as a hostage.[72] Upon returning to Galloway, however, Gilbert is said to have 'commanded that all foreigners who held any holdings in Galloway through the king of Scotland should go into exile; and that those who refused to consent to this decree should undergo capital sentence'.[73] Coming as it does on the heels of Scottish campaigns in Galloway and his submission to Henry II, this statement is rather puzzling; it has been taken to mean that Henry II agreed that those expelled in 1174 should not be restored.[74] What is clear, however, is that Gilbert remained recalcitrant even after the events of 1176. Howden records, for example, that in the summer of 1184 King William disbanded an army that had mustered to campaign against Gilbert, 'who had wasted his land and slain his vassals, and yet would not make peace with him'.[75]

---

69 *Chron. Fordun*, i, 261.
70 William of Newburgh in *Chron. Stephen*, i, 186–87; trans in *SAEC*, 256, 257 n. 1; *Annals of the Reigns of Malcolm and William, Kings of Scotland AD 1153–1214*, compiled and ed. by Sir A.C. Lawrie [*Annals of Malcolm and William*] (Glasgow, 1910), 189–90.
71 *Acts of William I*, nos. 189, 216; see Duncan, *Scotland*, 183, n. 11 for further discussion.
72 *Gesta Henrici Secundi*, i, 126; trans. in *SAEC*, 268.
73 *Gesta Henrici Secundi*, i, 126; trans. in *SAEC*, 268.
74 Duncan, *Scotland*, 183.
75 *Gesta Henrici Secundi*, i, 313–14; trans. *SAEC*, 286.

The reign of William also saw a welter of new challenges from the far north, and the extension of royal authority in this troubled region has been regarded as 'the major domestic concern' of William's administration.[76] In 1179, King William and his brother Earl David (d. 1219) took a large army into Ross, presumably as a response to some threat. In conjunction with this campaign, the king built two new castles, at Redcastle, on the north shore of the Beauly Firth, and Dunskeath, at the mouth of the Cromarty Firth.[77] *Gesta Annalia* adds that this expedition was undertaken against a man named Donald MacWilliam – the first time, but by no means the last, that the name of MacWilliam enters the annals of resistance to the Scottish kings.[78] In 1181, a well-informed English chronicle recorded the arrival of Donald MacWilliam in Scotland, 'with a numerous armed host', adding that he 'had many a time made insidious incursions into that kingdom'.[79] While it is unclear whether the events of 1179 and 1181 are connected, this passage strongly suggests that the 1181 uprising was not the first, and that MacWilliam had been active prior to this. Whatever the case, the challenge was serious enough for King William, who was accompanying King Henry II in Normandy and England, to return to deal with it. Yet it is clear that the royal expeditions of 1179 and 1181 had done little to eliminate opposition in the north, and MacWilliam remained at large; the troubled situation in Galloway between 1174 and 1185 may well have prevented any serious campaigning against Donald. *Gesta Annalia* says that Donald 'for no little time held the whole of Moray', and a charter from between 1185 and 1190 indicates that the royal castle of 'Heryn' – probably Auldearn (Nairnshire) – had been betrayed to the king's enemies by Gillecolm the royal marischal, most likely in the course of the insurrection of 1179–87; there is also some evidence that the burgh was destroyed in the insurrection as well, and subsequently refounded at Nairn.[80] It is also interesting to note that the king's itinerary does not seem to have taken him to the north between the two campaigns of 1179 and 1187.[81] Taken altogether, this might show that Donald had managed to wrest a vast tract of territory in the north from the grasp of the Scottish king, whose hold on the region was tenuous at best; whether or not that was the case, it is clear that the MacWilliams commanded considerable support and represented a new force to be reckoned with by the Scottish monarchs.

Meanwhile, on 1 January 1185, Gilbert of Galloway, described as '*princeps*

76 K.J. Stringer, *Earl David of Huntingdon, 1152–1219: A Study in Anglo-Scottish History* (Edinburgh, 1985), 30.

77 *Chron. Melrose*, 42 (1179); trans. with identification of castle sites in *ES*, ii, 301–2 and n.6.

78 *Chron. Fordun*, i, 268; ii, 263.

79 *Gesta Henrici Secundi*, i, 277–8; trans. *SAEC*, 278.

80 *Acts of William I*, 291–2 and n.

81 See Barrow, *Acts of William I*, 96–8.

[chief man] of the Galwegians, the enemy of his lord the king of Scotland',[82] died. Roger of Howden relates that, immediately after Gilbert's death, Roland, the son of Uhtred,

> collected to his aid a numerous host of horse and foot, and invaded the land of Gilbert aforesaid; and slew all who would oppose him, and reduced all that land to himself. Moreover, he slew also all the most powerful and the richest men in all Galloway, and occupied their lands. And in them he built castles and very many fortresses, establishing his kingdom.

Other sources relate that Roland fought two battles in the course of 1185: one on 4 July against Gillepatrick and another on 30 September against Gillecoluim, in which a brother of Roland fell. Little is known of these individuals, who were obviously supporters of Gilbert. *Gesta Annalia* gives a brief account of Gillecoluim's activities as a freebooter who had been raiding in Lothian before attacking Galloway and setting himself up in Gilbert's lands.[83] In the context of these events it is interesting to note that extensive excavations at Whithorn in the 1980s revealed that a number of buildings had been destroyed by fire at the end of the twelfth century. Although the fire could have been accidental, the excavation report does not rule out the possibility of an otherwise undocumented raid, and it may be that this destruction of the late twelfth century should be linked to the turbulent events of the period 1175–85 in Galloway.[84]

Since Gilbert's son and heir, Duncan, was in the custody of the English king, Henry II instructed William of Scotland to subdue Roland, but Roland 'collected a numerous host of horse and foot and obstructed the entrances to Galloway and its roads to what extent he could, placing along the roads felled and half hewn trees'. Eventually, after another attempted campaign on the part of the Scottish king and no less than two diplomatic initiatives, Roland was brought into the peace of both the English and Scottish kings, and the consolidation of Galloway began in earnest. Roland of Galloway, who died in 1200, is certainly one of the more interesting figures in twelfth-century Scottish history; contemporary chroniclers regarded him as the avenger of his father, who successfully reclaimed his patrimony, while at least one modern historian has viewed Roland as a sort of quisling who sold out native Gallovidian traditions with his Anglo-Norman political affiliations and alignments.[85]

Galloway may have found a measure of stability under its native lord,

---

82 *Gesta Henrici Secundi*, i, 336.
83 See *Chron. Melrose*, 45 (1185); *ES*, ii, 309–10; and *Chron. Fordun*, i, 269; ii, 264–6.
84 P. Hill, *Whithorn & St Ninian: The Excavation of a Monastic Town, 1984–1991* (Stroud, 1997), 22, 211–16.
85 Brooke, *Wild Men and Holy Places*, 121–30, *passim*.

Roland, but it was a different story in the far north, where Donald MacWilliam remained at large. It was not until 1187 that he was finally hunted down and killed. Howden's detailed account of the campaign relates how a royal army, led by some of the Scottish earls and using Inverness as a base, set off in search of MacWilliam. The leaders of the army, however, soon fell to quarrelling among themselves, 'for certain of them loved the king not at all, and certain of them loved him'. Eventually 3000 'warlike youths' under the command of Roland, Lord of Galloway, were dispatched to seek out MacWilliam. Howden relates what happened next:

> And when they approached the army of the aforesaid MacWilliam, they made an attack upon them, and slew MacWilliam himself and many of his army; and the remainder they compelled to flee, and divided their spoils amongst them. And the head of MacWilliam aforesaid they cut off and carried it away with them, and presented it to the king of Scotland.[86]

The Holyrood chronicler placed the conflict in Ross, while the *Chronicle of Melrose* puts it at a moor called *Mam Garvia* near Moray (*Mam Garvia prope Muref*); the site has yet to be definitively identified but a good candidate is Strath Garve near Dingwall, which would seem to fit the description of the chronicles.[87]

Probably providing some important insight into how these events were regarded by the Scottish court,[88] Roger of Howden concluded his account of the death of Donald MacWilliam by commenting:

> And because of the evils he had wrought neither grief nor lamentation, neither even any sorrow was caused by his death. And no wonder: 'For the praise of the wicked is short, and the joy of the hypocrite as for a moment; if his pride ascend to the sky, and his head touch the clouds, like a dung heap shall he perish in the end.'[89]

Earlier, in December 1186, and possibly connected with the events of 1187, there occurred another episode of political violence. The *Chronicle of Holyrood* records how

> . . . the peace of the holy church was outraged at Coupar [abbey], by the violence of Malcolm, earl of Atholl; because Adam (surnamed also Donald's

---

86 *Gesta Regis Henrici*, ii, 7–9; see also *Chron. Melrose* (1187); *ES*, ii, 312–13.
87 *Chron. Melrose*, 45–6 (1187); *ES*, ii, 312–13; on the site of the battle, see G.W.S. Barrow, 'The reign of William the Lion, King of Scotland', in *Scotland and Its Neighbours in the Middle Ages*, 77.
88 See A.A.M. Duncan, 'Roger of Howden and Scotland, 1187–1201', in *Church Chronicle and Learning in Medieval and Renaissance Scotland*, 141.
89 *Gesta Henrici Secundi* ii, 7–9; trans. *SAEC*, 295.

son), who was the king's outlaw, was seized, and one of his associates – a nephew – was beheaded before the altar; and the rest, fifty-eight in number, were burned and killed in the abbot's dwelling.[90]

Although the identity of this Adam, the son of Donald, is not clear – the case can be made that he was either a son of Donald MacWilliam, or else that he was a son of the Donald who was captured at Whithorn in 1156 – there can be little doubt that the incident is related to the MacWilliam insurrection of 1181–87: was Adam leading a warband on a raid into the heartland of Scotia? Whatever the case, incineration was a not uncommon method of dispatching enemies, and the burning of Adam's followers (the wording of the chronicle seems to suggest that Adam himself was captured but not slain) at Coupar Angus in 1186 finds parallels both in the saga literature[91] and in historical episodes of political violence in Scotland between 1000 and 1300. Thus, the mormaer of Moray, Gillacomgain, was burned alive with fifty of his men in 1032, and, lest we regard the famous Cenél Loairn feud (Benjamin Hudson calls it a 'civil war'[92]) of which this episode was a part as belonging to a brutal and distant past, Adam, the third Scottish bishop of Caithness, was burned alive in his dwelling by angry farmers in 1222.[93]

Unfortunately for the Scottish king, the elimination of Donald MacWilliam did not spell the end to opposition from the far north, and in the 1190s a new and potentially even more dangerous opponent appeared on the scene: Harald Maddadsson, Earl of Orkney and Caithness. There is good reason to think that Earl Harald was involved in the 1187 insurrection of Donald MacWilliam, but, be that as it may, he certainly moved into the forefront of events in the 1190s. Roger of Howden, whose text provides the most detailed account of events, records how, in 1196, 'William, king of Scots, collected a large army and entered Moray to subdue Harald MacMadit [Maddadsson], who had occupied that land. But before the king entered Caithness Harald fled to his ships, refusing to enter into battle against the king'. King William then sent his army to Thurso, where one of earl Harald's castles was destroyed. The earl, 'seeing that the king would wholly destroy his land', submitted to William and promised to deliver hostages. As a result of this agreement, the king allowed Harald to hold half of Caithness, and the other half was given to a rival named Harald Ungi. Later in the year, Howden says,

90 *Chron Holyrood* 170; *ES*, ii, 311; see also *Acts of William I*, 11–12.
91 The burning of Njal forms the central episode of *Njal's Saga*, and *Orkneyinga Saga. The History of the Earls of Orkney*, trans. H. Palsson and P. Edwards [*OS*] (Harmondsworth, 1978), contains several instances of enemies being burned alive: see chapters 20, 78.
92 *Kings of Celtic Scotland*, 134, 138.
93 For the Moray feud, see *ES*, i, 551, 571; for the death of bishop Adam see below, pp. 44–45.

William returned to Nairn in Moray, but when Earl Harald failed to deliver the required hostages, including his son, Thorfinn, William 'took Harald with him to the castle of Maidens [Edinburgh] and held him in chains, until his men brought from Orkney his son Thorfinn, and giving him as hostage to the lord king, released Harald from the king's prison'. Harald then returned to the north and eliminated his rival in a brief but bitter struggle, following which, Howden says, he offered to buy back Caithness from William. The king responded positively to this suggestion, but only on the condition that Harald dismiss his wife, the daughter of Malcolm MacHeth, which the earl refused to do. Caithness was then given to Rognvald, son of Godfrey, the king of Man (Howden calls him the son of Somerled, although Professor Duncan has shown that this is an interlineation[94]), and administered by stewards, a detail which is supported by the early thirteenth-century *Orkneyinga Saga*.[95]

The Melrose chronicle describes a campaign against Earl Harald by the king and the earl's subsequent incarceration, but places these events in 1197;[96] it is, therefore, a matter of some dispute as to whether this account and that of Roger of Howden refer to the same year (and if so, which), or whether there were royal expeditions in both 1196 and 1197.[97] In fact, Professor Duncan has shown that 'the events of 1196 in Howden's account patently did not all happen in that year'.[98] A series of royal charters shows the king at Elgin in late July 1196 and again in early May and the fall of 1196 or 1197 (probably the latter), which suggests at least two northern expeditions, while the death of Harald Ungi is placed in 1198 by Icelandic annals.[99]

There is also confusion over the resolution of the situation. It seems that in 1201 Harald launched a bid to recover his mainland possessions, possibly at the instigation, or with the help, of King John of England (1199–1216), and in which the bishop of Caithness, John, was mutilated (either with or without Harald's consent, depending upon which source is to be believed). According to the *Orkneyinga Saga*, Harald then

> imposed severe punishments and heavy fines on all those he thought most guilty of treason against him and had all the men of Caithness swear oaths of

---

94 Until Professor Duncan's study, Howden's comment created confusion as to which ruler was granted Caithness. Sellar, 'Hebridean Sea Kings', 196–7, favoured the identification of a son of Somerled, but see now Duncan, 'Roger of Howden and Scotland', 155 n. 51.

95 Roger of Howden, *Chronica Magistri Rogeri de Houedene*, ed. T. Arnold [*Chronica*] (4 vols. London, 1868–71), iv, 10–12; *OS*, ch. 110–12.

96 *Chron. Melrose*, 49 (1197); *ES*, ii, 347–48.

97 Topping, 'Harald Maddadson', 117.

98 'Roger of Howden and Scotland', 143.

99 Charters in *Acts of William I*, nos. 388, 391, 392, 394, 395; see also *ES*, ii, 350 for Icelandic Annals; further discussion in Duncan, 'Roger of Howden and Scotland'.

allegiance to him whether they liked it or not. Then he took over all the property belonging to the stewards, who had now gone back to the king of Scots, and he settled in Caithness with a very large army.

In response, King William undertook yet another campaign to Caithness in an effort to bring Harald to heel; in 1202, it seems that the bishop of St Andrews was able to broker a deal by which, for a payment of £2000, Harald was restored to the earldom. His son, meanwhile, was less fortunate: he was blinded and castrated by the king, probably in 1201, for his father's intransigence. Harald himself died in 1206. He was reckoned by the author of the *Orkneyinga Saga* as one of the three most powerful earls, while a modern historian has regarded him as 'a great survivor',[100] surely an appropriate description.

From the death of Donald in 1187 until 1211, little is heard of the MacWilliams, although the activities of Earl Harald Maddadsson meant that the north was never far from King William's mind in the 1190s. Then, in 1211, the MacWilliams reappear, this time in the person of Guthred, a son of Donald MacWilliam, who is said to have landed in the north from Ireland. The fifteenth-century chronicler Walter Bower is our major source for Guthred's activities and the campaigns against him, which are known in considerable detail since Bower was relying on a contemporary source – possibly a detailed itinerary – for his information. We are told that:

> In 1211 William king of Scotland sent a huge army together with all the nobles of the kingdom into Ross against Guthred MacWilliam. The king himself followed when he was able to come . . . On the way he built two castles, laid waste pretty well all of Ross, and took or killed as many of the said Guthred's supporters as he could find. But Guthred himself always avoided the king's army, meanwhile laying ambushes for it whenever he could by night or day, and driving off booty from the lord king's land.[101]

In similar fashion to what happened at Mam Garvia nearly 25 years before, a force of 4000 soldiers was sent out from the royal army. This detachment skirmished with Guthred's forces and forced their retreat. At this point – it was by now late September – the campaigning season drew to a close. The royal army withdrew and King William appointed Malcolm earl of Fife as guardian of Moray. Guthred, however, soon besieged, captured, and destroyed one of the royal castles in Ross that King William had constructed earlier in the year, demonstrating that he had not yet been decisively defeated. The next year, in June 1212, the king's son, Alexander, set out for Ross with the royal army, with the king himself intending to follow when he was able; an English chronicle

---

100 *OS*, chapter 112; Cowan, 'Caithness in the Sagas', 41.
101 Bower, *Scotichronicon*, iv, 464–5.

adds the important detail that King John of England had supplied Brabantine mercenaries to the Scottish king to assist with the campaign.[102] But before King William arrived, Guthred was betrayed by his own followers, placed in chains, and taken to William Comyn, earl of Buchan, who was acting as guardian of Moray for the earl of Fife. Bower continues:

> The justiciar [Comyn], who wanted Guthred brought before the king alive, got as far as Kincardine. There when he learned the king's will, which was that he did not want to see him alive, they beheaded Guthred, dragged him along by the feet, and hung him up. He was already very close to death for he had refused food ever since his capture.[103]

An English chronicle omits mention of Guthred's betrayal, relating instead merely that he was seized by the army and hanged on the gallows.[104] Bower concludes his account of Guthred with the remark that, 'He trod underfoot everything he encountered and plagued many parts of the kingdom of Scotland', while the *Chronicle of Melrose* remarked on an 'incalculable slaughter of men in every district . . . universally' in that year. The chronicler went on to note that this was very evident in Scotland, where 'the king of Scotland left behind him the lifeless corpses of many men, when he pursued the son of MacWilliam, Godfrey, and destroyed those responsible for perverting him'.[105]

A year earlier, in 1210, there would appear to have been a conspiracy against King Willliam, although details remain elusive. The Melrose chronicle records how Thomas de Colville was imprisoned in Edinburgh castle 'because of the sedition which he had plotted against his king and lord', but he successfully ransomed himself in November and his death was recorded in 1219.[106] This individual is presumed to be identical with Thomas de Colville, nicknamed 'the Scot', who was a landholder in Galloway and a dependant of Duncan of Carrick; he witnessed a number of royal charters between about 1185 and 1210, and he is also on record in 1190 as constable of Dumfries castle.[107] As usual, the chronicle that records the event is frustratingly sparing of details, and there is nothing to suggest that Thomas was in any way connected with the MacHeths or MacWilliams. It is interesting to note, however, that even though he is said to have ransomed himself in November of 1210 and lived until 1219, Thomas

102 *Annales Sancti Edmundi* in *Memorials of St Edmund's Abbey*, ed. T. Arnold (3 vols., London, 1890–96), ii, 20; trans. in *SAEC*, 330.
103 Bower, *Scotichronicon*, iv, 466–7.
104 Walter of Coventry, ii, 206; trans. in *SAEC*, 330 n. 1.
105 *Chron. Melrose*, 55–6 at 56 (1211); *ES*, ii, 389.
106 *Chron. Melrose*, 54, 71 (1210, 1219); *ES*, ii, 383, 437.
107 Barrow, *Acts of William I*, nos. 263, 328, 367, 382, 400, 426, 427, 430, 447, 462, 486, 489 and n; *The Register of the Priory of St Bees*, ed. J. Wilson (Durham and London, 1915), no. 60; see also Barrow, *Anglo-Norman Era in Scottish History*, 31.

witnessed no further charters after 1210, suggesting, perhaps, a fall from grace.

The year 1214 saw the king, by now elderly and in failing health, back in the north yet again. This time, according to *Gesta Annalia*, he came in August to Moray, where he made a treaty of peace with the earl of Orkney/Caithness and took his daughter as a hostage.[108] Some historians have suspected that yet another insurrection lies behind this episode, although *Gesta Annalia* makes no mention of this; the more likely explanation is that this incident belongs in the broader context of relations between the earls of Orkney/Caithness and the Scottish kings, and the drawing in of the northern reaches of the Scottish mainland toward the centre of the kingdom after the death of Earl Harald in 1206.

Considering the scope of the challenges that William faced in the north, it is fitting that one of the last acts of his reign should have been played out there. *Gesta Annalia* describes William's return from Inverness in 1214 'by short stages, and in great bodily weakness' to Stirling, where he lingered for some time, 'failing in strength from day to day' until he died on 4 December.[109] As with his brother, Malcolm IV, one of the most fitting testimonials to William's reign is to be found in Irish annals, where he was described as William 'Garbh', 'the rough' or 'the harsh' – surely an appropriate designation for one of the most vigorous of the Canmore kings, who had pressed royal authority steadily northwards and triumphed, sometimes with difficulty, over several formidable Gaelic and Norse opponents.[110]

Yet William's energetic activity in the north had not succeeded entirely in quashing opposition, and the succession of his son Alexander, a boy of sixteen with little experience in government, opened a further Pandora's box of resistance in the north. Thus, soon after William's death and the succession of Alexander II (1214–49), the MacWilliams and MacHeths united and entered Moray. There can be little question that the rising was timed to coincide with the death of William and the succession of Alexander, and it thus bears close affinity to the insurrections of 1124–34 and 1153, which also occurred at critical moments in the succession. This time, the leaders were Donald Bàn, the son of MacWilliam, and Kenneth MacHeth, as well as an (unnamed) Irish prince. Perhaps the most significant aspect to this uprising was that, for the first time, the MacHeths and MacWilliams seem to have joined forces in their opposition to the kings of Scots. Nevertheless, they were met and defeated by one of the native dignitaries of the north, Ferchar Maccintsacairt ('son of the priest'), in mid-June, with a local levy but apparently without the royal army. The defeat

---

108 *Chron. Fordun*, i, 279; ii, 274.
109 *Chron. Fordun*, i, 279; ii, 274.
110 *Annals of Loch Cé*, ed. and trans. W.M. Hennessy [*ALC*] (2 vols., Rolls Series, London, 1871), i, 251; *ES*, ii, 398; see also Barrow, 'Reign of William', 73.

of the united force is described in dramatic fashion by the *Chronicle of Melrose*: 'Machentagar attacked them, and mightily overthrew the king's enemies; and he cut off their heads, and presented them as gifts to the new king [Alexander II] . . . And because of this, the lord king appointed him a new knight'.[111] This episode is doubly interesting, for 'it shows a Celtic leader in the north now on the side of the royal house descended from Malcolm and Margaret; and, because of his services, the Celtic [i.e. Gaelic] leader is made a . . . knight'.[112] This incident also reveals just how hopeless opposition to the Scottish kings was becoming by the early thirteenth century: when native northern magnates like Ferchar were supporting the royal house instead of resisting it, it could only be a matter of time before the opposition faltered completely. Twilight was falling on the MacHeth and MacWilliam resistance as a new order, loyal to the Scottish kings, took root in the north, and as Scottish royal authority pressed steadily northwards.

The events of 1215 may have been significant ones, but they did not mark an end to insurrections against the Scottish kings: the 1220s were a troubled decade, particularly in the north. A brief notice preserved in an inventory of documents from the late thirteenth century indicates that the king had been with his army at Inverness in 1221, where he had campaigned against a certain Donald MacNeil. This individual is otherwise unknown, although there seems no reason to doubt the episode. Given the fact that the king had been at Inverness, the base of operations for the royal army against Donald MacWilliam in 1187, it is possible that these events are somehow connected to the persistent MacWilliam uprisings that frequently wracked Moray and Ross, but, on the other hand, Alexander is known to have campaigned in Argyll and the Isles in 1221 and/or 1222 (for which see below), and it is also possible that the events of 1221 ought to be linked to these campaigns instead. When the king returned to Perth, fines were levied against those who absented themselves from the army.[113]

The next year, in 1222, a grisly scene was played out at Halkirk, a few miles south of Thurso in Caithness, where the Icelandic annals laconically recorded 'the burning of bishop Adam . . .'[114] The full story can be gathered from a variety of other texts. Adam, a Cistercian monk who had been abbot of Melrose before being appointed bishop of Caithness in 1213, had been at odds with his parishioners over his zealous levying of tithes (teinds) and strict enforcement of other rights of the

111 *Chron. Melrose*, 59–60 (1215); *ES*, ii, 403–4.
112 W.C. Dickinson, *Scotland from the Earliest Times to 1603*, 3rd ed., revised and edited by A.A.M. Duncan (Oxford, 1977), 74; see also McDonald, 'Ferchar Maccintsacairt', forthcoming.
113 *Acts of the Parliaments of Scotland*, ed. T. Thomson and C. Innes [*APS*] (11 vols., Edinburgh, 1814–75), i, 398 c. II.
114 *ES*, ii, 451–2 (Icelandic Annals, 1222).

church in Caithness. Although a settlement had been achieved in the presence of the king, once the bishop returned to his see and the king had departed for England, the parishioners are said to have risen against their bishop 'like wolves against the shepherd'. Following the murder of his aide, Adam was stripped of his vestments, stoned, wounded with an axe, and finally burned to death in his own dwelling. Some sources implicated the earl of Orkney/Caithness, John, the son of Earl Harald Maddadsson, saying that it was he who ordered or even carried out the killing, while other sources go out of their way to exonerate him. Whatever the truth of the matter, the result was predictable: the king gathered an army and marched north, where he imposed a harsh settlement on those who had participated in the killings: 'the king of Scots caused eighty men who had been present at the burning to have their hands and feet cut off, and many of them died'. According to some accounts, Earl John was forced into exile, where he 'roamed about the isles of the sea' before eventually submitting to Alexander II; the Scottish king, on the other hand, was held up by the Pope as an avenger of Christian blood and a champion of the Faith.[115] In fact, of course, the Scottish king was also interested in the consolidation of royal authority in the north of his realm, and the episode offers up a potent reminder of how the extension of royal and ecclesiastical authority often progressed in tandem.

The closing scenes of the MacWilliam drama also occurred in the 1220s, although the precise sequence of events proves difficult to reconstruct because of the nature of the source material. Appended to his account of events that took place in 1223, Bower tells how Gillescop MacWilliam and his sons and a certain Roderic appeared 'in the furthest limits of Scotland' until they were delivered into the king's hands and 'brought summarily to justice'.[116] Unfortuantely, this uprising receives no corroboration from other sources, and it remains doubtful whether it belongs to 1223 or, as seems more likely, to events that were played out later in the decade. In 1228, Bower tells how

> a certain Scot named Gillescop set fire to some wooden defensive works in Moray and killed a certain thief called Thomas de Thirlestane after attacking his castle unexpectedly during the night. Afterwards he burned a large part of Inverness, and about [the time of the feast of] the Nativity of the Blessed Mary he plundered some neighbouring lands belonging to the lord king.[117]

After journeying to the north himself, the king entrusted custody of the region to William Comyn, the earl of Buchan, and provided him with 'a large number

---

115 The incident is well documented. See *ES* ii, 449–52, including the notes; *SAEC*, 336–7; *Chron. Melrose*, 75–6; *Chron. Fordun*, i, 289–90, ii, 284–85, and the account from Flateyjarbok in *Icelandic Sagas*, ed. Dasent and Vigfusson, iii, 232–3.
116 *Scotichronicon*, v, 117.
117 *Scotichronicon*, v, 143.

of troops' to fulfill his mission.[118] It is not clear what happened next, but Bower relates that, in 1229, Gillescop and two of his sons were killed and their heads taken to the king.[119] Unfortunately it is not known whether Gillescop's death occurred as a result of a clash of arms between Comyn and MacWilliam, or whether Gillescop, like some of his unfortunate predecessors, was betrayed by his own men. It is curious that the Comyns were accorded such a prominent role in these events, while no mention is made of Ferchar Maccintsacairt's involvement: not only had he proved himself to be an enemy of the MacWilliams in 1215, but by the late 1220s (probably by 1226) he had also been made earl of Ross, and was surely a power to be reckoned with in the north. It is, on the whole, difficult to avoid the suspicion that Ferchar played some role in these events (which was perhaps suppressed by the pro-Comyn stance of the chronicler), but, as is the case with so many of the episodes under consideration here, we can do no more than speculate.

The *Chronicle of Lanercost*, of northern English provenance and well-informed on Scottish affairs, records a MacWilliam insurrection in 1230, when 'certain wicked men of the race of Mac-William; and his son; and one Roderic . . . raised up treachery in the remotest territories of Scotland'.[120] It is hard to know whether the chronicler is here relating yet another incident of MacWilliam insurrection, separate from the events described by Bower in 1228–29, or whether in fact we are dealing with the same events simply misplaced by a year. But while the precise sequence of events in the late 1220s may remain murky, the Lanercost chronicler, alone among our various sources, recorded one gruesome detail that marked the end of the MacWilliams as the inveterate opponents of the Scottish kings:

> the same Mac-William's daughter, who had not long left her mother's womb, innocent as she was, was put to death, in the burgh of Forfar, in view of the market-place, after a proclamation by the public crier: her head was struck against the column of the [market] cross, and her brains dashed out.[121]

There can be no doubt that the killing of the infant MacWilliam at Forfar in 1230 – exactly a century after the death of Angus of Moray at Stracathro – represents a watershed in Scottish history, marking not only the end of the

---

118 *Scotichronicon*, v, 143 and notes on 256; see also G.W.S. Barrow, 'Badenoch and Strathspey, 1130–1312. 1: Secular and Political', *Northern Scotland* viii (1988), 6.
119 *Scotichronicon*, v, 145.
120 *Chron. Lanercost*, 40–1; trans. in *ES*, ii, 471. See Gransden, *Historical Writing in England c.550–c.1307*, 487–8, 494–96 on the Lanercost chronicle, which incorporated a chronicle by a Franciscan friar named Richard of Durham in the late thirteenth century; not only was it based on earlier annals and other sources, but Richard may have been connected with the friary at Haddington, East Lothian.
121 *Chron. Lanercost*, 40–1; trans. *ES*, ii, 471.

dynastic challenges to the Scottish kings, but also the virtual completion of the programme whereby those same kings extended their authority into the far north.

If the north had been pacified – or nearly so – by 1230, other regions of Scotland remained to be fully tamed and integrated into the fold of the Scottish kingdom. First, there was Galloway. The succession of Roland and his consolidation in power as Lord of Galloway (1185–1200) following the death of Gilbert in 1185 seem to have stabilised the situation in that region and to have begun the undoing of the effects of the reign of terror of 1174–75; nevertheless, the region continued to maintain a reputation for instability and unrest into the early thirteenth century. Thus, in 1223, when the Cistercians of Vaudey abbey in Lincolnshire transferred some lands on the borders of Galloway and Carrick to Melrose abbey, it was because the lands were 'useless and dangerous to them, both on account of the absence of law and order, and by reason of the insidious attacks of a barbarous people'.[122]

Both Roland and his son and successor, Alan (1200–34), were well integrated within the Scottish kingdom, and although they retained much of their autonomy as semi-independent Lords of Galloway, they were also, as Keith Stringer's study of Alan has shown, staunch supporters of the Crown's policies, especially when their own interests were served at the same time.[123] It is noteworthy that it was none other than Roland of Galloway who defeated and slew Donald MacWilliam in 1187, and Thomas, Alan's brother, was active in maritime expeditions against MacWilliam bases in Ireland in 1212 and 1214.[124] In short, although Galloway was far from fully integrated in the early thirteenth century, processes of colonisation and acculturation were at work and were moving the traditionally semi-autonomous region closer toward the centre of the medieval Scottish kingdom. It was, however, military action that saw the final incorporation of Galloway in the mid-1230s.

In February 1234 Alan, son of Roland, the Lord of Galloway and Constable of Scotland, a man admired by even Scandinavian writers as 'the greatest warrior', died.[125] He left three daughters, who were considered legitimate under canon law, and a son, Thomas, who was not. Alan's inheritance was therefore partitioned among the co-heiresses, all of whom were married to English noblemen. According to the *Chronicle of Melrose*, our main source for events in Galloway in 1234–35, the Gallovidians petitioned King Alexander II to reject the partition and take over the lordship himself,

---

122 *Liber S. Marie de Melros* (2 vols., Edinburgh, 1837), i, no. 195; trans. in Barrow, *Anglo-Norman Era*, 32.
123 Stringer, 'Periphery and Core', 82–113.
124 *AU* (Hennessy & McCarthy), ii, 252, 256 (1212, 1214); *ES*, ii, 393, 395–6.
125 *ES*, ii, 464.

thus preserving its unity, but the king refused. The episode is interesting because it demonstrates how much headway had been made in the integration of Galloway in the sixty years since the great uprising of 1174. Then, the Gallovidians had expelled royal representatives and destroyed symbols of royal authority; now, they had turned to the Scottish monarch himself and requested that he should take over the lordship. Only when the petition was refused did what some historians have regarded as a separatist party move into the forefront. Its aim, as the English chronicler Matthew Paris put it, was to 'restore Galloway to the baseborn son of Alan [i.e. Thomas]'; while illegitimacy might prove an obstacle in the eyes of twelfth- and thirteenth-century canon lawyers, it was no barrier at all to succession in the contemporary Celtic world. Thomas himself had achieved considerable status within Alan's maritime empire. During his father's lifetime he had married a daughter of the Manx king, Ragnvald (1187–1229), and, as one historian put it, 'his parentage, his marriage to a Manx princess, and his part in his father's maritime ventures, had built up for him respect and goodwill in parts of the Hebrides, and . . . in Man as well as in Ireland'.[126] The network of Irish Sea connections built up by both Thomas and his father paid dividends in 1235, for Matthew Paris relates how 'many noble and bold men of the different regions of the western provinces', including Ireland and Man, rallied to Thomas's cause; Paris alone also records the involvement of Hugh de Lacy, earl of Ulster, who was Alan's father-in-law and whose role in these events has been linked to both his concern over control of the Galloway lands in Ulster as well as his own military activities in Tir Eogain.[127]

Violence soon broke out again in Galloway: in the words of the Melrose chronicler, 'the Galwegians became angry beyond measure and prepared themselves to resist. Moreover also they laid waste with sword and fire some of the lands of the lord king that were nearest them'.[128] Matthew Paris tells a grisly story that was no doubt calculated to impress the barbarity of Gallovidians upon his Anglo-Norman readers:

. . . that . . . they might more surely attain to their desire, they made an unheard-of covenant, inventing a kind of sorcery, in accord nevertheless with a certain abominable custom of their ancient forefathers. For all those barbarians, and their leaders and magistrates, shed blood from the precordial vein into a large vessel by blood-letting; and moreover stirred and mixed the blood after it was drawn; and afterwards they offered it, mixed, to one another in turn, and drank it as a sign that they were thenceforth bound in a hitherto

---

126 Brooke, *Wild Men and Holy Places*, 134.
127 Matthew Paris, *Chronica Majora*, ed. H.R. Luard [*Chron. Majora*] (7 vols., London, 1872–83), iii, 364–6; trans. *SAEC*, 341; Oram, *Lordship of Galloway*, 144.
128 *Chron. Melrose*, 83 (1234); *ES*, ii, 494–5.

indissoluble and as it were consanguineal covenant, and united in good fortune and ill even to the sacrifice of their lives.[129]

Here, Paris works simultaneously within two closely related literary traditions that were well-established by his day: the first portrayed the Gallovidians as barbarians and subjected them to ridicule, while the second was a broader literary phenomenon related to what John Gillingham has called 'English imperialism' that portrayed the various Celtic neighbours of the English as barbarians from the middle of the twelfth century onward.[130] Both of these traditions and their ramifications are considered in greater detail later in the book.

With the south-west in turmoil, the Scottish king summoned the royal army in 1235, and marched into Galloway. The *Chronicle of Melrose* tells how, at midsummer:

> . . . he [Alexander II] came to a place sufficiently fair to the eye; where, since the day was now spent, he proposed to fix his tents. But the Galwegians, knowing better the site of the place, after lurking the whole day in the mountains, now on the contrary gave battle to the king. The aforesaid place had given them great confidence; because it was full of marshes, covered over everywhere with grass and flowers; and in these [marshes] the king's army for the greater part had sunk.[131]

The day was only saved for the Scots when the earl of Ross, Ferchar Maccintsacairt, arrived on the scene in timely fashion with reinforcements and took the Gallovidians in the rear, 'making a great slaughter', and pursuing the shattered army into the woods and mountains. Thomas and one of his key supporters named Gilrod (possibly an Irishman but more likely a Carrick chieftain[132]) are said to have escaped to Ireland, while, on the day following the confrontation, the king, 'with his accustomed piety, granted peace to all who came to him. Therefore the Galwegians who had survived came to the king's peace, with ropes put around their necks'. Matthew Paris presents a rather different version of events, in which the king gives battle to the Gallovidians in the open, without any mention of intervention by the earl of Ross. Alexander's response is also less benevolent in Paris's account: those who were taken alive were put to death, but those who threw themselves on his mercy were

---

129 *Chron. Majora*, iii, 364–6; trans. *SAEC*, 341–2.
130 See Brooke, *Wild Men and Holy Places*, 116–20 for Galloway, and J. Gillingham, 'The Beginnings of English Imperialism', *Journal of Historical Sociology* v (1992), 392–409 (reprinted in *The English in the Twelfth Century*), on English attitudes toward the Celtic peoples in general.
131 *Chron. Melrose*, 84–5 (1235); *ES*, ii, 496.
132 Brooke, *Wild Men and Holy Places*, 136.

imprisoned and had their lands forfeited.[133] Some historians have seen in Ferchar's defeat of the Gallovidians in 1235 retribution for the 1187 killing of Donald MacWilliam by Roland of Galloway,[134] but such a view, although it might apply to the rank-and-file of the armies involved, seems to miss the point entirely. Ferchar and Roland had much in common: both had proven themselves to be enemies of the MacWilliams and supporters of the Scottish crown, and in the final analysis what links the events of 1187 and 1235 is not a Galloway-Ross feud, but rather the fact that, in each case, a native magnate on the side of the Scottish kings faced their enemies and crushed a potentially deadly insurrection in a remote region of the realm.

In the wake of the Gallovidian defeat, the king promptly departed Galloway, leaving Walter Comyn, earl of Menteith (the son of William Comyn, earl of Buchan, who subdued Guthred MacWilliam in 1211–12) in charge of bringing order to the region. Comyn's appointment to this task emphasises what one historian has regarded as the role of the Comyn family as 'the official 'trouble-shooters' of the Scottish monarchy in the first three decades of the thirteenth century'.[135]

At this point the Melrose chronicler tells how the royal army, or at least certain elements of it, went on a rampage:

> But after the king's departure, certain Scots, not masters of knighthood, but servants of wickedness, despoiled the abbeys of that land with so wicked and villainous madness that they even denuded of the frock in which he was wrapped a monk who had, at the point of death, been placed in the infirmary of Glenluce, and laid up on a hair-cloth. Also at Tongland, they killed the prior, with the sacrist, in the church.[136]

Since parts of the chronicle that describe the atrocities were modelled upon incidents that took place in 1216, it is difficult to know precisely what happened and how widespread was the devastation, but some scholars have argued that, since the attacks seem to have been directed toward monasteries patronised by the Lords of Galloway, there may have been a political element to these events (a point which is developed further in Chapter 2). Whatever the case may be, Thomas appears to have seized the moment to make yet another attempt at claiming the Lordship. An invasion was launched from Ireland, and, although our information is unclear, it seems that Gilrod was captured after a rout of Irish forces. Thomas himself was compelled to seek peace, apparently through the intervention of the bishop of Galloway and the abbot of Melrose.

133 *Chron. Melrose*, 84–5 (1235); *ES*, ii, 492–9; *Chron. Majora*, iii, 364–6; trans. in *SAEC*, 341–2.
134 Brooke, *Wild Men and Holy Places*, 136.
135 A. Young, *Robert the Bruce's Rivals: The Comyns, 1212–1314* (East Linton, 1997), 36.
136 *Chron. Melrose*, 84 (1235); trans. *ES*, ii, 497.

The *Chronicle of Melrose* relates that Thomas was detained in Edinburgh castle and then released, but this is only part of the story: the Lanercost chronicle tells how he was released into the custody of John Balliol, the husband of Alan's eldest daughter, and subsequently remained in captivity at Barnard castle in Northumberland 'till decrepit old age'. This was no exaggeration, since Thomas was still alive when King Alexander III died in March of 1286: on the very day that the king perished, his Council was discussing a petition to release Thomas from imprisonment. Evidently, however, Thomas endured a further decade of confinement, for in 1296, aged eighty-eight, he was cleaned up, shaven, given new clothes, released from captivity, and restored to his lands in Galloway, where he was no doubt intended by Edward I to serve as a counterbalance to Balliol loyalties in the southwest.[137] Though it is difficult to disagree with the frequent characterisations of the aged Thomas as a pathetic figure, there is also a certain irony in the fact that one of the last enemies of the Scottish kings managed to outlive the dynasty of Malcolm III and Margaret itself: by 1296 Thomas must indeed have seemed like a ghost from the past,[138] though it seems doubtful that the circumstances of his incarceration were much more than a distant memory by then. His cause ended in defeat and incarceration, but old Thomas of Galloway nevertheless stands as a potent symbol of the resistance faced by the Canmore kings across some two centuries of Scottish history.

Historians have always regarded the events of 1234–35 as significant, delineating as they do the incorporation of the last great Celtic province south of Ross into the Scottish kingdom. Yet even a dozen years later it was still possible for violence to flare up: when one of Alan's daughters, Christina, who had married William de Fortibus, died without children in 1246, half of her lands were transferred to the husband of Alan's eldest daughter, Roger de Quincy. This seems to have triggered yet another uprising in 1247, when Roger, who was alleged to have 'oppressed by tyranny the nobler vassals of that land more than was customary and otherwise than he ought', was besieged in one of his strongholds. Armed to the teeth, Roger fought his way out of the besieged stronghold and rode to the Scottish king, who 'punished the rebels and established the earl peacefully in his possessions'.[139]

---

137 *Chron. Lanercost*, 116–7, 177; *Calendar of Documents Relating to Scotland Preserved in Her Majesty's Public Record Office, London*, ed. J. Bain [*CDS*] (4 vols., Edinburgh, 1881–88), ii, nos. 728–9. See also R.D. Oram, 'Bruce, Balliol and the Lordship of Galloway: South-West Scotland and the Wars of Independence', *Transactions of the Dumfriesshire and Galloway Natural History and Antiquarian Society* [*TDGNHAS*], 3rd ser. lxvii (1992), 34.

138 G.W.S. Barrow, *Robert Bruce and the Community of the Realm of Scotland*, 3rd ed. (Edinburgh, 1988), 112.

139 *Chron. Majora*, iv, 653; trans. in *SAEC*, 358–9. See also Duncan, *Scotland*, 532, and Brooke, *Wild Men and Holy Places*, 140.

Like Galloway, Argyll and the Isles were home to a vigorous native dynasty that occasionally found itself at odds with the Scottish kings. Without question the most significant challenge occurred in 1164, when Somerled invaded the Scottish mainland only to perish at the head of a formidable army in the battle of Renfrew. It is difficult to see any of Somerled's descendants (commonly referred to as the MacSorleys) as the same kind of threat to the Scottish kings as either their progenitor or the likes of Donald MacWilliam, although this is not to say that they did not present their own, sometimes unique, problems for the Scottish monarchs even if invasions like that of 1164 and uprisings like those of 1181 or 1234–35 were rare. Thus, not only did internecine strife among the descendants of Somerled sometimes spill over into the Scottish kingdom, but some branches of the MacSorleys almost certainly aided and abetted the MacWilliams in the 1220s, and the efforts of Somerled's descendants to maintain their status and independence aggravated the Scottish kings and ultimately brought the Scottish and Norwegian monarchs to odds over the western seaboard.

In fact, the story of Somerled's descendants in the century after his death is largely the story of increasing Scottish aggression against the western seaboard rather than challenges launched by the Hebridean chieftains against the Scottish kings. Following the demise of Somerled in 1164, his insular and mainland kingdom was divided among his sons; perhaps inevitably, the result was intense internecine strife, and the internal history of the west in the later twelfth century is largely the history of the struggles among Somerled's sons and grandsons. In 1192, for instance, the *Chronicle of Man* describes a battle between Ranald and Angus, two of Somerled's sons, in which many men were slaughtered, while another conflict between Ranald and the men of Skye took place in 1209 according to Irish annals. Little wonder, then, that the Icelandic annals laconically record 'warfare in the Hebrides' under the year 1210.[140]

At first the Scottish response to this situation appears to have been largely reactive and defensive, as suggested by the construction of a new castle by King William between the Doon and the Ayr in 1197, strategically placed to control the western seaways.[141] The failure of the Scottish kings to capitalise on the opportunity presented by the demise of Somerled and the infighting among his sons might appear surprising, but the dominant feature of William's reign was his preoccupation with the north of England in the form of his endeavours to recover the earldom of Northumbria for the Scottish crown, and he seems to have demonstrated little interest in the western frontiers of his realm. With the

---

140 *Chron. Man*, f. 40 v (1192); *AU* (Hennessy & McCarthy), ii, 248 (1209); *ES* ii, 327, 378, 382 (1210).

141 *Chron. Melrose*, 49 (1197); *ES*, ii, 348; see Duncan, *Scotland*, 187, for strategic significance.

latter years of William's reign dominated by MacWilliam uprisings in the north, it was not until the 1220s that the Scottish monarchs began to take an active interest in the western seaboard, an interest that was no doubt due in large measure to the chronic disorder in the region. *Gesta Annalia* records that Alexander II raised an army in Lothian and Galloway and set sail for Argyll in 1221, only to be thwarted by adverse weather conditions. The same source relates that the next year, however,

> . . . he [King Alexander] led the army back into Argyll, for he was displeased with the natives for many reasons. The men of Argyll were frightened: some gave hostages and a great deal of money, and were taken back in peace; while others, who had more deeply offended against the king's will, forsook their estates and possessions and fled. But our lord king bestowed both the land and the goods of these men upon his followers, at will; and thus returned in peace with his men.[142]

The fifteenth-century chronicler Andrew of Wyntoun also mentions a campaign to the western seaboard, although he describes only one expedition and places it in the year 1222.[143] Although the specific details are murky, there can be no doubt of at least one and possibly two royal campaigns against the descendants of Somerled in the 1220s. *Gesta Annalia* seems to be supported by other evidence, which suggests that the Scottish king may well have forced the redistribution of some lands between Ruairi and Donald, two grandsons of Somerled. It is also surely significant that in the summer of 1222 the king established a burgh at Dumbarton, symbolising the consolidation of royal authority in the Clyde estuary.[144]

It is unclear why the Scottish king was, as the author of *Gesta Annalia* put it, 'displeased with the natives' of the western seaboard in 1221/22, and it is to be regretted that the chronicler did not see fit to elaborate upon the 'many reasons' that he cited. Although there is no evidence that the MacSorleys had been directly involved in uprisings against the Scottish kings, it is quite likely that turbulence from their internecine strife had spilled over into the Scottish kingdom itself – this might explain the reference to the construction of a new castle by King William in 1197 – and there is also the suspicion that some branches, at least, of Somerled's descendants may have been aiding the MacWilliams and MacHeths in their uprisings of the 1210s and 1220s. Evidence for this association is to be found in references to the MacWilliam risings of the

142 *Chron. Fordun*, i, 288–9; ii, 284.
143 *Orygynale Cronykle*, iii, 240.
144 For the founding of Dumbarton, see *Registrum Magni Sigilli Regum Scotorum*, ed. J.M. Thomson *et al* [*RMS*](11 vols., Edinburgh, 1882–1912), vii, no. 190 (1); on the redistribution of some MacSorley lands, see McDonald, *Kingdom of the Isles*, 84.

1220s, where both the *Chronicle of Lanercost* and the later chronicler Walter Bower mention a 'Roderick' who joined the MacWilliam incursions of 1223 and 1228–30. This individual was quite likely Ruairi, a son of Ranald, the son of Somerled, who may well have been one of those dispossessed by the Scottish king in 1222.[145] If Ruairi had aided and abetted the MacWilliams in their uprising of 1215, then this might explain, in part, at least, the Scottish campaign of the early 1220s. On the other hand, there is no mention of Ruairi's involvement in this particular uprising, and it seems equally likely that his association with the MacWilliam in the 1220s stemmed from his expulsion from the western seaboard in 1222. Whatever the case might have been, we are left with the lingering impression that some, at least, of Somerled's descendants showed sympathy and support for the cause of the MacWilliams, and thereby provided the Scottish kings with further cause to expand their authority into the western seaboard.

One of the main problems for the Scottish kings who wished to extend their authority into the west was the danger of arousing the enmity of the Norwegian kings. Technically, the western Isles had been ceded to King Magnus of Norway by the Scottish king, Edgar, in 1098, an episode vividly described by the *Orkneyinga Saga.*

> King Magnus was making his way north along the Scottish coast when messengers from Malcolm [*recte* Edgar] of Scotland came to offer him a settlement: King Malcolm [*recte* Edgar] would let him have all the islands off the west coast which were separated by water navigable by a ship with the rudder set. When King Magnus reached Kintyre he had a skiff hauled across the narrow neck of land at Tarbert, with himself sitting at the helm, and this is how he won the whole peninsula.[146]

Civil war in Norway, however, coupled with the preoccupation of the Scottish monarchs with English affairs in the twelfth century, meant that a power vacuum ensued – and it was into this void that Somerled and his descendants (as well as the Manx rulers descended from Godred Crovan (d. 1095)) opportunely stepped. The intensification of Scottish claims to the western seaboard thus not only risked rousing the anger of the Norwegian monarchs; it also meant that the Hebridean sea-kings descended from Somerled were forced to walk an increasingly narrow and treacherous path between the two rival and expansive powers of Scotland and Norway in the thirteenth century.

---

145 See McDonald, *Kingdom of the Isles*, 82, 84.
146 *OS*, chapter 41. Professor Cowan thinks the legalistic-looking phrase 'the Scottish king will let him have all the islands off the west coast separated by water navigable by a ship with the rudder set' might preserve a fragment of the actual treaty: Cowan, 'Hakon IV and Alexander III', 111.

By the second half of the 1240s, with a brief period of turbulent Anglo-Scottish relations, as well as the MacWilliam uprisings of the 1220s and the Galloway insurrection of 1234–35, behind them, the Scottish kings were free to turn their attention to what one scholar has ominously referred to as 'a final solution to the west highland problem'.[147] In 1244 a diplomatic mission aimed at winning the west was launched. By then, a new generation of MacSorleys had appeared on the scene; the most important of them were Ewen of Argyll and Dugald MacRuairi, great grandsons of Somerled. Both had been in Norway in 1248, where Ewen was granted the title of 'king'; when the Manx ruler accidentally drowned later in the same year, Ewen was dispatched to 'go west as quickly as possible, and be [the ruler] over the islands'.[148] Ewen's presence in Norway, his homage to the Norwegian king Hákon IV Hákonsson (1217–63), and, finally, his assumption of the kingship of the Isles all seriously tried Alexander's patience. Diplomatic efforts ground to a halt, and the Scottish king summoned an army to teach the Hebridean chieftain a lesson.

Details of the relations between Alexander and Ewen are preserved in *Hakon's Saga* and also in Matthew Paris's chronicle.[149] Alexander seems to have demanded that Ewen surrender the territory granted to him by the Norwegian king, in return for the Scottish king's friendship and an even larger dominion within Scotland. According to Matthew Paris, Ewen refused to break his oath to the Norwegian king, responding to Alexander's accusation of treason that 'he should render entire the service due both to the king of Scots and to the king of the Norwegians' – in other words, Ewen sought to serve two masters, which sounds suspiciously like an attempt to play both ends against the middle. This only enraged Alexander, however, who mobilised his army and pursued the unfortunate Hebridean chieftain to 'near Argyll' where Alexander grew ill and died on Kerrera in 1249. It is interesting that both English and Norwegian accounts are particularly sympathetic to Ewen, who is described by Matthew Paris as 'one of the noblest of his realm . . . a vigorous and very handsome knight'. Alexander, on the other hand, was depicted as greedy and aggressive – the author of *Hakon's Saga* said he was 'very covetous of dominion in the Hebrides'.[150]

Despite his death at Kerrera, Alexander II's campaign had not been a complete failure, and had, in fact, probably managed to displace Ewen of Argyll. The major difficulty was that the death of Alexander II created an environment in which it was not possible to undertake a swift follow-up campaign. Alexander's successor was his eight-year-old son, also named

147 Barrow, *Kingship and Unity*, 115.
148 *ES* ii, 554–5 (Saga).
149 *ES* ii, 554–7 (Saga); *Chron. Majora*, v, 88–9; trans. in *SAEC*, 360–1.
150 Quotations in *Chron. Majora*, v, 88–9; trans in *SAEC*, 360, and *ES* ii, 555 (Saga).

Alexander (Alexander III, 1249–86), and his twelve-year minority was a turbulent period for the Scottish kingdom. Once he assumed personal control of the government in 1260 (or 1261), however, he quickly acted to raise the issue of Scottish control of the islands again, but diplomatic initiatives launched that same summer came to naught.

In the summer of 1262 word arrived in Norway that disorder was again rampant in the Hebrides, this time the result of an attack on Skye by the earl of Ross with a Scottish army, which 'burned a town and churches, and slew very many men and women'. *Hakon's Saga* related how 'they said also that the Scots had taken the little children, and laid them on their spear-points, and shook until they brought [the children] down to their hands; and so threw them away, dead'. The earl of Ross was none other than William, the son of earl Ferchar who had crushed the MacWilliam uprising of 1215 and rescued the Scottish king from a Gallovidian ambush in 1235. His involvement in the attack on Skye suggests that this was orchestrated by the Scottish king, no doubt as a 'direct challenge to Norwegian authority in the western seaboard'.[151] Indeed, the word carried to the Norwegian king was that 'the Scottish king intended to lay under himself all the Hebrides'.[152] Such a challenge could not go unanswered.

The ensuing naval expedition launched by Hákon IV has been well chronicled by historians and need not detain us here.[153] What has rather grandly been called the battle of Largs (30 September to 3 October 1263), fought between Scottish and Norwegian forces on the Ayrshire coast, was in reality a series of disorganised skirmishes, later elevated by both sides into a great victory. King Hákon died at Orkney, en route back to Norway, and diplomatic negotiations began within a few months of the conflict. These negotiations culminated in 1266 in the Treaty of Perth, which stipulated that '. . . Magnus, King of Norway . . . granted, resigned and quit-claimed . . . for himself and his heirs forever, Man with the rest of the Sudreys and all other islands on the west and south of the great sea . . . to be held, had and possessed by the said lord Alexander [III], King of Scots . . .' The inhabitants of the islands were not to be punished for the 'misdeeds or injuries and damage which they have committed hitherto while they adhered to the said king of Norway', and 'if they should wish to remain in the said islands under the lordship of the said lord king of Scots, they may remain in his lordship freely and in peace, but if they wish to retire they may do so, with their goods, lawfully, freely, and in full peace . . .'[154]

---

151 McDonald, *Kingdom of the Isles*, 106.

152 *ES* ii, 605 (Saga).

153 See G. Donaldson, *A Northern Commonwealth: Scotland and Norway* (Edinburgh, 1990), chapters 8 and 9; Cowan, 'Hakon IV and Alexander III', 103–31; and McDonald, *Kingdom of the Isles*, chapter 4.

154 *APS*, i, 420; trans. G. Donaldson, *Scottish Historical Documents* (Edinburgh, 1970; repr. Glasgow, n.d.), 34–6.

The events of 1263–66, then, finally forced the MacSorleys to choose either a Scottish or a Norwegian allegiance. Ewen, who, as we have seen, attempted to play both ends against the middle in a bid to retain his position in 1249, tried the same strategy in 1263, giving his firm support to neither side. I have argued elsewhere that Ewen remained an opportunist right to the end, since a Norwegian victory might have offered the prospect of a restored status quo, and that it was only after the events of 1266 that Ewen finally trimmed his sails to the winds of change and made a firm commitment to the Scottish cause.[155] Then, on the other hand, there was Ewen's cousin and rival, Dugald MacRuairi, who had no intention of submitting to Scottish authority and who appears as a freebooter in the Hebrides and Irish Sea both before and after the events of the 1260s. In 1258, for instance, Irish annals record that a fleet led by Dugald plundered in the west of Ireland, and when the English sheriff of Connacht attempted to intercept the fleet, he was killed for his trouble in the ensuing sea-battle. Dugald held fast to a Norwegian allegiance, being rewarded by Hákon with Ewen's territories in the immediate aftermath of Largs in 1263. In 1264 he was active in leading attacks against Scottish forces in Caithness, where he is said to have 'killed many of them, and . . . taken the great treasure that they were carrying with them. He slew there the law-man of the Scots'.[156]

Dugald MacRuairi, who died in 1268 – still styled king of the Hebrides by Irish and Icelandic annalists[157] – was one of the last adversaries that the Scottish monarchs had to face from the autonomous or semi-autonomous Atlantic-facing zones of their kingdom. By the time the Treaty of Perth was sealed in 1266 there had been no serious threats for over thirty years – the last really serious challenges were probably those of the late 1220s from Ross and the Gallovidian insurrection in 1234/35 – and the acquisition of Argyll and the Isles ('the winning of the west' as Professor Barrow called it) is generally regarded as marking the territorial completion of the medieval Scottish kingdom.[158]

Unquestionably one of the most striking characteristics of the uprisings against the Scottish kings is their recurring nature. Taken cumulatively, the frequency and persistence with which they unfolded is staggering: apart from the campaigns against the Moravians in the reign of Malcolm III, there were challenges or military actions in the 1110s, 1124, 1130, 1134, late 1140s, 1153–60, 1164, 1174/75, 1179, 1187, 1196–97, 1201/02, 1211/12, 1215, the 1220s,

---

155 See *Kingdom of the Isles*, 117–8.
156 *ES* ii, 648–9 (Saga).
157 *ALC*, i, 458 (1268); *ES*, ii, 660.
158 Orkney and Shetland were, of course, added some two centuries later, in 1468/69.

1230, 1234/35, 1247, 1262, 1263 and 1264. Whether or not the removal of the men of Moray referred to in the Holyrood chronicle in 1163 or King William's expedition to Moray in 1214, for instance, should be included in such a catalogue of challenges is unclear, but the doubt itself indicates that the list is probably not comprehensive. What is clear is that every decade of the twelfth century, as well as many of the thirteenth, witnessed confrontations of some sort between the kings of Scots and various opponents. Some were, of course, more serious than others, but the timing of many of these challenges is itself significant. Many coincided with the succession of a new monarch, including those led by Angus and Malcolm in 1124, Somerled and the sons of Malcolm between 1153 and 1157/60, and the MacHeths and MacWilliams in 1215, thus highlighting the essentially dynastic nature of these particular uprisings. Others were carefully timed to coincide with moments when the Scottish king was out of the kingdom. Thus, David I was absent from Scotland when Angus and Malcolm invaded in 1130, and half a century later, when Donald MacWilliam appeared in the far north, William I was far away in England or Normandy. Still others bear the stamp of sheer opportunism. This is most notoriously apparent in the Gallovidian insurrection of 1174, which followed the capture of William I by the English, but is also evident in Donald MacWilliam's challenges of the 1180s which may have been timed to take advantage of royal preoccupation with the situation in Galloway. Similarly, it has to be more than mere coincidence that Harald Maddadsson's campaigns against the Crown in 1196 occurred at a time when the king lay seriously ill and the nobles were divided over the potential succession. Guthred MacWilliam chose an opportune moment to land in the far north in 1211, since the king was ageing and increasingly feeble: an English chronicle even made a direct link between William I's age and his inability to pacify 'the interior districts of his kingdom, disturbed by revolt' in 1212.[159] Here, then, were no random events, but carefully timed, and presumably orchestrated, predatory strikes against the Canmore kings in some of their weakest and most vulnerable moments.

A second and perhaps very obvious point is the manner in which opposition spans virtually the entire history of the dynasty descended from Malcolm III and Margaret: this dynasty, which was born in strife, only sustained its grip on power with considerable effort and numerous bloody struggles against a variety of formidable opponents. With the exception of the reign of Edgar (about which little is known in any event), every single successor of Malcolm III had to deal with potentially lethal uprisings at one time or another; not only that, but many of the most serious insurrections took place on the death of one monarch and the succession of the next, as in 1124–34, 1153, and 1215. There is no doubt that by the time of Alexander III – and arguably from late in the reign of Alexander

---

159 Walter of Coventry, ii, 206 (1212); trans. *SAEC*, 330 n. 6.

II – the Scottish monarchs were firmly entrenched, and that Ewen and Dugald were hardly adversaries of the same calibre as Somerled, Donald MacWilliam, or Earl Harald of Orkney/Caithness. It is also instructive to note that, on one level at least, the opponents of the Canmore kings actually outlived the dynasty itself: we have already seen how old Thomas of Galloway was hauled out of retirement, after some sixty years of captivity, by Edward I. It can, therefore, be argued that a defining feature of Scottish kingship in the twelfth century and the first half of the thirteenth century was the seemingly fierce and almost incessant resistance with which the descendants of Malcolm III and Margaret were faced; when viewed from this perspective, instability and violence are much more prominent themes in twelfth- and thirteenth-century Scottish history than has been allowed over the past half-century of historical writing. Certainly the role of the Canmore kings in suppressing dynastic rivals and other disgruntled native warlords is one of the better-kept secrets of medieval Scottish history.

Finally, it almost appears as though resistance to the dynasty actually intensified as the kings descended from Malcolm III became more entrenched in the kingship. It is true that Malcolm III defeated his Cenél Loairn opponents three times over the course of twenty years, but even this pales in comparison with the impressive record of MacWilliam persistence and aggression, which encompassed no fewer than five insurrections over the fifty years between 1181 and 1230. If, in the end, the MacWilliam risings of the 1220s appear feeble and doomed to failure, that of 1181–87, led by Donald MacWilliam, posed a substantial danger to the Scottish king. Not only in 1187 but also in 1235 is it possible to envision a very different outcome to events – one in which the royal lineage was extinguished by one or another of its rivals.

Professor Barrow, with the MacWilliams in mind, has contended that the Scottish kings descended from Malcolm and Margaret can hardly be regarded as firmly established much before the 1180s.[160] Herein lies one facet of the significance of the challenges to these kings: it acts as a convenient gauge for the limits of the consolidation of the dynasty and its accompanying phenomena, Scottish regnal solidarity and the territorial consolidation of the realm. The survival of the Scottish kings in this period, their monopoly on the kingship, unity under these kings, and even the inclusion of marginal regions like Orkney, Caithness, Ross, Moray, Galloway, and Argyll and the Isles within the emerging Community of the Realm – these were all more closely-run things than is often admitted, and certainly should not be regarded as foregone conclusions much before the death of William I in 1214 and the suppression of the MacHeth/MacWilliam insurrection in 1215. In the final analysis, consideration of the challenges faced by the Scottish kings between the eleventh and thirteenth centuries is a potent reminder, if one is needed, that in dealing

160 Barrow, 'Some Problems', 100.

with the descendants of Malcolm and Margaret we are also dealing, in one respect, with the 'winners' in history. On the other hand, the recurrent challenges launched by the likes of the MacWilliams might also be viewed as the ultimate tribute to the power and endurance of these kings: the ending of the crises in the north and the defeat of their rivals mark the triumph of these rulers once and for all. As Professor Robin Frame so aptly summed it up, 'The weight of the house of Canmore was irresistible, and its brand of kingship inimitable'.[161]

161 Frame, *Political Development*, 104.

TWO

'THE KING'S ENEMIES':
The Origins and Nature of Resistance

On that day, in Scotland, Somerled and his nephews, the sons of Malcolm, allied with themselves very many men, and rebelled against King Malcolm, and disturbed and disquieted Scotland to a great extent.

With these words the Holyrood abbey chronicler described the uprising of Somerled and the sons of Malcolm against King Malcolm IV in 1153.[1] The brevity of this account – in the Latin text a mere twenty-five words are used – highlights the difficulties inherent in attempting to penetrate beyond a mere narrative of opposition to the Scottish kings and to probe more deeply into the circumstances, causes, and individuals involved. In this account, for instance, neither Somerled nor Malcolm is clearly identified; the 'many men' who joined them remain anonymous; and the impact of the insurrection is painted in the most general terms (they 'disturbed and disquieted Scotland to a great extent'). Most frustrating, however, is the chronicle's silence on the subject of the motivation behind the insurrection.

As the first chapter demonstrated, it is possible, despite the jejune nature of the sources, to construct a reasonably coherent narrative of challenges to the Scottish kings from the late eleventh to the mid-thirteenth centuries; such challenges appear as a central, perhaps even a defining, theme in the history of Scottish kingship and political culture in this period. Yet, as with the entry in the Holyrood chronicle cited above, the causes for these conflicts remain mysterious: was Somerled making a bid for the kingship, or merely seeking an opportunity for plunder? And what was the nature of his association with the children of Malcolm? This chapter attempts to unravel the mystery surrounding the nature of opposition to the Scottish kings. It proceeds by examining the leaders of opposition and the motivation behind their challenges, paying particular attention to the MacWilliam and MacHeth kindreds as well as individuals like Fergus of Galloway, Somerled of Argyll, Harald Maddadsson and Wimund. Moving beyond the élite leadership, the problem of ecclesiastical and popular facets to opposition is also addressed. The chapter concludes with an examination of the extent of connections among the leaders of the challenges, and an assessment of whether there existed what has been described as an 'anti-feudal faction' in twelfth- and thirteenth-century Scotland.

1 *Chron Holyrood*, 124–5, 187.

'Long hostility against the modern kings': the MacWilliams

For much of the twelfth and a good deal of the thirteenth century, resistance to the Scottish kings crystallised around the MacWilliam and MacHeth families: between 1124 and 1134 a Malcolm, usually identified as Malcolm 'MacHeth', led several uprisings against David I, while the last MacWilliam was slain at Forfar in 1230, the grisly conclusion to more than half a century of tenacious opposition from her predecessors. Yet, notwithstanding the frequency of these names in the annals of resistance to the Scottish kings, the ancestry of these families has long puzzled historians, and the basis for their opposition has also proved elusive. This is hardly surprising, given the patchy nature of the evidence and the major problems that exist in interpreting it. Yet there remain many unanswered questions about these two enigmatic kindreds, not the least of which revolve around the identities of Malcolm 'MacHeth' and Donald MacWilliam, their aims and claims, and the basis for the considerable support that they garnered for their actions against the Scottish kings.

Without doubt the most tenacious opponents of the Scottish kings were the MacWilliams, who first appear on the record about 1180 and whose opposition was almost endemic down to 1230. Donald MacWilliam was first mentioned by name in 1181, although it is quite possible that he was the target of a campaign launched by King William and his brother, Earl David, in the north in 1179. Roger of Howden, a well-informed source for the MacWilliam uprisings, gave Donald's descent as 'Donald son of William son of Duncan',[2] while an annalist at St. Edmund's described one of Donald's descendants as a 'certain relative of the king of Scots'.[3] Scandinavian sources, remarking upon the marriage of Malcolm III to his first wife, Ingibjorg of Orkney, noted that 'their son was Duncan, King of Scots, father of William . . .'[4] Donald's identity as a son of William, the son of King Duncan II, the son of Malcolm III and his first wife, Ingibjorg, who reigned briefly in 1094, is well established and not seriously in doubt, and it is clear that any discussion of MacWilliam resistance must begin with William fitz Duncan himself.[5]

Of all the shadowy figures of twelfth-century Scotland, none deserves to be better known than William fitz Duncan. Modern historians have shown surprisingly little interest in him, and the best account of his life remains that

---

2 *Chronica*, ii, 263.

3 *Annales Sancti Edmundi*, in *Memorials of St. Edmund's Abbey*, ii, 20: *'quidam cognatus regis Scotiae'*.

4 *OS*, ch. 33.

5 David Bates errs in stating that Duncan II died without male heirs to succeed him: D. Bates, 'Kingship, government, and political life to c. 1160', in *The Twelfth and Thirteenth Centuries 1066–c.1280*, ed. B. Harvey (Oxford, 2001), 89. In fact, Duncan II was the only one of Malcolm III's sons to be survived by a son (David was predeceased by his own son, Earl Henry, in 1152 and was succeeded by his grandson, Malcolm IV).

hidden away in the notes to Sir A.C. Lawrie's *Early Scottish Charters*, originally published in 1908.[6] Beyond his status as a son of King Duncan II, the eldest son of Malcolm III and his first wife, Ingibjorg, it is known that William fitz Duncan was a close companion of King David I, whose charters he frequently witnessed as *Willelmus nepos Regis* or simply *Willelmus filius Duncani*; in one of his own charters to the Priory of St Bees, he similarly identifies himself as 'William the nephew of the Scottish king'.[7] His high status in contemporary society is indicated clearly enough by his prominent position in those charters that he attests, where his name usually appears behind members of the immediate royal family like Earl Henry (son of David I) or important ecclesiastical witnesses, but almost always ahead of Scottish earls like Duncan of Fife.[8] William was an important figure on the battlefield as well as at court: he played a prominent role in King David's military campaigns in the north of England in the late 1130s, leading a division of the army that invaded Northumbria in 1137, and he commanded part of the Scottish contingent at the battle of the Standard in 1138. It therefore seems entirely fitting that the English chronicler Ailred of Rievaulx lauded him as 'a man of high spirit and the chief provoker of war' for his role in the invasion of northern England in 1138, and that the author of *Orkneyinga Saga* described him as 'a great man'.[9] William was married to Alice de Rumilly, the daughter of William Meschin, a prominent landholder in Cumbria.[10] Although the couple had one son, William (commonly known as the Boy of Egremont), and three daughters, Donald was not a son of William by Alice de Rumilly, but rather, perhaps, of an earlier marriage.[11] It is certainly noteworthy that Donald's naming style 'marked him as a product of a Gaelic upbringing quite at odds with his father's obvious preference for Anglo-French cultural traditions'.[12]

Although William became a landholder of some status in England after the late 1130s, acquiring, by the time of his death in about 1151, the lands of Allerdale, Coupland, Skipton and Craven, the extent of his Scottish lands remains unknown: it seems inconceivable that he held no lands in Scotland, and

6 Lawrie, *ESC*, notes on 271–2.
7 *The Register of the Priory of St. Bees*, ed. J. Wilson (Surtees Society, Durham and London, 1915), no. 16.
8 See *ESC* nos. 32, 35, 50, 57, 82, 83, 99, 100, 109, 117, 121, 141, 142, 153, 163, 172, 176, and notes at pp. 271–2; also *Acts of Malcolm IV*, nos. 2, 22, 29, 35, 41.
9 *De Standardo*, in *Chron Stephen*, iii, 195; *OS*, ch. 33.
10 Ritchie, *Normans in Scotland*, 400–1; Lawrie, *ESC*, 271–2. See also P. Dalton, *Conquest, Anarchy and Lordship: Yorkshire 1066–1154* (Cambridge, 1994), 211–6 for extensive comments on William's English lands.
11 Duncan, *Scotland*, 193; Barrow, *Acts of William I*, 12–13; Ritchie, *Normans in Scotland*, 400–1; and *ESC*, 271–2.
12 Oram, 'David I and . . . Moray', 9; see also Barrow, 'Macbeth and Other Mormaers', 119. Most of the chronicles describe the members of the family simply as 'MacWilliam'.

yet none can be firmly associated with him. The issue of his lands as well as his status is complicated, however, by a reference in a thirteenth-century Cumbrian document known as the 'Chronicon Cumbrie' to William fitz Duncan as 'earl of Moray' (*comes de Murray*), [13] a title which is not used to describe him elsewhere. This reference has led some scholars to conclude that William may have held the earldom of Moray for a brief period following the defeat of Angus and Malcolm at Stracathro in 1130, possibly through an earlier marriage to a sister or daughter of Earl Angus. Such a marriage alliance, it is proposed, may have represented an attempt by David I to vest the claims of the Moray dynasty in a man who had proven himself uninterested in his own claims to the kingship. It would also have given any offspring a claim not only to the Scottish kingship but also to the earldom of Moray – which might go a long way toward explaining why the MacWilliam insurrections were often associated with Moray beyond the Great Glen and with Ross.[14]

It has to be admitted that the reference to William fitz Duncan as 'earl of Moray' in the Cumbrian genealogy is indeed difficult to explain. While this document was apparently intended to provide claims to stand up to an inquiry in a court of law in the period 1275–1316,[15] not all historians have expressed overwhelming confidence in it. One example of the difficulties presented by this document is evident in its opening assertion that King William the Conqueror (1066–87) granted the earldom (lordship) of Cumbria to Ranulf Meschin; this is followed by the statement that his brother Geoffrey was given Chester and another brother, William, Coupland.[16] In fact, it is now generally agreed that Cumbria did not pass under English control until 1092, in the reign of William II 'Rufus' (1087–99), and that Ranulf Meschin did not receive Cumbria until circa 1102–06; his brother's infeftment in Coupland is placed later still.[17] Similarly, there is no evidence for the use of the title of earl by

13 *Register of St. Bees*, no. 498.
14 *Acts of William I*, 12–3, see also Oram, 'David I and . . . Moray', 10; compare Duncan, *Scotland*, 119.
15 *Register of St. Bees*, xviii-xix; J. Wilson, 'Introduction to the Cumerland Domesday, Early Pipe Rolls, and Testa de Nevill', in *Victoria History of the County of Cumberland*, ed. H.A. Doubleday [*History of Cumberland*] (2 vols., *Victoria History of the Counties of England*, London, 1901, repr. 1968), i, 297–8.
16 *Register of St Bees*, no. 498.
17 There is now a considerable body of literature dealing with Cumbria in this period. In addition to the *History of Cumberland*, i, 297–8, 303–07, see also C. Phythian-Adams, *Land of the Cumbrians* (Aldershot, 1996), 24–38; G.W.S. Barrow, 'The pattern of lordship and feudal settlement in Cumbria', *Journal of Medieval History* (*JMH*) i (1975), 117–38 (especially 121); Kapelle, *Norman Conquest of the North*, 200; H. Summerson, *Medieval Carlisle: The City and the Borders from the Late Eleventh Century to the Mid Sixteenth Century* (Cumberland and Westmorland Antiquarian and Archaeological Society Extra Series, Kendal, 1993), i, especially 14–24.

Ranulf, which is ascribed to him in the chronicle. Not surprisingly, then, historians have generally been sceptical of the significance of the document and placed little value upon its reliability without external corroboration.[18] Unfortunately, such documentation is not to be found. In all of his charter attestations William was styled simply *Willelmus nepos Regis* or *Willelmus filius Duncani*, and it is surely more than a little puzzling that he would not have been styled 'earl of Moray' in the charters if there had been cause to so designate him – although it is just possible that his identification as a kinsman of the king was considered to override his territorial designation in those charters that he attested.[19]

Despite this enigmatic reference, and the persuasive explanation of Mac-William claims set out by Professor Barrow, it remains difficult to discard the notion that Donald MacWilliam's claims to the kingship must have come from his royal grandfather, Duncan II, who ruled briefly in 1094. The vexing question here is, as Professor Barrow has rightly pointed out, explaining why Donald MacWilliam, in the 1180s, 'pressed a claim to the Scots throne which . . . had lain dormant for over sixty years'.[20] Indeed, there is little reliable evidence that either William fitz Duncan or his son William of Egremont ever put forward a claim to the kingship,[21] so the emergence of MacWilliam opposition to the Canmore kings in the 1180s proves even more baffling. We can perhaps best begin with the nature of the claim: the first wife of Malcolm was Ingibjorg, widow of Thorfinn, earl of Orkney; his second wife was Margaret, a Saxon princess, the sister of Edgar Ætheling who had fled north following the Norman conquest of England in 1066. By his first marriage Malcolm had at least one son, Duncan (the Donald who died in 1085 might have been another), and by his second marriage six sons: Edward, Edmund, Æthelred, Edgar, Alexander, and David. Now, there is a strong possibility that Malcolm and Margaret's eldest son, Edward, had been recognised as heir before his death (and that of his parents) in 1093. He is described in the *Anglo-Saxon Chronicle* as Malcolm's son, 'who would have been king after him if he had survived',[22] suggesting that Malcolm and Margaret had excluded Duncan from the succession.[23] In the turmoil surrounding the deaths of Malcolm, Margaret

18 *History of Cumberland*, i, 297 n.3; Lawrie, *ESC*, 271.
19 The situation of William fitz Duncan might bear some resemblance to that of David's own son, Earl Henry, who is never styled 'earl of Northumberland' in his charter attestations, but is described as 'son of the king': see Barrow, *Charters of David I*, for example, nos. 71, 120, 179. I am indebted to Alex Woolf for this suggestion.
20 *Acts of William I*, 12.
21 *Acts of William I*, 13; see also Barrow, 'Some Problems', 99–100.
22 *ASC*, 228 (1093).
23 Phythian-Adams, *Land of the Cumbrians*, 158.

and Edward within a few days of each other in November 1093, Malcolm's brother Donald Bàn was either chosen as king or seized the kingship (the sources use vastly differing terminology on the matter). Duncan, however, clearly regarded himself as the rightful heir. It was he, after all, who had been handed over as a hostage to William the Conqueror in 1072 to ensure that the Abernethy agreement was kept.[24] On the death of the Conqueror in 1087 Duncan was released and knighted by William Rufus, [25] but he does not seem to have visited Scotland after his release, and he might have been in Normandy until about 1090 or 1091.[26] In 1094 he moved against his uncle with the support of the English king: 'and thus with his [King William II's] consent [Duncan] went to Scotland with such support of English and French as he could get, and deprived his relative Donald of the kingdom, and was received as king'.[27] He has been regarded as an adventurer hoping for an improvement in his fortunes,[28] but his position was stated clearly in a charter from 1094, in which he styled himself 'hereditarily undoubted king of Scotland'.[29] By then, as the reference to 'infantibus meus' in his charter shows, Duncan had also fathered several children.[30] His reign was short lived, however, and he was slain later in1094, following which Donald again took the kingship. But although Duncan himself had been removed from the scene, his line continued: 'in his own person, or through any 'son,' Duncan has . . . to be seen as posing a serious threat to the pretension of the sons of Malcolm and Margaret as early as 1091/92'.[31] By the time Duncan's son(s) had grown to maturity, the descendants of Malcolm and Margaret had entrenched themselves firmly in the kingship and, perhaps just as importantly, had secured the backing of the English king for themselves.

The consolidation of the kingship in the line of Malcolm III and Margaret broke with longstanding tradition of Scottish succession practices. From the ninth to the eleventh century there operated in Scotland a system of alternating succession. By such a system, two rival but related segments took turns in the kingship so that each held power in alternating reigns. In the later tenth century this largely inclusive system broke down as Kenneth II (971–95) and Malcolm II (1005–34) attempted to restrict the kingship to their nearer descendants. This led in turn to the accession of Macbeth, a representative of the Cenél Loairn line of Moray – proving that exclusion from the succession was worthy of a

---

24 *ASC*, 208, 228 (1072, 1093).
25 William of Malmesbury, ed. Mynors *et al*, i, 724–5 (Bk. V, 400).
26 F. Barlow, *William Rufus* (London, 1983), 295.
27 *ASC*, 228 (1093).
28 Barlow, *William Rufus*, 295.
29 Lawrie, *ESC*, no. 12.
30 Lawrie, *ESC*, no. 12.
31 Phythian-Adams, *Land of the Cumbrians*, 158.

fight.[32] But the restoration of a rival segment was short-lived, and, after the turmoil of the years 1093 to 1097, the descendants of Malcolm III and Margaret were responsible for transforming the structures of the royal kin so that the dynasty acquired the attributes of a lineage: from 1097 to 1286 the kingship passed smoothly through this line, and Scottish kingship 'parted company with one aspect of its Gaelic past'.[33] Whether this happened through biological accident or through careful planning has never been satisfactorily explained. It is noteworthy that Malcolm III might have designated his eldest son by Margaret as his heir, to the detriment of his eldest son by his first marriage, and there is little doubt that by the mid-1140s David I seems to have intended that his own son should succeed him directly: Earl Henry was styled *rex designatus* or 'king-designate' in two St Andrews charters of the mid-1140s.[34] This meant that the claims of rival segments, including the descendants of Duncan II, had been pushed aside – thus setting the stage for segmentary strife and resistance to the descendants of Malcolm III and Margaret into the early thirteenth century. As D. Ó Corráin has noted in the Irish context, 'The passing of the kingship from one segment to another, from one dynastic power base to another, upset as many as it satisfied'.[35] In assessing the opposition to the Canmore dynasty, then, the profound transformation of kingship taking place in the twelfth century cannot be overlooked, as the descendants of Malcolm and Margaret consolidated their grip on the royal office, thereby squeezing out the claims of other contenders.

If it is hard to deny that MacWilliam claims were genuine, derived as they were from Duncan II, it is more difficult to say why Donald's father, William fitz Duncan, apparently made no effort to seize the kingship when, under a system of primogeniture, he had the better claim.[36] In this matter, however, several often-overlooked facts are crucial. First, William must have been very young when his father was killed in 1094, and he was also probably in England.[37] This, combined with the ensuing environment of claimants and counter-claimants seizing the Scottish kingship, some of them with military assistance from the Norman kings of England, makes it highly unlikely that William would have been able to set forth his own claim. In this he may resemble the Anglo-Saxon prince Edgar the Aetheling, whose youth and political isolation caused him to be overlooked for the English kingship on

---

32 A.P. Smyth, *Warlords and Holy Men: Scotland A.D. 80–1000* (London, 1984; repr. Edinburgh, 1989), 218–27; Barrow, *Kingship and Unity*, 24–6.

33 Frame, *Political Development*, 106.

34 *ESC*, nos. 163 and 164.

35 D. Ó Corráin, 'Irish Regnal Succession: A Reappraisal', *Studia Hibernica* xi (1971), 8.

36 Dickinson and Duncan, *Earliest Times to 1603*, 60.

37 Lawrie, *ESC*, no. 12 and notes on 271; Dickinson and Duncan, *Earliest Times to 1603*, 64 n. 12.

the death of Edward the Confessor in 1066.[38] Second, there remains the clouded issue of legitimacy. It is tempting to suppose that the various opinions voiced by contemporaries about the illegitimacy of William's father, Duncan II, represented a propaganda campaign on behalf of the sons of Malcolm and Margaret designed to discredit any claims to the throne from that quarter.[39] This would also have had the effect of casting aspersions on any claim of William to the throne. However, 'irregular' marriages – irregular from the perspective of members of the contemporary reform movement in the church – did not debar a candidate from seeking the kingship in Ireland and Wales.[40] Certainly Duncan was in no doubt about his own status when he styled himself 'hereditarily undoubted king of Scotland'.[41] Third, it also appears that William achieved an honourable and prominent position within the new order of Scottish society. He married a wealthy heiress, acquired significant landholdings in Cumbria, and was a frequent companion of the king.[42] Given the entrenchment of the sons of Malcolm and Margaret by the time of David I, he may have been happy to let his claim lapse; the king, for his part, would have been able to keep a watchful eye on a potential source of trouble. When the Norman form of his name, as well as what is known about his later career, when he was one of David's foremost military leaders, is considered, it would appear that William fitz Duncan achieved accommodation within the new Scottish society, not unlike the contemporary earls of Fife.[43] If his son, Donald, as his name suggests ('MacWilliam' rather than 'fitz William'), had grown up in a Gaelic environment, possibly through fosterage,[44] then his assimilation be-

---

38 On Edgar, see N. Hooper, 'Edgar the Aetheling: Anglo-Saxon Prince, rebel and crusader', *Anglo-Saxon England* xiv (1985), 197–214, especially 202–03, 212.

39 A passage inserted into the *Chronicle of Melrose* regarded him as illegitimate, as did William of Malmesbury, who was a great admirer of the sons of Malcolm and Margaret: see *ES*, ii, 89, and William of Malmesbury, ed. Mynors *et al*, i, 724–5 (Bk. V, 400). While it is possible that Malcolm III and Ingibjorg were within the forbidden degrees of consanguinity (Dickinson and Duncan, *Earliest Times to 1603*, 64 n. 12), most historians accept Duncan's legitimacy. In one of his charters, Duncan styled himself *constans hereditarie rex Scotie*, 'hereditarily undoubted king of Scotland': see A.A.M. Duncan, 'The Earliest Scottish Charters', *SHR* xxxvii (1958), 119–20.

40 See Frame, *Political Development*, 108–25.

41 Lawrie, *ESC*, no. 12 ; see note 34 above.

42 Again, the case of Edgar the Aetheling may offer some useful parallels: in the wake of the Norman Conquest in 1066 he seems to have come to some accommodation with William, receiving lands and honours, and after a flirtation with rebellion between 1068–74, returned to William's favour: see Hooper, 'Edgar the Aetheling', especially 204–05.

43 For whom see Bannerman, 'MacDuff of Fife', in *Medieval Scotland*, 20–38.

44 On fosterage, a legally defined relationship by which a boy or a girl lived with foster parents who provided care, instruction and education until about the age of puberty, see T.M. Charles-Edwards, *Early Irish and Welsh Kinship* (Oxford, 1993), especially 79–82; note however that these comments pertain to the earlier middle ages in Ireland.

comes less likely. The most plausible explanation for the various challenges by the MacWilliams, then, is that they were based upon the descent of Donald MacWilliam from his grandfather, Duncan II, and there are also some compelling reasons why the claim to the throne put forth by Donald Mac-William in the second half of the twelfth century may have lain dormant in the person of his father. Unquestionably, the MacWilliams represent a cast-off, alienated segment of the royal kindred; their challenges were attempts to reclaim the royal office, to which they no doubt felt they had a legitimate claim.

None of this, however, satisfactorily explains why Donald MacWilliam waited until the late 1170s or early 1180s to take action against his kinsman, King William; indeed, this might be regarded as an even greater mystery than why William fitz Duncan neglected to raise his own seemingly good claims to the kingship in the first place. Although there is no single event or outstanding dynastic factor that indicates why the MacWilliams emerged when they did, there is no shortage of considerations that might go some way, at least, toward explaining the matter. Not the least of these is sheer opportunism. In July 1174 King William was captured by the English at Alnwick, inaugurating a period of crisis that saw Scotland subjected to England. As if that were not bad enough, soon after William's capture Gilbert and Uhtred of Galloway launched their reign of terror against agents of royal authority, after which Gilbert had Uhtred mutilated so badly that he subsequently died. Once King William had performed homage to Henry II of England at York in 1175, he was given leave to take an army into Galloway and subdue Gilbert, and there is good evidence that the southwest remained turbulent and that many subsequent royal campaigns were undertaken there until 1185. Even more significant is the fact that both King William and his brother Earl David (who seems to have played a role as a military commander and accompanied William on the 1179 campaign into Ross) departed for Normandy and England in 1181, where they met with Henry II; in fact, they appear to have been absent from Scotland for some months, between about April or May and September.[45] It was during their extended absence from the kingdom that the insurrection of 1181 broke out. By timing an uprising in the late 1170s or early 1180s, Donald MacWilliam may well have been taking advantage of the interrelated crises posed by King William's capture and the turbulent situation in Galloway, as well as the immediate circumstance of the absence of the king and his brother from the realm in the summer of 1181. In respect of timing, the rising of 1181 resembles that of 1130, when the king was also away in the south. This reinforces the suspicion that the timing of many insurrections was carefully calculated to coincide with the movements and activities of the Scottish monarchs – which, in turn, implies a certain amount of intelligence information on the part of the leaders.

45 *Chron Melrose* 43 (1181); see also the royal itinerary in Barrow, *Acts of William I*, 97.

Galloway aside, the Scottish king had other problems in the 1170s and 1180s. The most significant of these was without doubt the nature of Anglo-Scottish relations and the submission of Scotland to its southern neighbour, a circumstance that arose from the capture of William at Alnwick in July 1174 and the subsequent treaty of Falaise by which he performed homage and fealty to his English counterpart, Henry II. Not until the death of Henry and the accession of Richard I in 1189 was King William able to purchase his freedom 'from all compacts which . . . Henry . . . extorted from him' in the quitclaim of Canterbury.[46] Even the *Chronicle of Melrose*, which expresses a viewpoint that is more Anglo-Norman than Scottish for this period, states that Henry laid a 'heavy yoke of domination and of servitude' upon the Scottish kingdom; this included the surrender of Edinburgh, Roxburgh, and Berwick castles.[47] Now, it may be that this 'yoke of domination and servitude' that had been laid upon the Scottish kingdom contributed to the support that Donald MacWilliam received – or, as Professor Barrow put it, 'led to a positive fever of insubordination along the fringes of the Scottish realm'.[48] Roger of Howden said that Donald made his incursion with the 'consent and counsel of the earls and barons of the kingdom of Scotland', and he also tells how, when the royal army set out against Donald in 1187, its leadership was divided, because 'certain of them loved the king not at all, and certain of them loved him'. It does not require a huge effort of imagination to suppose that Donald MacWilliam garnered support from magnates who were irritated with the submission to England, and it is possible that he was perceived as a more gaelicised candidate for the kingship, one who would be able to avoid the entanglement in northern English affairs that had preoccupied William throughout his reign and ultimately cost him so dearly. Perhaps, then, the MacWilliam rising could be regarded not only as a dynastic insurrection, but one that was made in favour of a more gáelicisied candidate, not unlike that of Donald Bàn in 1093.

Still another context for the MacWilliam challenges must be the turbulent affairs of the northern Irish Sea and the southern Hebrides in the late 1170s and the 1180s, in particular, developments in Ulster. It is clear that later MacWilliam insurrections were closely linked to Ireland: Guthred's invasion of 1211/ 12 is explicitly stated to have originated there, while that of 1215 was accomplished with the aid of an unnamed Irish prince. Roger of Howden described Donald MacWilliam's 1181 attack in terms that strongly suggest it was launched from outwith the kingdom of Scots: 'Donald, who . . . had many a time made insidious incursions into that kingdom . . . landed in Scotland with a

---

46 *Anglo-Scottish Relations 1174–1328: Some selected documents*, ed., E.L.G. Stones (London, 1965; 2nd ed. Oxford, 1970), 1–5, 6–8.
47 *Chron Melrose* 47 (1189), and Stones, *Anglo-Scottish Relations*, 1–5.
48 Barrow, 'Reign of William the Lion', 76.

numerous armed host', while an alternate manuscript adds the detail that 'he despoiled it along the sea-coast'.[49] The phrase 'landing in Scotland' makes it sound as though the invasion had been launched from somewhere else, while the fact that Donald 'despoiled [Scotland] along the sea-coast' (Wester Ross, perhaps?) as well as our knowledge of later MacWilliam links to Ireland all seem to point to an Irish connection for Donald MacWilliam as well as his descendants.

It can hardly be coincidence that the beginning of MacWilliam opposition to the Scottish kings occurred at precisely the moment when the legendary and energetic Anglo-Norman adventurer John de Courcy was carving out an empire for himself in Ulster between 1177 and 1182, defeating Ruaidri Mac Dunn Sleibe and the men of Ulster with their Cenél nEogain allies in the process.[50] De Courcy, who had come to Ulster from Cumbria, was a kinsman of Donald MacWilliam: his father was married to Avice de Rumilly of Coupland, whose sister, Alice, had wed William fitz Duncan, Donald's father. It is thus plausible that de Courcy's position of strength in Ulster gave the MacWilliams their opportunity in the late 1170s and early 1180s. As a *quid pro quo*, de Courcy probably needed supporters in Scotland for his position in Ulster; certainly by the 1190s he was allied with Duncan of Carrick, the son of Gilbert of Galloway. Indeed, the Ulster-Carrick-MacWilliam triumvirate may have provided a potent alliance versus Roland of Galloway, the MacSorleys, and intensifying Scottish authority in the southwest.[51] Yet the de Courcy-MacWilliam axis cannot be the whole story of MacWilliam links to Ireland, for it is clear that the kindred continued to draw on Irish support even after the fall of de Courcy in 1205. It is therefore almost certain that the MacWilliams garnered native Irish support as well, and it has been argued that the diminishing Gaelic offences against de Courcy after 1181 may indicate the diversion of military resources into MacWilliam activities.[52] Most likely there is an element of truth in both viewpoints, but we can hardly escape the conclusion that the profound shifts in the political landscape of Ulster and the northern Irish Sea in the last quarter of the twelfth century go some way toward accounting for the timing of the MacWilliam challenges.

49 *Gesta Henrici Regis*, i, 277–8; *Chronica*, ii, 263; trans. in *SAEC*, 278.
50 For John de Courcy see *Medieval Ireland 1169–1534*, ed. A. Cosgrove (*New History of Ireland* Vol. 2, Oxford, 1987), 114–6; S. Duffy, 'The First Ulster Plantation: John de Courcy and the Men of Cumbria', in *Colony and Frontier: Essays Presented to J.F. Lydon*, ed. T.B. Barry, R. Frame and K. Simms (London and Rio Grande, 1995), 1–28.
51 See Duffy, 'First Ulster Plantation', 5–6, on de Courcy's ancestry. I am grateful to Dr. Duffy for discussing the points developed in these paragraphs with me in some detail.
52 Oram, *Lordship of Galloway*, 104–6.

Or it may be that the timing of the MacWilliam insurrections needs no special explanation at all, and that the apparent commencement of hostilities around 1180 is more illusory than real. It is usually assumed that the MacWilliams appeared on the scene only in 1179/81, but how valid is that assumption? Certainly it is true that Howden names MacWilliam only in 1181, while *Gesta Annalia* appended to the chronicle of John of Fordun associate him with the events of 1179 as well. But Howden also states that Donald 'had many a time made insidious incursions' into Scotland – the use of the plural 'incursions' might be significant - and in this case the chronicler was well placed to know the truth of the matter. That is because Howden had visited Scotland on a number of occasions between 1174, when he had been a diplomatic envoy to Gilbert of Galloway, and the 1190s: 'The mission to Gilbert of Galloway in November 1174 began a close involvement with Scottish business which was to last the rest of his life, and involve him in many journeys to Scotland'.[53] It is no doubt significant that on one occasion in the 1190s Howden is found at Melrose in the company of, among others, Reginald, the new bishop of Ross (1195–1213). It has been sensibly suggested that 'presumably Roger used a meeting with the new bishop of Ross . . . to brush up his knowledge of both ancient and modern Scottish church history'.[54] But there is no reason to think that Howden's briefing was limited to ecclesiastical history: a bishop of Ross was in a good position to provide information on the MacWilliams, particularly when Donald's defeat at Mam Garvia in 1187 represented a recent memory.[55] If, as it seems, Howden was well informed when he stated that Donald MacWilliam had made many incursions against the Scottish king, then it may be that we need to regard the MacWilliam insurrections as commencing earlier than the late 1170s or early 1180s. It is true, of course, that nothing is heard of Donald or his kindred prior to his appearance at this time, but we are not so well informed that we can afford to rule out the possibility of earlier attacks that have gone unrecorded in the often jejune Scottish sources for the 1150s to 1170s.[56]

Underlining the simultaneously dynastic and opportunistic nature of Mac-William activities is the invasion of Guthred MacWilliam in 1211. Guthred was a son of Donald,[57] but the fact that his rising is largely ignored by the Melrose abbey chronicler and is detailed only in contemporary English sources as well

---

53 J. Gillingham, 'Travels of Roger of Howden', 151–69, quotation at 167. See also the more detailed study by Duncan, 'Roger of Howden and Scotland', 135–59.

54 Gillingham, 'Travels of Roger of Howden', 157.

55 See A.A.M. Duncan, 'Sources and uses of the Chronicle of Melrose, 1165–1297', in *Kings, clerics and chroniclers in Scotland 500–1297*, ed. S. Taylor (Dublin, 2000), 146–85, at 149 where it is suggested that the bishop of Ross sent information to both Melrose and Roger of Howden.

56 See Duncan's comments in 'Sources and uses of the Chronicle of Melrose', 153–9.

57 *Chron Melrose* 55–6 (1211); *ES*, ii, 389.

as the work of the later writer Bower (who had access to a contemporary source for this part of the chronicle) means that it has been largely ignored or at best underestimated. In fact, Guthred's rising has been regarded as a serious threat to the inheritance of King William's line, and the whole episode needs to be viewed in the broader context of the Scottish succession at a crucial juncture.[58] The crisis began in 1195, when William, having fallen ill and still lacking a son, proposed that his daughter should marry Otto of Brunswick, who would then succeed to the kingship. The plan did not meet with unqualified enthusiasm, however, and encountered opposition from those within the ranks of the Scottish nobility who championed the cause of William's brother, Earl David.[59] In the end, William recovered from his illness, and the birth of a son, Alexander, followed in August 1198, substantially altering the situation. In 1201 William had the magnates swear an oath of fealty to the three-year-old heir,[60] an action which has puzzled historians but which is probably explicable in terms of William's age – by then the king was nearing sixty – and the presumed fear that there were those among the magnates who would still prefer to exclude Alexander in favour of David. Relations between the two brothers might have cooled noticeably from this time, and it is probably significant that Earl David did not perform homage to the young heir until 1205.[61] After 1209 he remained in England, but within two years a new threat had emerged on the scene: in 1211 Guthred MacWilliam 'replaced [David] in William's fear that Alexander might be excluded from the throne'.[62] Guthred was said by the Barnwell annalist to have been 'of the ancient line of Scottish kings' and to have enjoyed the aid of both Scots and Irish, while Bower remarked that his invasion was part of a conspiracy by the nobles of Ross. This suggests that, as in the 1180s, there were still those among the Scottish magnates who favoured a MacWilliam claim over that of King William's line: this may have been what the Barnwell annalist was getting at when he contrasted Guthred's descent from the ancient kings with the 'more recent kings of Scots' who 'profess themselves to be rather Frenchmen, both in race and in manners, language and culture'.[63] Whatever the case, the threat was real and was reflected in a February 1212 meeting between the two kings, John and William, at Durham. The conference, the terms of which are recorded by Bower, resulted in a mutual accord whereby the young Alexander was to be provided with a wife by John; each king swore to protect the other in his just disputes; and, perhaps most tellingly, 'whoever of the two

---

58 A.A.M. Duncan, 'John King of England and the Kings of Scots', in *King John: New Interpretations*, ed. S.D. Church (Woodbridge, 1999), 261–4.
59 *Chronica*, iii, 298–9.
60 *Chron Melrose* 51 (1201); *ES*, ii, 354.
61 Duncan, 'John King of England', 262–3.
62 Duncan, 'John King of England', 263.
63 Walter of Coventry, ii, 206.

outlived the other should protect the other's heir as if he were his own son, should support him and make every effort to put him into possession of his kingdom'.[64] This has been regarded as a desperate measure on the part of the ageing king, and one that highlights the essential insecurity of William's line in the Scottish kingship: though we may be inclined to view the birth of Alexander in 1198 as rendering the dynasty invulnerable, the insurrection of Guthred, its timing and its context clearly warn us otherwise. Indeed, the thirteenth-century Barnwell annalist remarked that 'Guthred was of the ancient line of Scottish kings; and, supported by the aid of Scots and Irish, had practiced long hostility against the modern kings, now in secret, now openly, as had also his father Donald'[65] – surely a fine summary of MacWilliam claims and activities, if not quite yet an obituary for the dynasty as a whole.

After Guthred the MacWilliams become more obscure, their challenges to the Scottish kings more desperate and less threatening. But they had yet to play their final hour upon the stage of Scottish history. In 1215 a son of Donald MacWilliam named Donald Bán, accompanied by Kenneth MacHeth and the son of an Irish king, landed in Moray, and was defeated by Ferchar Maccintsacairt. The timing of the insurrection is significant, following as it did on the heels of William's death and the succession of the sixteen-year-old Alexander to the kingship, but the fact that it could be quashed without the mobilisation of the royal army is even more telling and speaks of diminishing support for their cause. Finally, in the 1220s, Gillescop, stated to have been of the 'race of MacWilliam' by Bower, caused trouble in the north. Little is known of him, although he seems to have been active in at least 1228/29 and possibly as early as 1223. It is hard to say whether this Gillescop was a son or a grandson of Donald MacWilliam, but given the time frame and allowing for a thirty-year generation gap, the latter is surely more likely. As for the daughter of MacWilliam who had her head smashed at Forfar, since she is described as having been out of her mother's womb for but a short time, it seems unlikely, if not impossible, that she was the daughter of Donald Bàn, killed in 1215. Almost certainly she would have been a daughter of Gillescop.

In the end, the MacWilliams were as luckless as their unhappy forbear, Duncan II, in pressing their claims to the kingship. Yet for half a century between 1179/81 and 1230 several generations of MacWilliams (whether two, three, or four is hard to say) harassed the Scottish kings, plundering and burning in the north as well as capturing and destroying royal strongholds. There is even the possibility that Donald MacWilliam succeeded in wresting Moray and Ross from the grasp of William the Lion between about 1181 and 1187, and it

---

64 *Scotichronicon*, iv, 466–69; see also *Chron Fordun*, i, 278.
65 Walter of Coventry, ii, 206.

seems more than likely there were some, at least, in Scotland who were prepared to see both Donald and his son Guthred attain the kingship in preference to William's line. In sum, the MacWilliam achievement was not inconsiderable (especially given the vastly superior resources available to the Scottish kings), and it was certainly an effort worthy of descendants of King Malcolm III.

'The heir of paternal hatred and persecution': Malcolm MacHeth and the MacHeths
The second kindred that figures prominently in the annals of resistance to the Canmore kings is the MacHeths. They seem to have been active from the 1120s right through to 1215, when they allied themselves with the MacWilliams and invaded Moray. In contrast to the MacWilliams, the aims and claims of this kindred are much more controversial; indeed, the identity of Malcolm Mac-Heth has been called 'one of the important unsolved problems of early Scottish history'.[66] Historians have for long accepted that the Malcolm who instigated two wars against David I in 1124 and 1130 and was subsequently incarcerated at Roxburgh from 1134 is identical with the Malcolm, styled 'MacHeth', who was reconciled with the king of Scots in 1157 and died as earl of Ross in 1168. But how sound is this identification?

There are some difficulties with linking the Malcolm of the 1120s and 1130s with that of the 1150s and 1160s. How, for example, are we to reconcile the statement of Orderic Vitalis that the Malcolm of 1124 was an illegitimate son of Alexander I with the patronymic 'MacHeth' – 'son of Heth'? In this regard it may be noteworthy that none of the sources relating the activities and fate of the Malcolm of 1124–34 style him 'MacHeth'. Thus, the Melrose abbey chronicler relates the capture and incarceration of 'Malcolm' in 1134, and the entry for 1156 describes the capture and imprisonment of Donald, Malcolm's son – but in neither case does the name 'MacHeth' appear. It is, in fact, modern editors and translators of these texts who have assumed that this individual must be identical with the 'Malcolm MacHeth' who was reconciled with the king in 1157: even the otherwise conscientious editor and translator of Orderic Vitalis supplies the surname 'MacHeth' in parenthesis when this does not appear in the original Latin text of the events of 1124 and 1130.[67] The patronymic 'MacHeth' actually appears on the record for the first time only in 1157, when the Holyrood chronicle described the reconciliation between the king and a Malcolm 'Mabeth' – a scribal error for 'MacHeth'.

---

66 Duncan, *Scotland*, 166.
67 *Ecclesiastical History of Orderic Vitalis*, iv, 276–7. Orderic's Latin text reads: 'Melcofus autem nothus Alexandri filius regnum patruo preripere affectauit, eique duo bella satis acerrima instaurauit'.

The first medieval writer to so designate the prisoner of Roxburgh was the author of *Gesta Annalia* appended to the chronicle of John of Fordun and composed by circa 1285.[68]

The identification of not one but two Malcolms – an illegitimate son of Alexander I who was imprisoned at Roxburgh, and a 'son of Heth' whose identity remains contentious – as enemies of the twelfth-century Scottish kings seems to be making headway in some academic circles.[69] It is certainly not outside the bounds of possibility that an otherwise unknown son of Alexander I led several insurrections against his uncle, David I, and such antagonism might square well with what is known of the rather uneasy relations between the two brothers Alexander and David. David claimed Lothian from his brother by threat of force in 1113,[70] and it is probably this sibling rivalry that was referred to in a Gaelic quatrain:

> It's bad, what Mael Coluim's son has done,
>   dividing us from Alexander;
> he causes, like each king's son before,
>   the plunder of stable Alba.[71]

Similarly, the identification of the prisoner of Roxburgh with an illegitimate son of Alexander I would also help to make sense of the otherwise problematic statement found in the contemporary Cistercian chronicler Ailred of Rievaulx that Malcolm was the 'heir of paternal hatred and persecution' – which, on this view, should be read as a reference to the antagonism between David and Alexander.[72]

There is much to recommend this interpretation, based as it is upon a close and careful reading of the original texts and the elimination of modern editorial assumptions. But it does not explain everything, and several key objections remain. First, this hypothesis owes much – indeed, almost everything – to the statement of Orderic Vitalis that Malcolm was an illegitimate son of Alexander I. Yet Orderic, although a contemporary, was writing at a remove of several hundred miles from Scotland, and is a very uneven authority for Scottish affairs. He is, for instance, the only source to mention Margaret's patronage of the religious community on Iona, and he also relates a bizarre anecdote about how a Norwegian priest with prosthetic limbs slew David's first-born child as an

---

68 See *Chron. Holyrood* 129 (and notes), 151; *Acts of Malcolm IV*, no. 157; see also *ES* ii, 232, n. 3 for the various forms of the name.

69 A. Woolf, 'The Prisoner at Roxburgh: Earl or King?' Paper presented at the International Medieval Congress in Leeds, England, July 2000; see now Oram, *Lordship of Galloway*, 70–1, and Duncan, *Kingship of the Scots*, 65–7 and 71–2.

70 Duncan, *Scotland*, 134.

71 'A Verse on David son of Mael Coluim III,' trans. Clancy, *Triumph Tree*, 184.

72 *de Standardo*, in *Chron. Stephen*, iii, 193.

infant.[73] But both episodes are problematic. Moreover, his identification receives no corroboration from other sources closer at hand: it is surely striking that the two Scottish chronicles of Holyrood and Melrose, as well as Irish annals and various other English chronicles, all remained silent on this important matter. If Alexander I did have an illegitimate son who engaged in a struggle with his uncle over the kingship, Orderic is our only source for him.[74] Thus, the case that the prisoner at Roxburgh was a son of Alexander I ultimately rests upon foundations of dubious strength.

In fact, it is by no means clear that there were two different Malcolms who acted as enemies of the Scottish kings in the twelfth century. The known events of 1124 to 1168 are entirely consistent with the activities of a single individual. The rising of Somerled with his nephews, the sons of Malcolm in 1153, the capture of Donald son of Malcolm in 1156 and the reconciliation of Malcolm MacHeth with the king in 1157 all fit nicely as links in a single chain of events. Moreover, it cannot be objected that an imprisonment of over twenty years, from 1134 until 1157, represented an impossibly long incarceration: Robert Curthose, eldest son of William I of England and brother and rival of William II and Henry I, languished for twenty-eight years from his capture at Tinchebrai in 1106 until his death in 1134, and an even more remarkable incarceration was endured by Thomas of Galloway between 1235 and 1296. Finally, the appearance of the name itself on the record for the first time in 1157 – if significant - does not necessarily mean that it was being used to distinguish Malcolm MacHeth from Malcolm son of Alexander. A contemporary of Malcolm MacHeth was Malcolm the earl of Atholl (c. 1153/59 – c. 1190), and it seems at least as likely that the designation MacHeth was intended to distinguish its holder from his namesake the earl of Atholl.[75]

---

73 *Ecclesiastical History of Orderic Vitalis*, iv, 272–3 on Margaret's patronage of Iona, and 274–7 for the killing of David's first-born son: 'David's wife bore him a son called Henry, and two daughters, Clarice and Hodierna. They had another boy, their first-born child, who was cruelly murdered by the iron fingers of a certain wretched clerk. This man was punished for an appalling crime which he had committed in Norway, by having his eyes put out and his hands and feet cut off . . . Earl David took him into his care in England for the love of God . . . Using the iron fingers with which he was fitted, he cruelly stabbed his benefactor's two-year-old son while pretending to caress him, and so at the prompting of the devil he suddenly tore out the bowels of the suckling in his nurse's arms. In this way David's first-born child was killed. The murderer was bound to the tails of four wild horses and torn to pieces by them, as a terrible warning to evil-doers'. Ritchie, *Normans in Scotland*, 252 n. 3, dismisses the story as 'mythical'.

74 Although Ritchie, *Normans in Scotland*, 252 n. 3, does note that Orderic had visited Crowland Abbey, which had connections to David's wife, Maud de Senlis.

75 The earl of Atholl witnessed charters between about 1154/59 and the 1190s, and so was contemporary with MacHeth after his release from imprisonment: see *Acts of Malcolm IV*, nos. 185, 173, 176, 264, 254, 292, and *Acts of William I*, indices, passim. As a case in point, it is unclear which 'Earl Malcolm' witnessed a charter of 1165: *Acts of Malcolm IV*, no. 292.

Whatever the case may be with regard to the thorny problem of one Malcolm or two, the question of exactly who Malcolm MacHeth was remains. Much naturally turns on the patronymic 'MacHeth', which undoubtedly represents the Gaelic 'son of Aed', *macc Aeda*, and it is the best evidence with which to refute Orderic's identification of him as an illegitimate son of Alexander I.[76] Several attempts have been made to explain this patronymic (which seems to have been used as a surname by 1215), and they may be divided into two main groups: those which would trace MacHeth's descent from a member of the Cenél Loairn dynasty of Moray, and those which would associate him with an important family from Ross. While the former is more commonly expressed than the latter, it is perhaps less accepted in recent scholarly circles. Its explanation would run something along these lines: when Lulach, Macbeth's stepson, was killed by Malcolm in 1058, the royal line of Moray did not die out but was represented by Lulach's son, Máelsnechtai. He died in 1085, and since he left no children his heir was his sister, Lulach's daughter. In the 1130 record of the death of Angus in the *Annals of Ulster*, he was styled 'the son of Lulach's daughter',[77] making him a nephew of Máelsnechtai and a grandson of King Lulach. Neither Lulach's daughter (Máelsnechtai's sister) nor her husband is anywhere named, but a reasonable conjecture would be that her husband's name was Aed (Aodh), and indeed a 'Beth' and a 'Head,' both styled *comes*, appeared in several early charters of Alexander I and David I;[78] these names probably represent scribal errors or Latinisations of Aed. Malcolm MacHeth would then have been either a son or a brother of Angus, obtaining his claims in direct descent from the Cenél Loairn Moray dynasty.[79] W.F. Skene postulated that Aed (Heth) might himself have been of a family closely associated with the dynasty of Moray. He argued that Heth should be identified with Teadh, a grandson of Gillechattan, founder of the clan Chattan, who, it was claimed, descended from the rulers of Moray.[80] Unfortunately, however, Aed cannot be definitely identified on the basis of the present evidence. No positive connection between the Aed of the charters and the Teadh of the Clan Chattan

---

76 *Chron Holyrood*, 129 n. 1. See also G.F. Black, *The Surnames of Scotland. Their Origin, Meaning and History* (New York, 1946), 357, 455.

77 *AU* (Hennessy), ii, 124 (1130); *ES*, ii, 173.

78 See Lawrie, *ESC*, nos. 36, 49, 94, and notes on 283–84.

79 E.g. Robertson, *Early Kings*, i, 184–90 (Malcolm, a brother of Angus); A. Mackay, *The Book of Mackay* (Edinburgh, 1906), 21–3 (Malcolm, a son of Angus); I. Grimble, *Highland Man* (Inverness, 1980), 97 and genealogy on 93; more cautiously, Duncan, *Scotland*, 166: 'It is likely that he was related to the line of mormaers and earls of Moray represented by Angus'.

80 Skene, *Highlanders*, ii, 162–4. The Clan Chattan genealogy is printed in Skene, *Celtic Scotland*, iii, 478–9, where 'Teadh', grandson of Gillechattan, does look like another attempt at rendering Aed.

genealogy can be proven; and as Aed was given no title in the three charters he witnessed, the matter cannot satisfactorily be resolved.

Another argument would follow some aspects of this pedigree while rejecting others. The meaning of the patronymic MacHeth as 'son of Aed' is accepted, and consequently the relationship of Malcolm to the Earl Aed of the charters is also accepted. It is at this point, however, that the two arguments diverge. By a second line of thought, Aed would not be identified as the earl of Moray but rather as an otherwise unknown earl of Ross. This argument would thus separate the MacHeth claims from descent from the Moray dynasty, but would regard them instead as agitating for the restoration of the earldom of Ross.[81] In a recent spin on this hypothesis, Alexander Grant has suggested that Aed was not only earl of Ross, but also a member of Malcolm III's kindred – perhaps a son of Donald, the son of King Malcolm who was slain in 1085, and who may himself have played some role in the north during Malcolm's reign. In further support of this hypothesis, it is significant that the names of the MacHeth kindred – Malcolm, Donald, Aed, Kenneth - are all names that were borne by the kings of Alba but that only seldom appear in the families of other twelfth-century earls, except those of Fife who were royally descended. [82] Whichever view is correct, one thing seems certain: MacHeth enjoyed a high status in contemporary society. This is most evident from the matrimonial alliance he forged: he married a sister of Somerled MacGillabrigte, probably before 1130.[83]

Subsequent events certainly suggest a Ross connection for the MacHeths. When he died in 1168, Malcolm was styled 'earl of Ross', and a royal document dating from between 1160 and 1162 was directed to 'Malcolm earl of Ross'.[84] The installation of Malcolm in the earldom of Ross must be connected with the events of 1157, when 'Malcolm MacHeth was reconciled with the king of the Scots'. Bearing in mind that Malcolm himself had been imprisoned at Roxburgh since his capture in 1134, that his sons had spearheaded an insurrection in 1153 (supported by their uncle Somerled), and that Donald, Malcolm's son, had been captured at Whithorn in 1156, it has been suggested that the laconic entry for the year 1157 represents an event of substantial importance, whereby Malcolm MacHeth was granted (or perhaps re-granted) Ross in return for abandoning his claims – a situation that can be regarded as mutually advantageous for both MacHeth and Malcolm IV.[85]

81 *Acts of William I,* 13, and genealogical table facing 12; Barrow, 'Macbeth and Other Mormaers', 118.
82 Grant, 'Province of Ross', 108–9.
83 *Chron Holyrood,* 124–5 (1153); *ES,* ii, 223–4; see Duncan, *Scotland,* 166.
84 *Chron Holyrood,* 151 (1168); *ES,* ii, 265–6; *Acts of Malcolm IV,* no. 179. An 'Earl Malcolm' witnessed another charter of 1165, but it is unclear whether this was Malcolm of Ross or Malcolm of Atholl: see no. 292.
85 McDonald, 'Treachery in the Remotest Territories', 174–5.

From the perspective of the king of Scots, not only would a buffer-zone be created between the province of Moray and the expansionist earl of Orkney/Caithness, Harald Maddadson, who was often hostile to Scottish authority, but the fact that its holder was of native stock and presumably well-known in the region would enhance his authority and might also have facilitated administration of an otherwise ungovernable and troublesome province (not unlike Ferchar Maccintsacairt half a century later). While the nature of the grant is unknown, it must have been similar in nature to that bestowing Fife upon the native earls of that province circa 1140, and was no doubt based upon dependent tenure. If this were the case, then the king would also have succeeded in binding a potentially troublesome magnate to his cause, entrapping him in obligations not unlike the earls of the east. If the king's aim was to reduce trouble in the north by binding MacHeth to his cause, then subsequent events must suggest that he was successful: it is a curious and overlooked fact that there was no further resistance from the MacHeths until at least 1186 and certainly 1215, and it must be significant that nothing more is heard of MacHeth's descendants for at least thirty years after his accommodation. From the MacHeth perspective such a settlement also had much to commend it. While it might seem odd, at first glance, that a rival for the kingship would come to terms with the king, the earldom of Ross and the title that accompanied it were perhaps as reasonable a reward as MacHeth could expect under the circumstances.[86] With the kingship monopolised by a dynasty that had already shown its ability to protect itself against rival claimants, the move by MacHeth must be regarded as extremely adroit: he may well have sensed which way the winds of change were blowing and decided to trim his sails accordingly. Such a situation is not without parallel in the Scottish kingdom: the earls of Fife, the premier native magnates, were likely descended from King Dub (d. 966), and may have obtained their status as inaugural officials by abandoning the claims of their kin to the kingship.[87]

What is not clear is whether the grant of 1157 represented the creation of the earldom of Ross, or merely the re-granting of a province that had presumably been held by the Crown since at least 1134 if not earlier. It has been suggested that the agreement of 1157 actually marked the creation of the earldom,[88] but this is a contentious point. The Earl Aed who appears in several charters of Alexander I and David I and who was probably the father of Malcolm MacHeth is sometimes also associated with Ross on the basis that the holders of all the other earldoms on the record in the early twelfth century are known and accounted for. If Alexander Grant is correct, this Aed might have been a

---

86 *Acts of Malcolm IV*, 8.
87 J. Bannerman, 'MacDuff of Fife', 20–38.
88 McDonald, 'Treachery in the Remotest Territories', 174–5.

kinsman of the Donald son of Malcolm who was killed in 1085 and who may also have had some connection with Ross, thus giving the earldom a much longer pedigree than has been allowed in the past. If Earl Aed had been at odds with David I, and had died sometime around 1130, this may also have provided a catalyst for the subsequent uprising of MacHeth and Earl Angus of Moray.[89] As Grant has argued, 'The troubles of 1130–34 may reflect MacHeth claims to the throne, as much as those of Oengus of Moray'.[90]

If little is known of Malcolm MacHeth, his descendants are cloaked in even deeper veils of mystery. Of his sons who joined forces with Somerled in 1153, Donald was imprisoned with his father in 1156. From this point on, his fate is unknown: was he, too, released in 1157, or did he remain in confinement? A reasonable suggestion, which would accord well with what we know in such circumstances, is that he was held as a hostage for his father's good behaviour. The fate of Malcolm's other son, or even his name, is unknown. It is also a point of some contention whether the Adam son of Donald who was seized at Coupar Angus in 1186 was a member of the MacHeth or the MacWilliam kindred. The case has been made, based on a close reading of the Holyrood Chronicle manuscript, that Adam was an alternate reading of Aed, and that Adam/Aed was a son of Donald MacHeth.[91] Chronology will certainly allow this, since if Adam had been born before his father's incarceration in 1156, then he would have been in the prime of life in 1186. If Adam's identity as a member of the MacHeth kindred proves correct, then this may provide yet another instance (along with that of 1215) of cooperation between the MacHeths and MacWilliams, since the events of 1186 are almost certainly related to the MacWilliam insurrection of the 1180s. Between the events of 1186 and those of 1215 there are no more references to the MacHeths. In 1215, however, Kenneth MacHeth appeared upon the stage, apparently allied with a son of Donald MacWilliam. His parentage is uncertain, although it seems likely that he was a son of the Adam/Aed taken at Coupar Angus in 1186 and therefore represented a fourth generation of the MacHeth kindred. With the death of Kenneth in 1215, it seems that the last of the MacHeths had played his final hour upon the stage.

It has been argued that when viewing the uprisings centred predominantly in the north of Scotland, two distinct claims to the kingship must be recognised: those of MacHeth, likely transmitted from the house of Moray, and MacWilliam claims, based upon descent from King Duncan II. In this respect the uprisings display a

89 And might also account for the remark of Ailred of Rievaulx about paternal hatred and persecution.
90 Grant, 'Province of Ross', 108–9, quotation at 109.
91 See *Acts of William I*, 11–2, and esp. n. 47.

strongly dynastic element. Further, these claims must be taken seriously. Whoever they were, and however modern historians regard them, both MacHeth and MacWilliam had some justice on their side. If their claims had not rested upon a sound genealogical basis, men of the twelfth and thirteenth centuries would scarcely have paid them any heed.[92] It is also significant to note the treatment accorded to Malcolm MacHeth after his capture in 1134: he was neither executed nor mutilated, but was imprisoned and reconciled with the king in 1157. Surely if MacHeth's cause had lacked a sound basis, David I would have taken steps to ensure that his rival would cause no more trouble. This is what apparently happened with the enigmatic Wimund in the late 1140s: he was blinded and castrated, and sent to Byland abbey to live out his last days as a monk there.[93] That David did not follow this route strongly suggests that MacHeth had some justice on his side, as does the 1157 accommodation and the grant of the earldom of Ross. In this context it is interesting to note that Donald MacWilliam and his descendants received much harsher treatment at the hands of the royal line they opposed. This could mean that, in the eyes of the Scottish kings, their claims were invalidated based upon the supposed illegitimacy of Duncan II, or it could simply represent the differing attitudes of the kings involved, since the MacWilliam insurrections began two decades after the reconciliation between the king and Malcolm MacHeth.

In assessing the problem of the resistance to the Canmore dynasty, it may also be of some significance to return to the question of the name MacHeth. It has already been noted that this probably means *macc Aeda*, 'son of Aed'. Aed or Aodh, meaning fire, was a fairly common name,[94] but it also appears to have carried very strong prophetic connotations in contemporary Gaeldom. One version of *Berchán's Prophecy*, for instance, alluded to an Aodh Eanghach from Cruachan who would win victories and inflict slaughter on both Irish and foreigners, while the *Annals of Loch Cé* preserve an enigmatic entry under the year 1214 about the appearance of a 'false Aedh, who was called 'the Aider".[95] In the Irish context, then, there was a 'popular expectation of a messianic king called Aodh, who would deliver his country from the Norman invaders . . .'[96]

---

92 Barrow, 'Some Problems', 99; see also W.D.H. Sellar, 'Highland Family Origins – Pedigree Making and Pedigree Faking', in *Middle Ages in the Highlands*, 103–16.

93 William of Newburgh, *Historia Rerum Anglicarum*, in *Chron Stephen*, i, 72–6.

94 See *Highlanders*, notes on 404–5.

95 A.O. Anderson, ed., 'The Prophecy of Berchan', in *Zeitschrift für Celtische Philologie* xviii (1930), cap. 72; *ALC*, i, 253. The enigmatic prophecy attributed to Berchan has been described by its most recent editor and commentator as 'a compilation of pieces of varying date': Hudson, *Prophecy of Berchan*, 14. The relevant section was composed during the reign of Malcolm III, before his marriage to Margaret in *c.* 1070.

96 K. Simms, *From Kings to Warlords: The Changing Political Structure of Gaelic Ireland in the Later Middle Ages* (Woodbridge, 1987), 27.

Other prophecies also circulated in the twelfth and thirteenth centuries which promised the expulsion of the Anglo-Normans from Ireland and Wales. Gerald of Wales recorded a tradition that 'almost all the English will be dislodged from Ireland by a king who will come from the lonely mountains of Patrick, and on the night of Our Lord's day will overrun a castle in the wooded region of Ui Fhaelain'.[97] In Wales, prophecies of Myrddin were also circulated which foretold that the Welsh would be rid of the Normans and English.[98] There seems no reason why prophecies like these, obviously widely known in the twelfth century, could not have become current in Scotland, especially given the close contacts that existed between northern and western Scotland and Gaelic Ireland in this period: lines from Berchán and attributed to him by name survive in a Scottish manuscript of fifteenth/sixteenth-century date.[99] Traditions like these could well have added strength and support to the MacHeth cause against the Scottish kings, closely allied as these kings were with contemporary European trends.

Implicit in the foregoing discussion is the thesis that the MacHeths and MacWilliams were excluded from competing for the kingship, succession to which had traditionally operated through an alternating system, by the descendants of Malcolm III and Margaret as they organised themselves into a lineage which monopolised the royal office. But underlying these changes in the succession was an increased southern influence, first English and then Anglo-Norman, promoted by the union of Malcolm III and Margaret around 1070. Although superficially dynastic in nature, at a deeper level the northern opposition must also be regarded as directed against fundamental cultural changes that affected succession practices. It is significant in this context that a contemporary English chronicle, recording the MacWilliam rising of 1211/12, went on to say that 'more recent kings of Scots profess themselves to be rather Frenchmen, both in race and in manners, language, and culture: and after reducing the Scots to utter servitude, they admit only Frenchmen to their friendship and service'.[100] This link between the Europeanising policies of the

97 Giraldus Cambrensis (Gerald of Wales), *Expugnatio Hibernica: The Conquest of Ireland*, ed. and trans. A.B. Scott and F.X. Martin (*A New History of Ireland Ancillary Publications* Vol. 3, Dublin, 1978), 233; see also notes on 351.

98 *The Black Book of Carmarthen*, trans. M. Pennar (Lampeter, 1989), 71; see also 76. The better-known but even more indecipherable 'Prophecies of Merlin' contained in Geoffrey of Monmouth's *History of the Kings of Britain*, trans. L. Thorpe (Harmondsworth, 1966) could also be cited as an indication of the popularity of such prophecies in this period.

99 Hudson, *Prophecy of Berchán*, 9 and note 18; I am grateful to Professor Hudson for pointing this out to me.

100 Walter of Coventry, ii, 206; trans. in *SAEC*, 330 n.6; see also Owen, *William the Lion*, esp. ch. 2 on this theme.

kings of Scots and the MacWilliam rising must therefore be regarded as more than just coincidence, and is, in fact, indicative of resentment and reaction against such policies. These uprisings, then, may be seen not only as attempting to restore the form of succession which gave collateral branches of the royal line access to the kingship, but also as resisting the Anglo-Norman penetration of Scotland – and particularly Moray and Ross – from within. Perhaps, then, if the Norman infiltration of Scotland is often regarded as a 'peaceful Norman conquest', it can no longer be held to have been exclusively so, as demonstrated by the military actions of the Scottish kings against their northern foes. Moreover, one of the valuable lessons to be learned from closer study of this northern resistance is that, despite the current characterisation of the twelfth- and thirteenth-century kingdom as a balance of 'old' and 'new',[101] the incidents of resistance to the Scottish kings show that there existed within this kingdom elements that were clearly alienated and disaffected – in contrast to the prevailing view of medieval Scottish historiography which emphasises unity and harmony.

If MacHeth and MacWilliam are seen as agitating for the same prize, namely, the kingship of Scotland, then the problem does arise of the apparent cooperation of the counter-claimants in seeking the same objective. In some interpretations this provides an important stumbling block for the acceptance of the genealogies outlined above.[102] A careful reading of the evidence, however, will not allow the conclusion that MacHeths and MacWilliams were cooperating continuously throughout the twelfth century. It is striking that for nearly thirty years, from the time of Malcolm MacHeth's reconciliation in 1157 to the events of 1186, there is no mention of the sons of Malcolm MacHeth being involved in any insurrections – and the identification of Adam, son of Donald, who was seized in 1186, with a son of Malcolm MacHeth is contentious. Not until the uprising of 1215 – and apparently only then – is there any hint of collaboration between MacHeths and MacWilliams; this might well be the first cooperative effort, perhaps born of desperation. *Gesta Annalia* recorded how 'the king of Scotland's enemies – namely, Donald Bàn, son of MacWilliam, Kenneth MacHeth, and the son of a certain king of Ireland – entered Moray with a numerous crowd of miscreants'.[103] This does seem to suggest a common cause, but can hardly be projected backward and thereby taken to indicate collaboration and cooperation over the previous eighty years. In fact, the issue of counter-claimants competing for the same prize can be better understood by turning to contemporary Irish and Welsh society, where it was by no means unusual to find two or more segments of the royal lineage competing for the

101 E.g. Barrow, *David I of Scotland, passim.*
102 *Acts of William I*, 13.
103 *Chron Fordun*, i, 282; ii, 278.

kingship; indeed, in Ireland, the dispossessed segments might unite in common opposition to that in possession of the royal office.[104] This might be exactly what happened in twelfth-century Scotland, where the MacWilliams represented the claims of the eldest son of Malcolm III and his first wife, Ingibjorg, while the MacHeths might have descended from a second or illegitimate son.

The sparse nature of the sources and the ambiguities in their interpretation mean that it is impossible to determine with certainty the identity of Malcolm MacHeth and the nature of his claims, or those of Donald MacWilliam, for that matter. But the validity of the claims made by these men need not be doubted: both leaders found men willing to fight and die with them, and it is clear that that their causes were taken seriously by contemporaries, including the Scottish kings themselves. In the final analysis, however, the MacHeths and the MacWilliams are best regarded as dynastic rivals – the representatives of cast-off segments of the royal kindred and the casualties of the consolidation of the kingship into a lineage by the descendants of Malcolm III and Margaret. They were, in a very real sense, the losers of twelfth- and thirteenth-century Scottish history.

Fergus, Somerled and Harald Maddadsson
There can be no doubt that the MacHeths and MacWilliams were the leading figures in opposition to the Scottish kings, or that the antipathy of these kindreds to the Canmore rulers was rooted in essentially dynastic causes. Indeed, opposition from these kindreds provides a unifying thread to the period between at least 1124 and 1230. Yet the MacHeths and MacWilliams by no means enjoyed a monopoly on opposition and insurrection, and from time to time other adversaries also appeared on the scene. One particularly troubled period, which saw several uprisings and a good deal of military campaigning in Scotland, was the 1150s and 1160s, a time dominated by the clashes of Malcolm IV with the formidable rulers of Galloway and Argyll, Fergus and Somerled.

With Fergus and Somerled we come to two of the most intriguing figures of the twelfth century. Less mysterious than the MacHeths and MacWilliams, and probably better known, their place in Scottish history seems assured: not only are they perceived as foremost among the king's enemies in the twelfth century, but they were also the progenitors of kindreds that played important roles in the subsequent history of Galloway, Argyll, and the Isles. Both seem to have emerged in the 1130s or 1140s as powerful figures in Atlantic regions that were only loosely attached to the Scottish kingdom. Fergus, designated simply 'de Galweia' (of Galloway) in his earliest appearance on the historical record as a witness to a charter of about 1136, was the progenitor of a powerful dynasty of native Lords of Galloway that endured until the death of Alan of Galloway in

104 Frame, *Political Development*, 108–25; Ó Corráin, 'Irish Regnal Succession', 8.

1234. Although his lineage remains uncertain and it has sometimes been argued that he must have been an outsider or a parvenu, the consensus among historians now is that he was in fact a member of a native Gallovidian dynasty into which some Scandinavian elements had probably intruded in the course of the tenth and eleventh centuries. Somerled, whose pedigree is known, was also of mixed Gaelic-Norse descent, a point nicely highlighted by considering his own name and those of his immediate forbears: his own name is Norse, but those of his father (Gilla Brigde) and grandfather (Gilla Adomnain) are Gaelic. A late medieval pedigree of Somerled traces his ancestry back to the ninth-century chieftain Godfrey MacFergus, a figure with Irish, Scottish, Hebridean, and Scandinavian associations. Like Fergus, Somerled was the progenitor of not just one but several prominent kindreds in the west highlands in the middle ages, including the MacDonalds, MacDougalls, and the MacRuairis.[105]

Though most commonly regarded as provincial rulers of subordinate status, it is now clear that both men possessed regal standing in an era when multiple kingships were only beginning to fade and when kingship itself was still relative in some parts of the British Isles. Eastern Scottish and English sources styled Fergus *princeps* or *comes*, even though he was never designated in this manner in the charters, while Somerled was *regulus*.[106] These terms are notoriously difficult to translate, however, and it would be anachronistic to render *princeps* as simply prince: literally 'chief man', 'ruler' or 'lord' might also be more accurate, while *regulus* also has the meaning of 'ruler' or 'underking'.[107] In general, the terms utilised by the Scottish and English chroniclers place Fergus and Somerled in a broad category of rulers including, but not limited to, kings who, as *principes*, determined the fate of their subjects and the church in their territories.[108] But it is also important to realise that Fergus and Somerled are really only known from the perspective of those whom they opposed – namely, the Scottish rulers descended from Malcolm III and Margaret. Since the chronicles and annals describing their status were composed at monastic centres patronised by the kings of Scots, an objective outlook is hardly to

---

105 See Oram, *Lordship of Galloway*, chs. 1 and 2, Brooke, *Wild Men and Holy Places*, ch. 4, and McDonald, *Kingdom of the Isles*, ch. 2 for more detailed accounts of the emergence of Fergus and Somerled as regional powers. On Somerled's pedigree, see W.D.H. Sellar, 'The Origins and Ancestry of Somerled', *SHR* xlv (1966), 123–42.

106 Fergus: *Chron Holyrood*, 137, 139; Richard of Hexham, *De Gestis Regis Stephani*, in *Chron Stephen* iii, 177–8. Somerled in *Chron Melrose*, 36 (1164).

107 R.E. Latham, *Revised Medieval Latin Word-List from British and Irish Sources* (London, 1965), 372; see also S. Reynolds, *Kingdoms and Communities in Western Europe 900–1300* (Oxford, 1984), 259–60.

108 See K.F. Werner, 'Kingdom and principality in twelfth-century France', in T. Reuter, ed., *The Medieval Nobility: Studies on the Ruling Classes of France and Germany from the Sixth to the Twelfth Centuries* (Amsterdam, 1979), 244.

be expected. It is probable that Scottish and English sources deliberately played down the regal status of rulers like Fergus and Somerled to conform with the new ideals of unitary kingship espoused by the Canmore kings.[109] There is, however, compelling evidence from outside Scotland that Fergus and Somerled both possessed royal standing. Irish annals that record the death of Somerled style him *rí Innse Gall & Cind Tíre*, 'king of the Hebrides and Kintyre', while Somerled's son, Ranald, styled himself 'king of the Isles and lord of Argyll and Kintyre'.[110] Irish annals also designate Fergus's descendants, but not Fergus himself, as *rí Gall-Gaidhil*.[111] But the most compelling evidence for the royal status of Fergus is to be found in a copy of a charter of the lord of Galloway granting Galtway in Balmaclellan, Kirkcudbrightshire, to the Knights of St John of Jerusalem (the Hospitallers), in which Fergus is described as *rex Galwiten-sium*.[112] The document, probably copied directly from Fergus's own charter, provides valuable insight into the style that he used to describe himself, proclaiming, as one modern authority has put it, his 'unconditional and hereditary right to rule Galloway'.[113]

There is little evidence on which to base any assessment of the relationships between Fergus and Somerled on the one hand and the Scottish kings on the other before the death of David I in 1153, but nothing seems necessarily to indicate hostility. Contingents of Gallovidians and Islesmen fought in the Scottish army that was defeated by the English at the battle of the Standard in 1138, for instance.[114] Although it has been argued that these might have been mercenary troops, the presence of contingents from the territories of Fergus and Somerled has often been taken to indicate peaceful, or at least cooperative, relations between these rulers and David I. Clearly, however, by the 1150s and early 1160s that situation had changed, when both Somerled and, it seems, Fergus joined the ranks of the enemies of the Scottish kings. Somerled's insurrection of 1153 is well known, as is his invasion of the Scottish mainland at the head of a formidable fleet in 1164. The Melrose chronicle, describing the invasion of 1164, states that Somerled had been in rebellion against the king for twelve years, suggesting that the events of 1153 to 1164 formed a single insurrection. In fact, there is good evidence for two distinct risings, the first from 1153 until 1160, and then a second in 1164 that resulted in Somerled's death. The rising of 1153 was undertaken on behalf of Somerled's nephews, the sons of

---

109 R.A. McDonald, 'Rebels without a Cause? The Relations of Fergus of Galloway and Somerled of Argyll with the Scottish Kings, 1153–1164', in *Alba*, 178–9.

110 *Annals of Tigernach*, ed. W. Stokes, in *Revue Celtique* xviii (1898), 195, and in *ES*, ii, 254.

111 *AU* (Hennessy and McCarthy), ii, 234–5, 240–1.

112 Stringer, 'Acts of Lordship', 212 (no. 1).

113 Brooke, *Wild Men and Holy Places* ,79.

114 Ailred of Rievaulx, *De Standardo*, in *Chron Stephen*, iii, 196–7.

Malcolm MacHeth who had been incarcerated since 1134. Although there is little evidence for the actual course of the insurrection, it does not seem to have gone well for the allied forces, in part because of Somerled's involvement in Manx affairs between 1154 and 1156, which must have entailed a diversion of attention, not to mention resources, to the Irish Sea, and also in part because of the capture of Donald, Malcolm's son, at Whithorn in 1156. Although it has sometimes been argued that hostilities ceased in 1157, when Malcolm MacHeth was reconciled with the king, *Gesta Annalia* observed that Somerled 'still wickedly wrought his wickedness among the people'.[115] This is probably correct. There is no evidence for a treaty between Somerled and the king until 1160, when a royal charter was dated 'at the next Christmas after the agreement between the king and Somerled' (*in Natali Domini proximo post concordiam Regis et Sumerledi*).[116] Unfortunately the terms of the agreement are not known, but its date, 1160, might be significant, since this was the same year in which the Scottish king campaigned against Galloway and brought its ruler, Fergus, to heel.

The evidence for Fergus's involvement in these events is much more circumstantial and subject to interpretation. A crucial clue in assessing the question is the capture of Donald MacHeth at Whithorn in 1156. Whithorn, the site of the bishopric of Galloway, was located close to one of the principal centres of power of the Lords of Galloway at Cruggleton. Thus, Donald's presence at Whithorn hints at some connection with Fergus, but was he an enemy or an ally of Somerled and the MacHeths? On the one hand, it might be argued that Donald MacHeth was apprehended by Fergus, who then turned him over to the king. It is difficult to imagine Donald being taken in Galloway without at least the tacit approval of the ruler of the region; moreover, since Godfrey, the Manx king against whom Somerled was struggling in the mid-1150s, was the grandson of the Lord of Galloway, Fergus, according to this line of reasoning, would have been no friend of Somerled. It is possible, then, that as late as 1156 Fergus and Somerled were in opposing camps. On the other hand, there is no evidence that Fergus was an active supporter of Godfrey; when Godfrey was driven out of Man, he is known to have sheltered for a while at the court of the Scottish king before journeying to Norway.[117] Indeed, Donald's presence at Whithorn might be construed as an indication that Fergus was somehow involved in the events of the 1150s; perhaps Donald was at Whithorn seeking the support of the powerful ruler of Galloway. Taken altogether, then, there is insufficient evidence for Fergus's involvement in the insurrection of the

---

115 *Chron Fordun* i, 255; ii, 250.
116 Barrow, *Acts of Malcolm IV*, no. 175.
117 *Chron Man*, f. 37v–f. 38r (1158); his presence in Scotland is proven by a charter attestation, probably from 1159: *Acts of Malcolm IV*, no. 131.

1150s. By 1160, however, it would appear that the stance of the Lord of Galloway had changed, which also brings us to consideration of the famous 'revolt of the earls' at Perth.

The events of 1160 have never been the subject of intensive scrutiny, although it has been rightly suggested that they represent an important moment in the history of both the reign of Malcolm IV specifically and, more generally, his entire dynasty.[118] The *Chronicle of Melrose*, the only contemporary source for these events, says that:

> In the year 1160, Malcolm, king of Scots, came from the army at Toulouse. And when [Malcolm] had come to the city that is called Perth, earl Ferteth and five other earls (being enraged against the king because he had gone to Toulouse) besieged the city, and wished to take the king prisoner; but their presumption did not at all prevail. King Malcolm went three times with a great army into Galloway, and at last subdued them.[119]

Gesta Annalia describes the episode as follows:

> At length the Scottish lords, seeing their king's too great intimacy and friendship with Henry, king of England, were sore troubled, and all Scotland with them. For they feared this intimacy had shame and disgrace in store for them; and they strove in earnestness to guard against this . . . Thereupon, he returned from the army at Toulouse and came to Scotland, on account of divers pressing matters; and by his authority as king, he bade the prelates and nobles meet at Perth. Meanwhile the chief men of the country were roused. Six earls – Ferchard, earl of Stratherne, to wit, and five others – being stirred up against the king, not to compass any selfish end, or through treason, but rather to guard the common weal, sought to take him, and laid siege to the keep of that town. God so ordering it, however, their undertaking was brought to naught for the nonce; and after not many days had rolled by, he was, by the advice of the clergy, brought back to a good understanding with his nobles. He then, thrice in the same year, mustered an army, and marched into Galloway against the rebels . . .[120]

To begin with, it is clear that the essential context for these events is the king's absence from the realm and his expedition to Toulouse in the entourage of King Henry II of England. Malcolm's journey to Toulouse is rooted firmly in Anglo-Scottish relations of the late 1150s, characterised by tension between Malcolm IV and Henry II over the northern counties, and also by Malcolm's ardent desire to receive knighthood at the hands of Henry. In 1157 Malcolm

---

118 Barrow, *Kingship and Unity*, 47–8.
119 *Chron Melrose* 36 (1160); *ES* ii, 244.
120 *Chron Fordun* i, 256; ii, 251.

was summoned to Chester where he performed homage to the English king, and was also deprived of Northumbria and Cumbria, territories which David I had striven to add to Scottish territory during the upheavals of Stephen's reign. In the following year a meeting between the two rulers at Carlisle ended when 'they departed not well pacified on either side, and in such a manner that the king of Scots was not yet knighted'. Henry II, it seems, was astute at manipulating Malcolm with the prospect of knighthood, and accordingly he induced the Scottish king and his brother William to join his campaign against the count of Toulouse in 1159. It was only in the course of this campaign that Malcolm finally attained knighthood at Perigueux.[121] It has thus been argued that the hostile response Malcolm received upon his return to Scotland was due in no small measure to his apparent subservience to the English king, which might have been regarded as a threat to the independence of the realm. While there can be little doubt that this must have been an important motive for insurrection, *Gesta Annalia* also raises the possibility that the 'revolt of the earls' needs to be set in the broader context of the disturbances of the 1150s.

Gesta Annalia relates how King Malcolm returned to Scotland 'on account of divers pressing matters' – matters which necessitated the summoning of a council of prelates and nobles at Perth and which threatened the common good of the realm. But what were these pressing matters? As we have seen, it is by no means certain that the insurrection against Malcolm IV that had begun in 1153 was quashed by the capture of Donald MacHeth in 1156 and the reconciliation between the king and Malcolm MacHeth in 1157. The evidence points instead to ongoing hostilities down to 1160, the year of a treaty between Somerled and the king. It can therefore be argued that the hostile reception King Malcolm received upon his return to Scotland in 1160 is directly related to the fact that, when he departed for Toulouse in the spring of 1159 (he crossed the channel in mid-June and the siege of Toulouse occupied three months from July to September[122]), Somerled and his allies had not yet been brought to heel. On this view, the anger of the earls was perhaps prompted not so much by Malcolm's relationship with Henry II as by the fact that the king had absented himself from the realm in the midst of a serious domestic crisis, possibly otherwise unrecorded attacks by the ruler of Argyll and the Isles and his allies. It is also possible that by this time Fergus of Galloway was allied with Somerled – thus providing a Gallovidian as well as an insular context for the events of 1160.
.   Much turns on the wording of the chronicles that record these events. The Melrose chronicler immediately follows his narrative of the revolt of the earls with the statement that 'King Malcolm went three times with a great army into Galloway, and at last subdued them'. The *Chronicle of Holyrood* omits mention of

121 *ES* ii, 243.
122 See *ES* ii, 240, n. 5.

events at Perth, but does mention royal campaigns into Galloway: 'In 1160 king Malcolm led an army into Galloway three times. And he conquered his enemies there, and made a treaty with peace; and he returned without loss'. Next, it says, 'Fergus, the prince of Galloway, received the habit of a canon in the church of Holyrood at Edinburgh'. *Gesta Annalia* explicitly links the events of 1160, the royal campaigns to Galloway, and Fergus's retirement: 'He [King Malcolm] then, thrice in the same year, mustered an army and marched into Galloway against the rebels. At last, when he had vanquished these, made them his allies, and subdued them, he hied him back in peace, without loss to his men; and afterwards, when he had thus subdued them, he pressed them so sore that their chieftain, who was called Fergus, gave up the calling of arms, and . . . donned the canonical garb at the monastery of Holyrood in Edinburgh'.[123]

Scholars have long assumed a direct, causal relationship between the events at Perth and the royal campaigns in Galloway that followed, and the view has often been expressed that Fergus must have been one of those who participated in the attack on King Malcolm, despite the fact that he was not commonly designated an earl in contemporary records. Daphne Brooke, however, has made a cogent and convincing argument that the Melrose chronicler has conflated two essentially unrelated pieces of information into a major military operation that begins with the attack on the king at Perth and ends in the three military campaigns in Galloway.[124] On this view, Fergus's involvement in the events at Perth in 1160 is dismissed. It is, for example, difficult to see why the rebel earls, having been bested by Malcolm at Perth, would have fled to Galloway in the southwest rather than dispersing to their native territories. Moreover, there is no evidence that any of the prominent native earls were punished for their role in events; most appear as witnesses in royal charters immediately after the events at Perth, suggesting their status remained un-changed. Brooke proposes instead an alternative scenario: the native earls, incensed with Malcolm's seeming dependence on Henry II of England, under-took a 'rough but fatherly carpeting of a young king', at Perth; Fergus meanwhile took advantage of the situation to engage in raiding on the frontiers between Scotland and Galloway, possibly in an attempt to smooth over internal dissensions by uniting the fractious parties in common military activity.[125] Malcolm's military campaigns in Galloway were therefore undertaken in response to these otherwise unrecorded attacks. Certainly the cession of Cumbria to Henry II by Malcolm IV in 1157 would have considerably loosened

---

123 *Chron Fordun* i, 256; ii, 251.
124 Brooke, 'Fergus of Galloway: Miscellaneous Notes for a Revised Portrait', *TDGNHAS* 3rd ser. lxvi [Hoddom Volume 2] (1991), 47–58; *idem*, *Wild Men and Holy Places*, 93–4.
125 *Ibid.*

Scottish control in the southwest, and this, combined with the absence of the king himself in 1159, could have provided a suitable environment for Gallovidian forays into Scotland proper in 1159/60. Two series of land transactions made post-1160 support this hypothesis. In the first, Fergus's son, Uhtred, parcelled out lands in the region of 'Cro' (between the Urr and the Nith), lands not usually regarded as belonging to Galloway proper in the time of Fergus, and possibly obtained by military activity. Second, at about the same time, Malcolm IV granted extensive territories around Biggar to Fleming colonists; these lands sit astride an important communication route in Clydesdale, and their distribution to Flemings must have been intended to close off this route to Gallovidian raiders and their allies.[126]

Taken altogether, then, the events of 1159/60 suggest that, by then, Fergus of Galloway was counted among the king's enemies, and that there had been Gallovidian forays into Scotland around that time. There can be no denying the fact of three campaigns against Galloway in 1160 that forced Fergus, in the words of the author of *Gesta Annalia*, to give up 'the calling of arms' and retire to Holyrood abbey. Although Fergus may well have been of advanced age by 1160, and was possibly facing domestic crisis in the form of internecine quarrels, his retirement was certainly brought about by military defeat: how else to explain the choice of Holyrood abbey near Edinburgh, founded by David I in 1128, when Fergus himself had acted as founder or patron of a number of reformed monastic houses within Galloway itself to which he might more fittingly have retired? Moreover, the events of 1159/60 also suggest an alliance between Fergus and Somerled. Is it mere coincidence that the campaigns against Galloway occurred in the same year as the treaty between Somerled and the king? One version of the *Chronicle of Holyrood* refers to the defeat of King Malcolm's 'confederate enemies'; this raises the suspicion that Fergus's Gallovidians had allied with Somerled's Argyllsmen and Islesmen. If Fergus and Somerled were allies by 1159/60, then it may be that the treaty mentioned by the *Chronicle of Holyrood* as having been made with the Gallovidians in 1160 was more or less the same agreement between Somerled and the king that is referred to in a Scottish charter of the same year. It thus seems possible that the fall of Fergus also prepared the ground for Somerled to come to terms. In support of this hypothesis, a land-based campaign against the Gallovidians would almost certainly have been more feasible than the sea-based sort of campaign that would need to be undertaken against Argyll and the Isles, for which the Scottish kings did not have the resources until the 1220s. Finally, whether or not Fergus and Somerled were cooperating in their actions against the Scottish king in 1160, Malcolm's achievement in 1160 is

126 Brooke, 'Fergus of Galloway', 54–55; *Acts of Malcolm IV*, 47.

surely remarkable – having defused the crisis at Perth, he managed not only to force the powerful ruler of Galloway into retirement, but also brought the mighty Somerled to heel as well.

From 1160 until 1164 Somerled disappears from the historical record; perhaps, if he, too, had been forced into submission in 1160, he was licking his wounds, or perhaps there were other demands on his attention. Then, in 1164, he appeared in the Clyde estuary with a fleet of no less than 160 vessels (if the often unreliable Manx chronicle is to be believed), filled with warriors from the Hebrides, Kintyre, Argyll, and Dublin. In the ensuing battle near Renfrew, Somerled, together with one of his sons, was killed, and his army routed. This invasion has long puzzled historians. The earliest attempts to explain it are confused and probably in-accurate. The Manx chronicler stated that Somerled's intent was to 'subdue the whole of Scotland'. *Gesta Annalia* gave the primary objective as plunder, appar-ently casting Somerled in the role of a latter-day Viking raider, while Buchanan, writing in the sixteenth century, suggested that Somerled's aim was nothing less than the kingship itself.[127] The seventeenth-century *History of the MacDonalds* implied that Somerled had been provoked to invade because the 'nobles were still in [King Malcolm's] ears, desiring him to suppress the pride of Sommerled [sic]' so that they could divide his kingdom among themselves.[128] None of these explanations is convincing, but most modern historians have been disinclined to consider the motivation behind the invasion.[129]

There are two important considerations in assessing the hostility of Fergus and Somerled toward the Scottish kings in the 1150s and 1160s. The first of these is the fundamentally westward orientation of their respective territories. It has been argued that both Fergus and Somerled were rulers who belonged not to the essentially eastern-oriented kingdom of Alba, but rather to marginal kingdoms located in the rugged outer Atlantic zone of north Britain.[130] These regions, connected by the western seaways, constituted a distinct cultural province with a history that extended hundreds, even thousands, of years into the past: prehistoric peoples, Celts, wandering saints and missionaries, and Viking raiders, traders, and settlers had all utilised the sea lanes and left their indelible imprint upon the lands ringing the shores of the Irish Sea. As Barry Cunliffe has put it, 'the unifying bond created by the ocean, for those who have lived around its edges, should not be under-

127 *Chron Man*, f. 39r (1164); *Chron Fordun* i, 257; ii, 252; Buchanan, *History of Scotland*, trans. J. Aikman (Glasgow 1827), i, 359–60.
128 *History of the MacDonalds*, in *Highland Papers*, ed. J.R.N. MacPhail (4 vols., Scottish History Society, Edinburgh, 1914–34), i, 8.
129 Although the suggestion has been made that Somerled's invasion might need to be viewed in the context of Henry II's foreign policy toward Scotland: *Medieval Ireland*, ed. Cosgrove, 62.
130 McDonald, 'Rebels without a cause?', 166–86.

estimated'.[131] Whithorn, for instance, an important ecclesiastical site in the early middle ages, was influenced and shaped by Romano-British, Brittonic, Anglian, and Scandinavian impulses; in the lifetime of Fergus it had even been gifted lands on the Isle of Man by the Manx kings.[132] Similarly, Iona, the premier ecclesiastical site within Dalriada, although isolated from the Scottish mainland by mountains and deep sea-lochs, had been, in its early medieval heyday, a bustling hub of trade and communication that maintained contacts as far afield as Ireland, Pictland, England, Gaul, and the Eastern Mediterranean. It also held lands in Galloway, and an Irish connection was very much in evidence when, in the very year of his death, Somerled attempted a reform of the religious community on Iona.[133] The westward orientation of Somerled's lordship can also be illustrated by the composition of the army with which he invaded the mainland in 1164 – it consisted of men from Argyll, Kintyre, the Hebrides, and the Foreigners from Dublin – as well as by the fact that the attempted church reform in 1164 was undertaken with the counsel of 'the men of Argyll and of the Hebrides'.[134] The simple fact of the westward orientation of Galloway and Argyll goes a long way toward explaining the antipathy between the Scottish king and the rulers of Galloway and Argyll in the 1150s and 1160s. While Fergus and Somerled remained firmly rooted in their westward-looking kingdoms, the Scottish kings were aligning themselves with European cultural models which included, among other things, the notion of a social hierarchy with room for only one king at its head. Eventually, of course, this model would prevail, and Alba would attain a strong unitary kingship – but this path was neither smooth nor certain, and in the middle of the twelfth century multiple kingships in north Britain were not yet anachronistic.

But it was also in the middle of the twelfth century that the eastern-looking kingdom of Alba began to intrude into the western-facing Atlantic zones of the kingdom, thrusting royal authority with its concomitant fiefs, knights and castles further into the margins of the kingdom. The process by which this occurred in the southwest and far west is imperfectly known, in part because the

131 This concept has been recently and powerfully articulated by Barry Cunliffe, *Facing the Ocean: The Atlantic and Its Peoples* (Oxford, 2001), quotation at 566; but see also E.G. Bowen's two books, *Saints, Seaways and Settlements* (Cardiff, 1969) and *Britain and the Western Seaways* (London, 1972), and McDonald, *Kingdom of the Isles, passim.*
132 Hill, *Whithorn and St Ninian*, ch. 1 and *passim*; on the Whithorn lands in Man, see B. Megaw, 'The Barony of St Trinian's in the Isle of Man', *TDGNHAS* 3rd ser. xxvii (1948–49), 173–82.
133 See A. Ritchie, *Iona* (London and Edinburgh, 1997), *passim*. Iona lands in Galloway in *Acts of William* I, no. 141; Somerled's attempted reform at Iona in *AU* (Hennessy), ii, 144 (1164); *ES* ii, 253–4; see discussion below, pp. 113–4.
134 The sources for Somerled's army are conveniently collected in *ES* ii, 253–6; for more on this theme, see ch. 3 below.

evidence is so thin in comparison with other parts of Scotland. Careful scrutiny of the distribution of lands to newcomers in the twelfth century suggests that the Scottish kings pursued a policy of isolating Galloway and Argyll with a ring of districts resembling nothing so much as the Welsh marcher lordships established by William I in the late 1060s. [135] The parallel is apt: from the perspective of the Scottish kings, Galloway and Argyll must have resembled frontier regions, and the motivation for surrounding them with a buffer zone probably included not only preventing disturbances from spilling over into the Scottish kingdom itself, but also the maintenance of important lines of communication. Professor Cowan's description of the Stewart Lordship on the Clyde as a 'bulwark against the wild Scots of the Inner Hebrides'[136] may be fitting.

The benefit of hindsight permits us to view the gradual infiltration of royal authority into the easternmost fringes of the Irish Sea world, but there is little doubt that by the 1150s and 1160s the trend was clear enough even to contemporaries like Fergus and Somerled. The process began early in the reign of David I, when Annandale, a vast lordship, was granted to Robert de Brus circa 1124. With its castles at Annan and Lochmaben, it was a key lordship; in the hands of a friend and loyal companion of the king, it both maintained a watch on Nithsdale[137] and Galloway, and also guarded a long stretch of the road from Carlisle to Glasgow. Another of the king's barons was Walter fitz Alan, a Breton who was granted extensive lands in Renfrew, Paisley, Pollock, and part of Kyle. These lands, forming part of what would become a far-flung Stewart lordship, constituted a buffer zone in equal parts against Galloway and Argyll. Still another large lordship, Cunningham and Largs, was granted out to Hugh de Morville, while Lanark remained in the hands of the Crown. Smaller holdings like those of Robert Avenel in Eskdale and Ranulf de Soules in Liddesdale rounded out the process. It is noteworthy, of course, that among the Anglo-Norman lords whose lands pushed westwards were none other than the Steward (Walter fitz Alan) and the Constable (Hugh de Morville) – trusted royal officials whose mailed fists no doubt served as a deterrent to border raiding, while at the same time extending and strengthening royal authority in the western fringes of the kingdom of Alba.[138]

135 See McDonald, *Kingdom of the Isles*, 63–6.
136 Cowan, 'Hakon IV and Alexander III', 112.
137 Nithsdale was ruled independently of Fergus by its own native lord, Dunegal of
     Strathnith, and his sons Ralph and Donald: see Barrow, *Charters of David* I, no. 16;
     Acts of Malcolm IV, 38 and nos. 138, 174, 195, 230, 254, 265.
138 This discussion draws upon: Ritchie, *Normans in Scotland*, 186, 188, 213, 279;
     Duncan, *Scotland*, 135–6; Barrow, *Anglo-Norman Era*, *passim*; Barrow, *Kingship and
     Unity*, 47; Barrow, 'Pattern of feudal settlement in Cumbria', 117–38; Barrow, 'The
     earliest Stewarts and their lands', in *Kingdom of the Scots*, ch. 12.

Corresponding with the extension of royal authority went a campaign of castle building. This is especially evident in areas where royal authority was less clearly acknowledged; the heavy concentration of the distinctive military fortification known as the motte (an earthen cone-shaped mound) in Galloway, for instance, is well known. It is significant that, by 1200, there were fortifications in the west and southwest at Annan, Ayr, Brantalloch, Buittle, Dumfries, Dundonald, Irvine, Lanark, Liddel, Lochmaben, Renfrew and Turnberry. Although it is difficult, in most cases, to assign precise dates to these fortifications, it is surely noteworthy that those at Annan (c. 1124) and Renfrew (c.1163–65) were both in place before 1165, while that at Lochmaben had been erected by 1173;[139] the fortifications at Annan and Renfrew were particularly important as the centres of the great networks of estates held by the Bruce and fitz Alan families respectively. As Professor Barrow has suggested, 'The symmetry of the fiefs between Clyde and Doon . . . suggests very strongly a deliberate and well worked out policy of defending a vulnerable coastline and doorway to Scotland against attacks from the Isles and Galloway'.[140]

Bearing all of this in mind, it is probably no coincidence that Somerled chose Renfrew as the beachhead for his invasion in 1164, and it is this choice of site for the landing that provides one of the strongest clues for the motivation behind the attack. Renfrew was both the *caput* of the fiefs held by Walter fitz Alan of the Scottish king[141] and the centre of a far-flung lordship that stretched from the Clyde valley to northern Northumbria. With its castle and burgh, Renfrew therefore symbolised both the Anglo-Norman penetration as well as the extension of royal authority west to the Clyde, pressing close on Somerled's insular and mainland lordship. But it is not only the geographical setting of the invasion that plays a role in establishing motive - the chronology of events in the 1160s is also significant, for westward expansion seems to have heated up then. Not only did King Malcolm IV confirm the grant of Renfrew (and other territories) by his grandfather to Walter fitz Alan in 1161 or 1162[142] (part, in fact, of a widespread process of expanding knights' fees and estates in Clydesdale), but the castle at Renfrew also seems to have been in existence by 1163 to 1165 at the latest (as noted above, a precise dating for the construction of the castles is impossible). In short, 'the feudal colonisation of the Clyde valley was a deliberate and forceful stroke of royal policy'.[143] Not surprisingly, then, it has been suggested that the king was threatening a campaign against Somerled,[144]

---

139 See G.G. Simpson and B. Webster, 'Charter Evidence and the Distribution of Mottes in Scotland', in *Essays on the Nobility of Medieval Scotland*, 1–24; G. Stell, 'Mottes', in *Historical Atlas of Scotland*, 28–29; Barrow, *Anglo-Norman Era*, maps at 51–60 and especially 52.

140 Barrow, 'Earliest Stewarts and their lands', 339.

141 Ibid.

142 *Acts of Malcolm IV*, no. 184.

143 G.W.S. Barrow, 'The beginnings of military feudalism', in *Kingdom of the Scots*, 290–1.

144 R.L. Bremner, *The Norsemen in Alban* (Glasgow, 1923), 177.

and although this moves beyond the bounds of the evidence, it is certainly instructive to note that only a few years earlier, in 1160/61, Malcolm IV had campaigned three times against Fergus and the Gallovidians. Whether or not King Malcolm was planning an attack on the mighty ruler of the Isles, Somerled's landing at Renfrew in 1164 certainly begins to look less like a plundering raid or an attempt at seizing the kingship than a pre-emptive, reactionary strike against the westward thrust of Scottish royal authority in the Clyde valley, close to the frontier with his insular and sea-girt kingdom.

I have argued in the past that Somerled's invasion of the Scottish mainland was aimed at the elimination of Anglo-Norman influence on the eastern frontiers of his lordship.[145] This view now seems overly simplistic. It is more likely that the goal was to check the westward expansion of Scottish royal authority, as represented by the extension of vast lordships in the Clyde valley and elsewhere in the west; the fact that these lordships were held by Anglo-Normans who were themselves newcomers to Scotland is probably of limited importance. Whichever view one takes, however, it is hard to see in the battle at Renfrew anything other than a clash of the Scoto-Norse periphery (with its firm connections in the Atlantic and Irish Sea) with the rapidly expanding core of the Scottish kingdom, closely linked, as it was, with European impulses. Indeed, considering that Somerled's invasion occurred in the heartland of Walter fitz Alan's lordship, it is tempting to suppose – especially as no leader of the Scottish forces is named – that it was fitz Alan himself who defeated Somerled: the former representing the dynamic forces of Europeanisation that were sweeping the Scottish kingdom; the latter representing what might be called the forces of Irish Sea conservatism.[146] Somerled, of course, paid the ultimate price for his invasion, but it took the Scottish kings another century to reap the harvest of Renfrew.

One of the mightiest enemies faced by the Scottish kings was without doubt Earl Harald Maddadsson of Orkney/Caithness (d.1206), who was the dominant figure in northern Scottish politics for over sixty years and who figured prominently in several insurrections and military activities of the 1190s.[147]

---

145 See, e.g., *Kingdom of the Isles*, 65–6.

146 Although it should probably be noted that the 'Carmen de Morte Sumerledi' highlights the role of the bishop of Glasgow in the defence against Somerled and makes no mention of Walter fitz Alan.

147 Important treatments of Earl Harald's career, which pay particular attention to his relations with the Scottish kings, are: Crawford, 'Earldom of Caithness', 25–43; Topping, 'Harald Maddadson', 105–20; and Cowan, 'Caithness in the Sagas', esp. 39–41; see also Duncan, *Scotland*, 194–6; Thomson, *History of Orkney*, ch. 7; and the older though still useful book by J. Gray, *Sutherland and Caithness in Saga-Time* (Edinburgh, 1922), esp. ch. 7.

Despite the fact that they are separated by the heavy seas of the Pentland Firth, Orkney and Caithness enjoyed considerable political unity: both had been settled by Scandinavians in the ninth century, and had, accordingly, fallen under the control of highly autonomous Norse earls. Caithness, as the pages of *Orkneyinga Saga* demonstrate, was frequently a battleground between Scots and Scandinavians, and from the middle of the twelfth century the Scottish kings pursued a policy designed to detach it from its Scandinavian orbit and draw it closer into the fold of their realm. This inevitably led to conflict with the earls, and it has been remarked that Harald had the misfortune to live at a time when both Scottish and Norwegian monarchies sought to expand and consolidate their power.[148]

In contrast to Fergus and Somerled, a good deal is known of Harald's life and career, thanks in large measure to the thirteenth-century *Orkneyinga Saga*, a history of the Orcadian ruling dynasty down to the death of Earl Harald in 1206.[149] Harald was the son of Maddad the mormaer/earl of Atholl and his second wife, Margaret, who was the daughter of Earl Hakon Paulsson of Orkney. Norse sources indicate that Maddad was a kinsman of the Scottish king Malcolm III - his father Maelmuire was said to have been a brother of Malcolm - which meant that Harald was related by blood to the Scottish ruling dynasty.[150] Harald came to power in a maelstrom of dynastic strife and intrigue in Orkney and Caithness: when he became nominal joint ruler of Orkney and Caithness in 1139 (at the age of five), it was through the connivance of his mother and with backing from David I, who saw an opportunity to increase Scottish influence in the northern mainland through the establishment of a half-Scottish earl, and one who was related by blood to the ruling house. The installation of Harald Maddadsson as earl of Orkney/Caithness has thus been called 'a triumph for Scottish diplomacy',[151] but it was short-lived, lasting only until Harald matured and became sole ruler in 1159. From then until the end of his life he pursued a policy of expansion and consolidation of his power in the north, and it is hardly surprising, although more than a little ironic, that the remainder of his tenure of the earldom should have been marked by clashes with the Scottish kings.

The evidence for Earl Harald's involvement in mainland Scottish politics is problematic, although generations of historians have rightly surmised that he was active in opposing the Scottish kings and quite likely was involved, perhaps tacitly, in the MacHeth and MacWilliam insurrections that characterise the 1180s in the far north.[152] Much turns on how much importance is attached to

---

148 Thomson, *History of Orkney*, 68–9.
149 Harald's life is traced in chs 75 to 112.
150 See *OS*, ch. 63; Duncan, *Scotland*, 164–5.
151 Oram, 'David I and . . . Moray', 11.
152 See also ch 3, below, pp. 158–9.

Earl Harald's second marriage, made sometime around 1168 to a daughter of Malcolm MacHeth named Hvarflod; Harald had earlier wed a daughter of Earl Duncan of Fife. The second marriage strongly suggests that the earl aimed at detaching himself from Scottish influence and sought instead to bind himself to those associated with resistance to the Scottish kings. It has also been argued that the marriage to MacHeth's daughter may have been made in order to associate Earl Harald directly with Malcolm MacHeth's title to Ross. This hypothesis is supported by the statement in *Gesta Annalia* that, up to this time, Earl Harald had been a trusty man, which seems to indicate that the marriage was accompanied by a shift in attitude on the part of the earl. It is also surely significant that the timing of the marriage (its precise date is not known, but it is placed with confidence about 1168) coincides with the death of Malcolm MacHeth himself, who, as we have seen, was described in his obituary as earl of Ross.

It is quite likely, then, that Earl Harald supported the MacHeth and MacWilliam factions, even though the evidence for this remains problematic. Thus, the expedition of King William and his brother, Earl David, to the north in 1179 which resulted in the construction of two new castles at Redcastle and Dunskeath may well have been as much a response to the activities of Earl Harald as to those of the MacWilliams. It has also been suggested that Earl Harald may have been involved in the events of 1186, when the earl of Atholl seized Adam, son of Donald, and slew his warband at Coupar Angus abbey. If Adam was a member of the MacHeth kindred (which remains doubtful at best), then his sister was Earl Harald's wife, and the events of 1186 might be related to a bid for Ross on the part of Earl Harald. On the other hand, the earl of Atholl himself was Harald's half-brother, which means that it is difficult at best to read much into the kin-relationships centring on the massacre at Coupar Angus.

There can be no doubt that Earl Harald viewed with great concern the expansion of Scottish royal authority in the far north in the wake of the suppression of Donald MacWilliam in 1187, and it was probably this concern that fuelled the conflicts between the Earl of Orkney/Caithness and the Scottish king in the 1190s. In fact, there were probably several factors that culminated in the clash between earl and king in 1196–1202. The first was simple timing, for the king had fallen seriously ill in the summer of 1195, prompting a crisis over not only the state of his health but also his desire to marry his daughter to Otto of Saxony, a move which was opposed by many members of the Scottish nobility.[153] Most significantly, however, there is good evidence for the infiltration of Scottish secular landowners and officials into Caithness and especially Sutherland in this period. This infiltration had, it seems, been spearheaded by the de Moravia family (as they would come to be

---

153 *Chronica* iii, 298–9; trans. in *SAEC*, 315.

known), who had received lands at Duffus in 1130 and had figured prominently since then in the consolidation of royal authority in Moray; Barbara Crawford has argued that they were almost certainly involved in the advance of royal authority to Cromarty in the years after the suppression of the MacWilliams in 1187.[154] Certainly Hugh son of William possessed lands in Sutherland, and between 1212 and 1214 he granted Skelbo (in Dornoch) and most of Creich parish to his relative Gilbert of Moravia (archdeacon of Moray); William son of Hugh was called *dominus de Sutherlandia* before 1222.[155] Although its outlines are sketchy, there is little doubt of the aggrandisement of agents of royal authority in the far north from the 1180s, which amounted to a process of Scottish conquest of Orcadian territory. In essence, and as Crawford so aptly put it, 'Harald Maddadson was not enthusiastic about the policy of spreading Scottish influence in Caithness'.[156] Earl Harald, therefore, was primarily a political opponent of the Scottish kings, one who was motivated by many of the same concerns that placed Fergus and Somerled in the camp of those opposed to the Scottish kings.

What is most striking about the struggles between earl and king, however, is how little permanent advantage the king gained, and how little the earl lost. It is surely significant that it was only in 1201 that Earl Harald submitted to the king – and even then it was a voluntary submission; while it is true that he had seen his earldom briefly redistributed in the late 1190s, he suffered no permanent alienation of his lands or rights, and ruled undisturbed until his death in 1206. Indeed, as Crawford has shown, the only really effective form of punishment used by the king was the imposition of fines, a pattern that continued even after the burning of Bishop Adam in 1222. These facts suggest that the Scottish kings remained relatively powerless to administer forfeited or confiscated lands in the far north, and royal authority consequently remained weak there: 'despite the royal expeditions of 1196–7, 1202 and 1222 and the submissions of the earls which followed, despite the installation of members of the Moravia family . . . the Scottish kings had no more than shaken the tight grip which the earls possessed over Caithness'.[157] That would take another fifty years, and was accomplished through means other than military.[158]

Without question the most shadowy rival of the Scottish kings, and therefore the most difficult to make sense of, is Wimund, the bishop of the Isles who led

154 Crawford, 'Earldom of Caithness', 31.
155 *Acts of William I*, no. 520; W. Fraser, *The Sutherland Book* (Edinburgh 1892), iii, 2; see Crawford, 'Earldom of Caithness', 32–3.
156 Crawford, 'Earldom of Caithness', 28.
157 *Ibid.*, 33.
158 Gray, *Sutherland and Caithness in Saga-Time*, ch. 9.

an army against David I in the 1140s and who managed to wrest territory in Cumbria from the grasp of the Scottish ruler before being mutilated and sent into retirement at Byland abbey in Yorkshire. Both Wimund's identity and the aims of his campaigns have proved baffling and contentious to generations of scholars who have considered them.[159] The English chronicler William of Newburgh, who is the most important source for Wimund's activities and who seems to have possessed first-hand knowledge of them, stated that Wimund 'feigned himself to be the son of the earl of Moray, and that he was deprived of the inheritance of his father by the king of Scotland'. This could mean that Wimund was a son of Angus, the earl or king of Moray who fell at Stracathro in 1130, even though William does not name Wimund's father. Angus was, of course, a grandson of Lulach, slain by Malcolm III in early 1058, and has been regarded as a member of the Cenél Loairn.[160] A Cenél Loairn connection certainly fits well enough with some aspects of Wimund's career, particularly his activities in the Isles, including Skye.[161] If this genealogy for Wimund proves to be correct, then the story of Cenél Loairn challenges to the kings of Scots needs to be carried beyond the insurrection of Angus of Moray in 1130 and even further into the reign of David I.[162]

Yet, as with other enemies of the Scottish kings, nothing is quite as simple as it seems and this proposed ancestry for Wimund proves difficult to square with other aspects of his career. William of Newburgh placed Wimund's birth in an obscure part of England (*obscurissimo in Anglia loco natus*), and stated that he entered religious life at Furness Abbey in Lancashire; neither location seems particularly appropriate for a member of the Moray dynasty. Then there is the landed settlement that Wimund wrung from David I: this clearly constituted lands in Cumbria, which the Scottish king had held from 1141.[163] Again, this seems an unlikely place to find a member of the Moray dynasty, but it is the

---

159 See, e.g., A.O. Anderson, 'Wimund, Bishop and Pretender', *SHR* vii (1910), 29–36, a much more sensible discussion than the now totally outdated arguments in T.E. Casson, 'Wymund', *Transactions of the Cumberland and Westmorland Archaeological and Antiquarian Society*, new series xxxix (1939), 1–14, where the notion persists that Wimund was identical with Malcolm MacHeth.

160 See Hudson, *Kings of Celtic Scotland*, 146.

161 *Chronica Pontificum Ecclesiae Eboracensis*, in *The Historians of the Church of York*, ii, 372; the account is problematic, however. William of Newburgh's account makes it clear that Wimund knew the language of the Islesmen: see McDonald, 'Place of Wimund', 257.

162 As suggested by Hudson, *Kings of Celtic Scotland*, 146.

163 See K.J. Stringer, 'State-Building in Twelfth-Century Britain: David I, King of Scots, and Northern England', in *Government, Religion and Society in Northern England 1100–1700*, ed. J.C. Appleby and P. Dalton (Stroud, 1997), 45; and *idem, The Reign of Stephen: Kingship, Warfare and Government in Twelfth-Century England* (New York and London, 1993), esp. ch. 3.

Cumbrian connection that raises another possible context for Wimund's activities. William fitz Duncan, whose career has been considered above, was styled earl of Moray in an admittedly problematic Cumbrian genealogy from the thirteenth century, and it has been suggested that this identification might stem from a brief career as earl of Moray in the 1130s. But whatever the nature of his involvement in the north, William can firmly be placed in a Cumbrian context, since by the time of his death he held Allerdale, Coupland, Skipton and Craven. The Cumbrian associations of both Wimund and William fitz Duncan raise the possibility that Wimund was in fact an otherwise unknown son of William. On the other hand, this identification would create at least as many problems as it resolves: William of Newburgh's statement that Wimund had been deprived of his father's inheritance by the Scottish king, for instance, is difficult to tally with what is known of relations between William fitz Duncan and David I.

At the end of the day, the motive for Wimund's insurrection remains frustratingly obscured by the significant problems surrounding his origins and ancestry. Yet it is clear that contemporaries took his claims seriously, for it is hard to see how he could have acquired such a substantial warband otherwise, and it is even more difficult to imagine why David I would have come to terms and given him a landed settlement. Moreover, Wimund's treatment at the hands of David strongly suggests that he stood in some relationship to the royal house: how else to explain the fact that, although mutilated, he was permitted to live out his last days as a monk of Byland abbey rather than being executed?

Xenophobia, Resentment, and Resistance

Considering the multiethnic nature of the twelfth- and thirteenth- century kingdom of the Scots, to what extent were the challenges to the Scottish kings fuelled by resentment of the infiltration of foreign colonists and customs? Certainly the influx of foreigners (conveniently termed Anglo-Normans, although their ranks included, in addition to English and Normans, Bretons and Flemings) was a notable characteristic of the twelfth century: so much so, in fact, that it has been famously regarded as the 'Anglo-Norman Era' in Scottish history.[164] Yet, despite the frequent assertion that race-relations in medieval Scotland were remarkably free of the xenophobia and ethnic tensions that characterised other areas of Europe, there is some evidence that in certain parts of Scotland the importation of foreigners did in fact cause resentment and ruffled the feathers of some members of the native nobility.

Scottish society was well aware of distinctions between natives and new-comers, particularly in the twelfth century. This can be seen in the royal

164 Barrow, *Anglo-Norman Era.*

charters of the age, which were often addressed to the king's French, English, Scottish, and sometimes even Gallovidian, subjects, highlighting the different ethnic groups within the Scottish kingdom.[165] Yet it would be dangerous to infer from this form of address that the French and English newcomers were favoured: all four groups were described as the king's 'worthy men' (*probi homines*), and native Scots continued, by and large, to enjoy the social standing that they had possessed before the influx of foreign settlers in the reign of David I. The existing aristocracy was not elbowed aside, disinherited, or annihilated, then, but the two groups, old and new, instead settled down shoulder to shoulder. In the words of Professor Duncan, 'In our preoccupation with the new men of David I and Malcolm IV, we must not lose sight of the native landowners whom they left undisturbed, whose importance may have declined at court, but who were neither submerged nor depressed in their own or the king's eyes as a local gentry and even aristocracy'.[166]

Nonetheless, it is clear that from time to time ethnic tensions bubbled to the surface of this multiethnic kingdom. Even before the colonisation under David I, and the inauguration of the 'Anglo-Norman Era' proper in Scotland, there is evidence of reaction against the English influences that accompanied the marriage of Malcolm III to Margaret circa 1070. Margaret was, of course, an Anglo-Saxon princess and a refugee (together with her sister and her brother, Edgar the Aetheling) from the Norman Conquest of England in 1066. According to her medieval biographer, she exercised considerable influence on the king and court,[167] although modern historians have tended to disagree about her overall influence beyond court circles.

One of the most famous examples of apparent xenophobia in medieval Scotland comes from the period before the 'Anglo-Norman' era proper, and relates to the dynastic conflict of the years 1093 to 1097 that followed the death of Malcolm III. The *Anglo-Saxon Chronicle*, an important source for Scottish affairs in these years, relates how, upon taking the kingship in 1093, Donald Bàn, Malcolm III's brother, 'drove out all the English who were with King Malcolm earlier . . .' The next year, 1094, Donald Bàn was himself driven out by Duncan, who took the kingship with the backing of William II of England and a force of English and French knights. Following the coup, however, many of Duncan's followers were in turn slain, and the luckless king only held onto the reigns of power on the condition that 'he never again lodged English men or French men into that land'.[168] He was slain in 1094 by Máelpetar, described as mormaer of

---

165 See, for example, Barrow, *Charters of David I*, nos. 44, 66, 70, 76, 120. No. 98
    addresses the French, English, and Cumbrians.
166 Duncan, *Scotland*, 141; see also Barrow, *David I of Scotland*.
167 Turgot's *Life of Queen Margaret*, in *ES*, ii, 59–88.
168 *ASC*, 228 (1093).

the Mearns. The overall impression of these events is that of a resentful native aristocracy reacting against foreigners and/or foreign influences, although the extent of foreign influence in Scotland during these years is notoriously difficult to gauge and remains contentious. Certainly Duncan II was essentially an outsider: between 1072 and 1087 he had been a hostage in England for the maintenance of the Abernethy agreement of 1072 between William the Conqueror and Malcolm III. Even after his release in 1087 he does not seem to have returned to Scotland; he has been viewed as an adventurer who was seeking to improve his fortunes – in this case, no doubt by securing the support of the English king, William Rufus. That support paid off when Duncan seized the kingship in 1094 with English aid, but the fact that he was an outsider, and one who was strongly Normanised at that, seems to have contributed to his demise: 'Duncan's own Normanized attitudes and sympathies . . . were clearly in part responsible for his own overthrow and death at the hands of the gaelicized anti-Norman interests in 1094.'[169] Duncan's uncle and rival, Donald Bàn, has been seen on the other hand as representing Gaelic interests since on the accession of Macbeth in 1040 he is said to have taken refuge in the Western Isles.[170]

The events of the 1090s form only a prelude to one of the more famous examples of xenophobic activity in medieval Scotland, however: the 'reign of terror' perpetrated by Fergus's sons, Uhtred and Gilbert, in Galloway in the mid-1170s. Taking advantage of the capture of William of Scotland by the English at Alnwick in 1174, the two brothers raged against royal officers and foreign settlers in their territory. The English chronicler Roger of Howden, who had first-hand knowledge of events in late twelfth-century Galloway, describes how Gilbert and Uhtred

> . . . expelled from Galloway all the bailiffs and guards whom the king of Scotland had set over them; and all the English and French whom they could seize they slew; and all the defences and castles which the king of Scotland had established in their land they besieged, captured and destroyed, and slew all whom they took with them.

William of Newburgh, writing of the same events, attributed them to the hatred of foreigners. 'The towns and burghs of the Scottish realm are known to be inhabited by English,' he said, and added that 'the Scots declared their hatred against them . . . and as many as they fell upon they slew'.[171] The context for this rampage is almost certainly to be found in both royal policy toward Galloway and the acceleration of foreign settlement there following the death

169 Phythian-Adams, *Land of the Cumbrians*, 158.
170 *Scotichronicon* ii, 426–27. Malcolm, of course, fled south to England.
171 *Historia Rerum Anglicarum*, in *Chron Stephen* i, 186; trans. *SAEC*, 256.

of Fergus in 1161. It has been argued that after Fergus's death Malcolm IV partitioned Galloway between his two sons, Uhtred and Gilbert, perhaps in an effort to weaken Gallovidian lordship. As a result, Scottish influence in the southwest might never have been so strong as it was in the decade of the 1160s. Moreover, there is at least some evidence for the incursion of Anglo-Norman settlers into eastern Galloway between 1160 and 1165; these included Hugh II de Morville, who obtained the lands of Borgue from Uhtred, and Walter de Berkeley, the Chamberlain, who held Urr from before 1165. [172] The closeness of men like these to the king might have singled them out for attack: Walter de Berkeley, for instance, 'could easily be labelled as a royal agent implanted into the local power structure'.[173] Presumably, it was men like these who were driven out or slain in the Gallovidian insurrection of 1174/75, a view that is strengthened by archaeological evidence, which indicates that Walter de Berkeley's fortification at Urr was burnt in the mid-1170s.[174] Urr might have been selected not only because of its association with a royal agent, but also because its lord was detained in England after the Treaty of Falaise for the good behaviour of the Scottish king, which meant he would have been unable to strengthen or defend his stronghold.[175] Whatever the case, ethnic violence was certainly not unknown in a contemporary insular context. Gerald of Wales, for example, reports how the natives of Waterford 'cruelly put to death any English they found in the streets and inside the houses, without respect for sex or age' in 1171. A similar plot in Wexford was foiled by the arrival of an English fleet.[176]

Also significant are the comments made by the Barnwell annalist in the context of Guthred MacWilliam's insurrection of 1211/12. After outlining the timing of the rising and the fate of Guthred, the writer remarked that 'More recent kings of Scots profess themselves to be rather Frenchmen, both in race and in manners, language and culture; and after reducing the Scots to utter servitude, they admit only Frenchmen to their friendship and service'.[177] As a statement of fact, the comment is exaggerated, although not entirely wide of the mark. The penetration of Anglo-Norman colonists and their pre-eminence in court circles in the twelfth century is widely acknowledged. Moreover, the Scottish royal house was deeply attached to the French way of life by the late twelfth century, and as Keith Stringer has put it, '[Earl] David and his elder

---

172 *Acts of Malcolm IV*, 13, and n. 2; see also Brooke, *Wild Men and Holy Places*, ch. 5.
173 Oram, *Lordship of Galloway*, 200.
174 B. Hope-Taylor, 'Excavations at Mote of Urr. Interim Report, 1951 season', *TDGNHAS* xxix (1950–51), 167–72.
175 Ibid. See *Gesta Henrici Secundi* i, 97–98.
176 *Expugnatio*, 140–41.
177 Walter of Coventry ii, 206: 'Moderniores enim Scottorum regis magis se Francos fatentur, sicut genere, ita moribus, lingua, cultu, Scotisque ad extremam servitutem redactis, solos Francos in familiaritatem et obsequium adhibent'.

brothers Malcolm and William were in fact very nearly as rich in French blood as Henry II of England'.[178]

The comments of the annalist, then, nicely capture the move away from a balance of old and new in the time of David I toward a more French affiliation by his successors Malcolm and William. Moreover, the annalist's juxtaposition of the 'more recent kings of Scots' with Guthred who is said to belong to the 'ancient line of Scottish kings' is a telling piece of social commentary, one that contrasts the Frankish cultural affiliations of the modern kings with the more conservative Gaelic orientation of the MacWilliam claimants. It is no doubt significant that the MacWilliams enjoyed strong connections with Gaelic Ireland, and that Guthred himself had landed in Scotland from Ireland in 1211. But it is also significant that the regions most closely associated with the MacWilliam insurrections – Moray beyond the Great Glen and Wester Ross – were locales where Scottish royal authority and its concomitant foreign influence were notoriously slow to penetrate. That may be why both Donald MacWilliam and Guthred are said to have enjoyed considerable support from the nobles of the region, and it was not until the appearance of Ferchar Maccintsacairt in 1215 that a native magnate of Ross took the side of the Scottish kings against their MacWilliam rivals. Thus, in the end, if the remarks of the Barnwell annalist do not provide clear evidence of xenophobia in early thirteenth-century Scotland, they at least provide 'a valuable indication of the feelings aroused by the gradual transformation of Moray and Ross into another feudalised province'.[179]

The insurrection of 1174/75 and the remarks of the Barnwell annalist provide the clearest indication that resentment of foreign influence might find expression in insurrection and resistance, yet they also urge caution. In the first instance, anti-foreign sentiment needs to be distinguished from resentment of territorial incursion by Anglo-Norman lords and the concomitant extension of royal authority; thus, the insurrection of 1174/75 was almost certainly fuelled as much by a reaction against royal pressure in the decade of the 1160s, not to mention sheer opportunism (taking advantage of the capture of the Scottish king), as it was by hatred of foreigners. There is also the very real danger of polarising these insurrections into a sort of 'Celt versus Norman' rugby match played on a grand scale, which would surely be too fatuous an explanation. As a warning against such an oversimplification, the royal armies that took the field against the king's enemies were every bit as 'Celtic' as the enemies themselves. In 1187, for instance, it was Roland Lord of Galloway with his three thousand Gallovidian warriors who defeated and slew Donald MacWilliam. Even more telling is the army that was assembled against Donald's son Guthred in 1211/12:

178 Stringer, *Earl David*, 10.
179 Duncan, *Scotland*, 197–8.

it included levies from Mar, Buchan, Atholl and Fife.[180] Similarly, we need look no further than the events following the Gallovidian insurrection for a warning against this sort of interpretation: no sooner had the sons of Fergus unleashed their reign of terror than Gilbert had his brother Uhtred mutilated so severely that he subsequently died. This led in turn to Uhtred's son, Roland, seeking vengeance upon his father's killers, thereby creating further turbulence in the southwest for another decade. Within the twelfth-century Scottish kingdom, rivalries within and between native kindreds also bubbled to the surface from time to time.

Incinerated Bishops and Warrior Bishops: Ecclesiastical Aspects of Resistance

It is noteworthy that clerics figured prominently in several episodes of political violence in the twelfth and thirteenth centuries. Apart from the uprising led by Wimund, the bishop of the Isles, two of the first three bishops of Caithness, for instance, found themselves embroiled in conflict with the earls of Orkney/ Caithness in the late twelfth and early thirteenth centuries, resulting in the mutilation of one bishop and the burning alive of the other in his residence. Conversely, in the wake of the violence that wracked Galloway in 1234/35, a royal army sacked several monasteries with strong connections to the Lords of Galloway, with the result that two monastic officials at Tongland were killed. Considering the close interrelationships that existed between secular and ecclesiastical spheres in our period, it is to be expected that the theme of opposition and resistance to the Scottish kings also resonates in the ecclesiastical arena.

Thanks to the efforts of Barbara Crawford, the ecclesiastical history of Caithness in the period under question has been fully illuminated, and it has been shown to represent an integral part of the struggle between the earls of Orkney/Caithness and the Scottish kings over control of the far north of the Scottish mainland. David I founded the bishopric of Caithness in the mid-twelfth century (before 1147–51), before which Caithness formed part of the bishopric of Orkney. The first Scottish bishop of Caithness was Andrew, who held the see from its inception before 1147–51 to 1184, but who was bishop in title only: there is no evidence that he ever visited his diocese.[181] The foundation of the bishopric of Caithness by the Scottish king is regarded as a precursor the establishment of royal authority in the region, and the extension of Scottish ecclesiastical rule coincided with Earl Harald's long rule in the north. Crawford has regarded the establishment of the bishopric as 'part of a

---

180 *Scotichronicon* iv, 464–7. See also Duncan, *Scotland*, 198.
181 D.E.R. Watt, *Fasti Ecclesiae Scoticanae Medii Aevi ad annum 1638* (Edinburgh, 1969), 58; 'Two Ancient Records of the Bishopric of Caithness . . . With a prefatory note by Cosmo Innes', in *Bannatyne Miscellany* (Edinburgh, 1855), iii, 5.

deliberate policy of detaching the area from the neighbouring Norse influence. The Church was to prepare the ground for succeeding royal authority'.[182]

It appears, however, that Earl Harald and the inhabitants of Caithness resented the establishment of a new bishopric, the appointment of a Scottish bishop, and the inevitable introduction of new customs. Sometime during the pontificate of pope Alexander III (1159–81), Earl Harald had made a grant to the papacy of one annual penny for every inhabited house in Caithness. The grant was made out of reverence for Sts Peter and Paul and also for the needs of the Roman Church, and it was probably of a type known as 'Peter's Pence' that was common in a northern European context but was unknown in the Celtic regions of Britain, including Scotland, at the time. It was made in the time of the first bishop of Caithness, Andrew, but is only known about because the second bishop, John, who held the see from 1189/99 to 1202, obstructed it. It is unclear why John acted in this manner, but it is thought that he was opposed to the Scandinavian custom that the grant represented. As a result of the bishop's interference, the earl wrote to the new pope, Innocent III, who responded with a letter ordering the bishops of Orkney and Rosemarkie (Ross) to restrain John from preventing the collection of the grant.

It was this bishop who was mutilated in 1201. *Orkneyinga Saga* relates how he was attacked in his stronghold at Scrabster by a large force led by Earl Harald. 'As the Earl's troops stormed up to the stronghold from the ships, the bishop set out to give the Earl some kind word of welcome, but what actually happened was that Earl Harald took the bishop captive and had his tongue cut out and a knife driven into his eyes, blinding him.'[183] It is difficult to disagree with the proposition that the expedition was directed principally at the bishop – the troops stormed up to his stronghold – but the Earl's animosity toward Bishop John was only partly rooted in ecclesiastical matters. *Gesta Annalia* relates that Earl Harald believed the bishop to be 'an informer, and the instigator of the misunderstanding between him and the king',[184] showing how ecclesiastical and secular matters could become blurred and overlap. Exactly what Bishop John had done to lead the earl to this conclusion is difficult to say, but it is known that Earl Harald had been in correspondence with King John of England, an enemy of the Scottish king, and 'the deliberate mutilation of Bishop John's eyes and tongue would appear to be a symbolic punishment, typical for the age, for a crime involving spying and informing'.[185]

---

182 B. Crawford, 'Peter's Pence in Scotland', in *The Scottish Tradition*, ed. G.W.S. Barrow (Edinburgh, 1974), 20; see also 'Norse Earls and Scottish Bishops', 129–47, and R.G. Cant, 'The Medieval Church in the North: Contrasting Influences in the Dioceses of Ross and Caithness', in *Firthlands of Ross and Sutherland*, ed. J. Baldwin (Edinburgh, 1986), 47–58.

183 *OS*, ch. 111.

184 *Chron Fordun* i, 276; ii, 271.

185 Crawford, 'Peter's Pence', 20.

The earl's actions naturally drew a response from both secular and ecclesiastical authorities. Earl Harald's attack on Caithness and the mutilation of its bishop prompted King William to launch a military campaign against the earl in 1201/02 – *Orkneyinga Saga* says that 'It was a truly massive army that the King of Scots led. He marched ahead to Ausdale near the boundary between Caithness and Sutherland, and there his camp extended from one end of the valley to the other, quite a distance'.[186] This campaign resulted in the eventual submission of Earl Harald in 1202. On the ecclesiastical front, a letter of pope Innocent III to the bishop of Orkney describes the penance to be laid on one of the earl's followers named Lumberd who had been involved in the attack on the bishop and was apparently the man responsible for actually mutilating the bishop.[187] Crawford has argued that Earl Harald successfully managed to escape any direct retaliation from the church by diverting blame on to his follower, and aptly notes that: 'It takes some effort of historical perspective to realise that a minor expedition of the earl of Orkney on the coast of Caithness in 1201 resulted in a letter being written by Pope Innocent III in August–September 1202 ordering the Bishop of Orkney to see that the above sentence was carried out'.[188]

Only twenty years later, in 1222, another clash between the people of Caithness and their bishop took place, when Adam was incinerated alive in his house at Halkirk. Like the events of 1201, this episode is best understood in the context of tense relations between earl and bishop, and it was also rooted in a deep-seated clash of cultures. Bishop Adam, the successor to the unfortunate John, aroused the animosity of the inhabitants of Caithness by his over-zealous attempts to collect increased tithes; these changes to traditional church payments were no doubt regarded as consequences of the imposition of Scottish customs and Scottish personnel on the Caithness church.[189] The bishop's efforts were rewarded with an attack by local farmers (*boendr*), in which Adam was stoned and eventually burned alive in one of his own buildings. The involvement of Earl John (son of Harald Maddadsson) is unclear, but he was implicated by some sources and was certainly blamed by others for not having done more to prevent the killing. As in the wake of the mutilation of Bishop John in 1201, the Scottish king fitted out a royal expedition to the north which resulted in the submission of Earl John; while the pope praised the king for his prompt action in mounting the retaliatory expedition, the king's actions in punishing the Caithness men lived in the memory of the inhabitants: an Icelandic saga writer noted decades later that 'The punishments inflicted by him [King Alexander]

186 *OS*, ch. 112.
187 Lawrie, *Annals*, 339–40.
188 Crawford, 'Norse Earls and Scottish Bishops', 135.
189 Crawford, 'Norse Earls and Scottish Bishops', 136.

for the burning of the bishop, by mutilation and death, confiscation and outlawry from the land, are still in fresh memory'.[190] In the wake of Adam's death, King Alexander ensured the appointment of Gilbert de Moravia as bishop of Caithness (1222–45); *Gesta Annalia* said that this took place while the army was still in Caithness, 'in the presence of our lord the king and the chief men of his host'.[191] Earlier in the thirteenth century, between 1212 and 1214, as archdeacon of Moray, Gilbert had received a grant of extensive lands in Sutherland, including Skelbo and 'Ferenbeuthlin' from his relative, Hugh de Moravia; the grant speaks of these lands as running to the 'boundaries of Ross' (*deuisas de Ros*) and leaves little doubt that its context is an essentially defensive one.[192] The bishop is also said to have engaged in castle building in the far north.[193] Sutherland was, by the 1220s, firmly under the control of the Moravia family and out of the sphere of influence of the earl of Orkney/Caithness; thus, it is hardly surprising that Gilbert soon reorganised the diocese and constructed a new cathedral at Dornoch, in a location much closer to the southern boundary with Ross and in the midst of the lands held by the new bishop himself.[194] As for Earl John, he was himself burned alive by his enemies in 1231, the irony of which did not escape medieval commentators like the Melrose abbey chronicler and the author of *Gesta Annalia*.[195] Bishop Adam's relics were transferred to Dornoch in 1239 where they were reburied: 'In their elevation (as it is reported), no few miracles were performed.'[196]

Like Caithness, the see of Galloway at Whithorn was also in many respects a frontier see, and by the 1230s royal ecclesiastical policy there was falling closely into line with secular policy for the subjugation of the region. It is noteworthy that the insurrection in Galloway following the death of Alan, Lord of Galloway, in 1234 was paralleled by a crisis in the election of a new bishop of Whithorn in 1235. When Bishop Walter died in early 1235, the election of two rival candidates ensued in what was quickly to become a 'highly charged and immensely politicised affair'.[197] The first candidate to emerge was Gilbert, a former monk of Melrose and abbot of Glenluce. He had been elected by the 'people and clergy' of Galloway, excepting the prior and convent of Whithorn. The election of a monk from the most favoured royal monastery in Scotland as

190 *Orkneyinga Saga*, trans. J.A. Hjaltalin and G.Goudie, edited with notes and an introduction by J. Anderson (Edinburgh, 1873; repr. 1973), 200–1 for the episode; quotation at 201.
191 *Chron Fordun* i, 289–90; ii, 285.
192 *Acts of William I*, no. 520.
193 Innes, 'Two Ancient Records', 11.
194 See Crawford, 'Earldom of Caithness', 30.
195 *Chron Melrose* 81 (1231); *ES* ii, 478–9; *Chron Fordun* i, 289–90; ii, 285.
196 *Chron Melrose* 86–7 (1239); *ES* ii, 516.
197 Oram, *Lordship of Galloway*, 181.

bishop of Whithorn has been seen as part of Alexander's policy for the settlement of Galloway following Alan's death, since the kings of Scots had exerted little influence in the succession to the see from its revitalisation in the 1120s, and since the bishop of Whithorn played a role in local politics as an immensely powerful and influential figure.[198] Shortly after Gilbert's election, however, the prior and convent at Whithorn elected a candidate of their own, Odo, and there ensued a lengthy crisis over the disputed election.[199] Odo was a canon of Whithorn and abbot of Holywood, a Premonstratensian monastery that had probably been founded by one of the lords of Galloway in the twelfth century. Although some scholars have viewed the disputed election primarily in terms of the complex history of the diocese of Whithorn and the long struggle to elect a canon of Whithorn as bishop, these events may also be related to the Gallovidian insurrection of 1234/35, and the two candidates probably represented the opposing sides in the conflict.[200] Certainly Gilbert's election was said to have been 'unfairly influenced from outside and by secular power', and it is also interesting to note that a letter from Whithorn to York referred to 'the war of the lord king of Scots against Galloway'[201] – leaving no doubt about which secular powers were involved. This has been interpreted to mean that the sympathies of the Whithorn clergy lay with 'popular demand', but whatever the case there is little doubt that the king of Scots was an insecure overlord 'who may well have felt that the loyalty to himself of a bishop of local background and sympathies could not be counted upon'.[202]

It is evident from the events in Caithness and Galloway in the 1220s and 1230s that Scottish ecclesiastical control was both a stepping-stone and a complement to the expansion of Scottish royal authority in the remote, frontier regions of the kingdom, where Scottish personnel and Scottish customs seem to have created a degree of resentment among either the inhabitants or the ruling

---

198 See K.J. Stringer, 'Reform Monasticism and Celtic Scotland: Galloway c.1140–c.1240', in *Alba*, 160.

199 Well-documented in *Historians of the Church of York and Its Archbishops*, ed. J. Raine (RS, London, 1894), iii, 144–9. See also A. Ashley, 'Odo, Elect of Whithern, 1235', *TDGNHAS* 3rd ser. xxxvii (1958–59), 62–9.

200 Brooke, *Wild Men and Holy* Places, 134–5. If that is the case, it is ironic that Whithorn itself was associated with the expansion of royal authority in the far north, since it planted a daughter house at Mid Fearn in Ross on the invitation of Ferchar Maccintsacairt. Crucially, the date of this plantation is elusive: while it might belong to the 1220s, it might also belong to the second half of the 1230s, after the insurrection in Galloway had been quashed. See Stringer, 'Reform Monasticism and Celtic Scotland',162, for some comment. Some of these problems are addressed in A.B. Scott, 'The Celtic Monastery and Roman Abbey of Fearn', *TGSI* xxviii (1912–14), 391–410, esp. 401–3.

201 Ashley, 'Odo, Elect of Whithern', 63–4.

202 Ashley, 'Odo, Elect of Whithern', 68.

élite (or both). However, it is also possible, given the close connections that could and did exist between local rulers and the church in their territories, that ecclesiastical personnel or institutions might show sympathy for, or else directly support, the rivals of the Scottish kings.

The most obvious instance of resistance perpetrated by an ecclesiastical figure is of course that of Wimund the bishop of the Isles, who may have been a member of the Moray dynasty and who was certainly an inveterate opponent of David I in the 1140s. Although Wimund was probably a dynastic rival of the Scottish kings, there may have been an ecclesiastical aspect to his insurrection as well. William of Newburgh, our chief source of information for the career of Wimund, describes an episode in which he strove to extract tribute from another bishop, with the result that a battle was joined:

> And while he succeeded in everything, and was even a terror to the king himself, a certain bishop, a very simple man, for a time miraculously checked his advance. For when [Wimund] proclaimed war against him and threatened him with destruction unless he paid tax, 'God's will,' said he, 'be done; for never by my example shall any bishop be made tributary to another bishop. So he gathered his people and went against [Wimund] . . . and he himself for the encouragement of his men, giving the first blow in battle, hurled a small axe, and, God willing, laid low his enemy, who was marching in the front. The people were reassured by this chance, and made a bold onset upon the marauders; and slaying a great part of them they compelled their savage leader timidly to flee.[203]

The chronicler identifies neither Wimund's opponent nor the location of the conflict, but modern historians have generally agreed that the battle took place in Galloway, and that the unnamed bishop was Gilla Aldan, the first bishop (circa 1128–51) of a revived see at Whithorn from the late 1120s. Indeed, there is even a local tradition relating to a conflict of warrior-bishops near Penninghame, site of an episcopal manor house.[204] It may be more than coincidental that Wimund's attack occurred at precisely the time when Whithorn was undergoing a revitalisation, and it has been suggested that Wimund's invasion represented a 'response to the erosion of the sphere of his see that the revival of Whithorn had entailed'.[205] Whatever the case may have been – and it is surely difficult to know whether, or how, Wimund's dynastic ambitions were related to his ecclesiastical aims – warrior-bishops and ecclesiastical violence were vivid realities in Wimund's world. In 1204, when a new Benedictine monastery was

---

203 William of Newburgh, in *Chron Stephen* i, 73–6; trans. in *SAEC* 225–6.
204 P.H. M'Kerlie, *History of the Lands and their Owners in Galloway* (Edinburgh, 1870–79), ii, 160.
205 Oram, *Lordship of Galloway*, 166.

built on Iona, 'in violation of the [rights of] the community of Iona', Irish clergy mustered and destroyed the new monastery. [206] In Scandinavia clerics could still be prohibited from carrying arms as late as the 1170s and 1180s, and the case of Wimund calls to mind another Scandinavian warrior-bishop, Gudmund Arason, bishop of Hólar in north Iceland (1203–37). Gudmund's episcopate was characterised by clashes with both powerful landowners and small farmers and was punctuated by periods of exile and captivity. He is reputed to have had a large and unruly household, and trouble followed him wherever he went. In 1208, for instance, his followers killed one of his main opponents in a skirmish, but then in 1209 he was driven from his diocese. On another occasion, after he had taken refuge with the famous saga-writer Snorri Sturluson at Reykholt, Gudmund's enemies killed his supporters and then entered Hólar cathedral, drove out the people, and killed them in the churchyard. Little wonder, then, that one modern commentator has remarked that 'unrest and anarchy flourished everywhere around him'.[207]

Not all forms of ecclesiastical resistance were as aggressive as Wimund's military campaigns, or the attack on Iona in 1204. Somerled's conservative policies in the secular sphere were mirrored by equally conservative tendencies in the ecclesiastical, if an entry in the *Annals of Ulster* for the year 1164 is anything to go by: 'Dignitaries of the community of Iona . . . came to meet Columcille's successor, Flaithbertach Ua-Brolchain, [asking him] to take the abbacy of Iona, by counsel of Somerled, and the men of Argyll and of the Hebrides . . .'[208] This may represent an attempt to reform the religious community on Iona in accordance with contemporary developments in Europe and other parts of the British Isles, which were often undertaken under the auspices of regional kings, as was the case in twelfth-century Ireland. Yet it is notable that Somerled turned not to a figurehead of modern, reformed religion, but rather to Flaithbertach Ua-Brolchain of Derry, an energetic northern Irish bishop and one whose sympathies were distinctly conservative in nature: in the 1150s and 1160s he had been involved in the reform of the church in the north 'in line with, or in opposition to, the organization of the new orders imported from abroad'.[209] Indeed, the north generally was slow to accept ecclesiastical innovation (although there were exceptions), and it seems likely that, in turning to this region and to Flaithbertach in particular, Somerled was making a

206 *AU* (Hennessy), ii, 240–2 (1204); *ES*, ii, 363.
207 For Bishop Gudmund, see *The Saga of the Icelanders*, in *Sturlunga Saga*, trans. J.H. McGrew, intro. R.G. Thomas (New York, 1970–74), i, 115–448. For some comments on his career and its context, see J. Byock, *Viking Age Iceland* (London, 2001), 333–5. Quotation is from J. Johannesson, *Islendinga Saga: A History of the Old Icelandic Commonwealth* (2 vols., Winnipeg, 1974), ii, 212.
208 *AU* (Hennessy), ii, 144 (1164); *ES* ii, 253–4.
209 *Medieval Ireland*, ed. Cosgrove, 38.

deliberately conservative gesture which drew upon the revival of Irish Christianity in the north and which was the 'ecclesiastical equivalent of his rebellions against the kings of Scots'.[210] It is also notable that, at a time when the reformed religious orders were putting down roots throughout Europe and Britain, Somerled, so far as is known, never acted as a patron of these avant-garde representatives of medieval monasticism. Although Somerled has sometimes been regarded as the founder of the Cistercian monastery of Saddell on the east side of the Kintyre peninsula, this identification rests on no firm basis, and the introduction of representatives of the reformed religious orders into the west highlands and islands was left to Somerled's descendants, the MacSorleys, some of whom, like his son, Ranald, were notable patrons of more contemporary forms of religious life.[211] Thus, on the one hand, it is clear that conservative tendencies and insurrections in the secular sphere could be matched by equally conservative policies in the ecclesiastical. On the other hand, it is not always possible to relate opposition to the Scottish kings in the secular sphere with conservative tendencies in the ecclesiastical: Fergus of Galloway, who was almost certainly an enemy of the Scottish kings from the late 1150s, was also an active patron of the Cistercians and Augustinians, and was obviously fully in tune with contemporary religious tendencies.[212]

That monasteries or monastic officials as well as bishops could play a role in insurrection is suggested by events in Galloway in 1234/35. It has been noted how, following the defeat of the Gallovidian army in 1235, the king placed Walter Comyn in charge of the pacification of the region. The Melrose abbey chronicler relates how this army, or at least certain elements of it, went on a rampage, despoiling the abbeys of Glenluce and Tongland and slaying the prior and sacrist at Tongland. Unless the action is attributed to rogue elements of the army, it becomes difficult to avoid the conclusion that these monasteries, or perhaps some of the monastic officials, had somehow played a role in the insurrection. In the first instance, the Melrose chronicle seems to go out of its way to exonerate the king from any responsibility for the attack: it emphasises the fact that Alexander II hastened to leave Galloway after the defeat of the Gallovidian army, leaving Walter Comyn in charge of the mopping-up operations. This in itself suggests some lingering contemporary suspicion about the king's role in events: it almost seems as though the chronicle protests a little too loudly about the king's distance from events (he was at Berwick on 1 August for the marriage of his sister to Gilbert Marshal[213]).

210 McDonald, *Kingdom of the Isles*, 205.
211 R.A. McDonald, 'Scoto-Norse Kings and the Reformed Religious Orders: Patterns of Monastic Patronage in Twelfth-Century Galloway and Argyll', *Albion* xxvii (1995), 187–219, especially 207–13 for Raonall's religious patronage.
212 Ibid.
213 *Chron Melrose* 85 (1235); *ES* ii, 498–9 and n. 2.

Secondly, it is noteworthy that the monasteries which were apparently attacked and despoiled both enjoyed solid connections with the native Lords of Galloway: Tongland was a foundation of Alan in about 1218, while Cistercian Glenluce was founded from Dundrennan by Roland in the early 1190s. Tongland, like Whithorn, was a Premonstratensian house, and it may be that the canons of Tongland had displayed solidarity with the prior and canons of Whithorn in their efforts to have one of their own chosen as bishop in the disputed episcopal election of 1235. Similarly, it may be significant that Gilbert, the monk of Melrose who was elected bishop by the clergy and people of Galloway in 1235, had been abbot of Glenluce but had resigned his office in 1233 and sought refuge at Melrose for reasons that are unknown.[214] All of this suggests a political dimension to the attack on the Gallovidian monasteries in 1235. Finally, it has already been demonstrated how the nomination of Gilbert as bishop of Whithorn in the disputed episcopal election of 1235 can be viewed as an attempt by the Scottish king to buttress royal authority in Galloway. In similar fashion, the Scottish king seems to have been eager to remove from office clerics who were in a position to provide local leadership for Gallovidian resistance. In 1236, for instance, a mere year after the cessation of violence in Galloway, the Cistercian General Chapter deposed abbots Jordan of Dundrennan and Robert of Glenluce, and their replacements were two former monks of Melrose, Leonius and Michael. When Leonius was elected abbot of Rievaulx in 1239, yet another monk of Melrose replaced him as abbot of Dundrennan.[215] Although the official explanation given for these changes in personnel was that the abbot of Glenluce had been improperly chosen, and the abbot of Dundrennan had colluded in his election, the replacement of the heads of these monasteries with monks from Melrose, the most favoured of the royal monasteries in Scotland, must surely be regarded as yet another facet of Alexander's royal policy in Galloway; indeed, it is tempting to suppose that the deposed abbots had even played some part in the insurrection of 1234/35. In sum, when all the evidence surrounding the despoiling of the Gallovidian monasteries by the royal army in 1235 is weighed, it seems difficult to avoid the conclusion that 'the murder of the prior and sacristan [of Tongland] . . . looks premeditated and political'.[216]

Beyond the Political and Military Élite: Popular Resistance
The story thus far has been confined to the élite: the political and military leaders or the discontented dynasts with axes to grind against the Scottish kings. Such a limitation is imposed by the sources, and highlights a difficulty all too

214 *Chron Melrose* 82 (1233); *ES* ii, 489.
215 *Chron Melrose* 85, 86–7 (1236, 1239); *ES* ii, 499–501, 514–5.
216 Brooke, *Wild Men and Holy Places* ,138.

familiar to the historian of medieval Scotland: namely, penetrating beyond the perspective of the ruling élite and into that of the lower social orders. Medieval chroniclers were not much concerned with the rhythms of everyday life, and reserved their attentions for those who mattered in contemporary terms: the kings, nobles, knights and bishops, abbots, and priors who constituted the first estate of medieval society, 'those who ruled'. Yet the question remains: what evidence, if any, is there for resistance to the Scottish kings beyond the level of the élite? What role, if any, was played by the lower orders of society in the challenges to the Scottish kings? There is some evidence of what might be called popular resistance: that is to say, episodes in which resistance does not appear to have been generated by or around a particular élite leader, but rather stemmed from the aspirations or frustrations of more ordinary folk. This seems especially evident in the burning of Bishop Adam in 1222 and in the Gallovidian insurrection of 1234/35.

The involvement of Earl John of Orkney/Caithness in the burning of Bishop Adam is questionable. In some sources he is said to have slain the bishop's aide personally and to have ordered the bishop's killing, but in others he is said to have stood by without interfering, while still other accounts go out of their way to exonerate him from the killing. The saga account of the episode, which may have been written within living memory of the events that it describes, [217] offers the most detailed outline of events surrounding the bishop's unfortunate demise, possibly obtained at first-hand. Significant is the fact that in this account the killing of the bishop is the work of an angry mob of farmers (*boendr*).[218] The account begins by noting that the people of Caithness 'found him [Bishop Adam] rather exacting in his office, and blamed a certain monk who was with him chiefly for that'. The bishop's attempts to increase tithes was something 'thought by all men most unreasonable'.[219] After consulting the earl, who gave no advice on how to deal with the matter, we are told that the *boendr* held an assembly on a hill above the village. The lawman, Rafn, attempted to persuade the bishop to moderate his demands, but the latter refused, objecting that 'the Boendr would become quiet of their own accord'. Another appeal to the earl proved futile, and then, suddenly, the violence began: 'the Boendr ran down from the hill in great excitement, and when Lawman Rafn saw it he warned the Bishop to take care of himself'. The saga relates that the bishop and his friends were drinking in a loft, and that 'when the Boendr arrived the monk went to the door, and he was immediately hewn across the face, and fell back

---

217 *OS* (Anderson), v, 201.
218 The term was used across the Scandinavian cultural world to denote a free farmer: *Medieval Scandinavia: An Encyclopedia*, ed. P. Pulsiano (New York and London, 1993), 51–2.
219 *OS* (Anderson), 200.

into the room dead'.[220] Another attempt at reconciliation between the bishop and the angry mob followed. But although moderate elements in the crowd welcomed further negotiations, more radical elements 'seized the bishop, brought him into a small house, and set fire to it, and the house burnt so quickly that those who wished to save the bishop could not do anything'.[221] The author of *Gesta Annalia* says[222] that the crowd numbered more than three hundred, but as no estimate of the size of the gathering is mentioned in any of the earlier sources that recount the event, this statement seems dubious at best, with the figure of three hundred probably best read as a 'sizeable' number of people.

The episode is instructive not least because the earl remained at arm's length from events. Perhaps having learnt something from the retribution visited upon his father, Earl Harald, for the mutilation of Bishop John in 1201, the saga-writer says that Earl John would have nothing to do with the complaint of the farmers, 'adding that the case was not a difficult one. There were two alternatives: this was not to be endured, yet he would not say what the other might be'.[223] Resentment among the farmers was directed toward the bishop and his adviser, a monk, no doubt in part because they represented Scottish personnel imposed upon the local population, but more importantly because of the bishop's insistence on trebling the tithes to be paid to the local church, thereby altering ecclesiastical custom and no doubt placing a harsh burden upon the farmers.[224] It was these farmers or *boendr* who were responsible for the incineration of the bishop and the killing of his aide, and it is also informative that an assembly preceded the killings where the farmers presumably debated what course of action to take. The whole episode has the ring of mob violence about it, and finds some striking parallels in contemporary Iceland, where Bishop Gudmund Arason of Hólar also managed to stir up resentment among the local *boendr*. They are said to have resented the fact that they were expected to support Gudmund's rag-tag retinue, and when the bishop came to a local farm called Múli, about forty of them, 'prepared as if for battle', barred his way. Even though the bishop moved on without a fight, the *boendr* sought assistance

220 *OS* (Anderson), 200–1.
221 *OS* (Anderson), 200–1.
222 *Chron Fordun* i, 289; ii, 284–5.
223 *Chron Fordun* i, 289; ii, 284–5.
224 The saga says that 'It was an ancient custom that the Bishop should receive a spann [24 marks, or 12 lbs] of butter of every twenty cows. Every Bondi in Caithness had to pay this – he more who had more cows, and he who had fewer less, and so in proportion. Bishop Adam wished to increase the impost, and demanded a spann of every fifteen cows; and when that was obtained, he demanded it of twelve; and when this too was conceded, he demanded it of ten. But this was thought by all men most unreasonable'. *OS* (Anderson), 200.

from several local strongmen who eventually came to blows with the mettle-some bishop and his followers.[225]

There is a similar aura of popular resistance surrounding the events of 1234/35 in Galloway. Although leadership of this insurrection eventually seems to have devolved upon Thomas, the illegitimate son of Alan of Galloway, with some role also being played by Hugh de Lacy, earl of Ulster, Alan's father-in-law, it is noteworthy that the origin of the insurrection lies in the rejected plea by the inhabitants of Galloway to Alexander II to preserve the unity of the Lordship. As the author of the English *Dunstable Annals* put it: 'because the people of the land refused to permit a division of the fief, a great slaughter took place'.[226] The insurrection appears, then, as a spontaneous uprising on the part of the Gallovidians, and at least one historian has regarded Thomas as a passive figure who was manipulated by other interests, and who 'appears to have been a convenient vehicle through which to answer the desire on the part of the Gaelic nobility to retain the integrity of the lordship . . .'[227] Daphne Brooke has gone one step further and argued that these native elements constituted a 'Community of Galloway', which gave expression to local opinion and which constituted the greater and lesser members of the nobility of the region, both secular and ecclesiastical.[228]

It is likely that this 'Community of Galloway', and especially its ecclesiastical members, had a substantial role to play in other events of 1234/35 as well. It has already been noted that the attacks inflicted upon Tongland and Glenluce by the royal army in late summer 1235 look politically motivated. This becomes easier to understand when the place of these monasteries in the local setting is evaluated. Although the reformed religious orders of the twelfth century had their origins on the Continent, and their expansion was part of an international phenomenon, with colonial implications, they were also (as Keith Stringer has so convincingly demonstrated for Galloway) successful in adapting to the local environment.[229] Thus, the new orders made use of old ecclesiastical centres, as at Whithorn, where a Premonstratensian chapter was established in the 1170s, and they also maintained and developed the reverence for local saints: again, the cult of St Ninian at Whithorn is a good example. The question of local recruitment is harder to answer, at least for Galloway, but there are hints that even as early as the twelfth century, and certainly by the thirteenth, these

---

225 *Saga of the Icelanders*, ch. 37. See also Byock, *Viking Age Iceland*, 335.
226 *Annals of Dunstable*, in *Annales Monastici*, ed. H.R. Luard (5 vols., London, 1864–69), iii, 143; trans. in *SAEC*, 340.
227 Oram, *Lordship of Galloway*, 141.
228 Brooke, *Wild Men and Holy Places*, 134–5; a good discussion of medieval concepts of community is Reynolds, *Kingdoms and Communities*, especially chs. 7 and 8. In a Scottish context the seminal work is Barrow, *Robert Bruce*.
229 Stringer, 'Reform Monasticism and Celtic Scotland',127–65.

religious houses were drawing recruits from local families. Walter Daniel, whose account of Ailred of Rievaulx's visit to Dundrennan abbey in 1159 is loaded with cultural élitism, nonetheless suggests that some native Gallovidians had entered the Cistercian abbey there: 'Some of the men of those parts are turned into monks of a sort if they have been formed into a religious house, though under the counsel and guidance of others ... Rievaulx made a plantation in this savagery, which now, by the help of God ... bears much fruit'.[230] Certainly at Whithorn in 1235 about half of the twenty-two canons who petitioned the archbishop of York on behalf of their candidate for the episcopal see had Gaelic names (including the prior, Duncan); later still, when Robert I confirmed grants to Whithorn, there were many local families among the benefactors.[231] All of this means that, although the reformed monasteries of Galloway never lost their international connections or their colonial aspects, it was also possible for them to become firmly rooted in the local environment and to reflect local sentiment accordingly. The actions of the royal army in 1235 and the replacement of the heads of two Gallovidian monasteries in 1236 strongly suggest that several of these religious houses did indeed play a role in the insurrection of 1234/35, possibly having identified with the forces of Gallovidian opposition.

Was there an 'Anti-Feudal Faction' in twelfth- and thirteenth-century Scotland?
Opposition to the Scottish kings of the twelfth and thirteenth centuries came in many different forms. The MacWilliams and MacHeths were essentially dynastic opponents, representatives of cast-off branches of the royal kindred, while others, including Fergus, Somerled, and Harald Maddadsson, were driven to resistance as a result of Scottish encroachment upon the largely autonomous Atlantic zones of the kingdom. Nevertheless, it would be something of an oversimplification to suggest that such neat distinctions between the two groups of opponents can always be maintained, and it is certainly within the bounds of possibility that the interests of the two groups might coincide from time to time, thus blurring distinctions between dynastic and political resistance.

In a seminal essay dealing with the historical Macbeth, Professor E.J. Cowan coined the term 'anti-feudal faction' to describe those who opposed the Canmore kings in the twelfth and thirteenth centuries, including not only the Cenél Loairn dynasty but also the likes of Somerled, Malcolm MacHeth, the MacWilliams, and Harald Maddadsson.[232] It is a striking phrase, suggestive

---

230 *Vita Aelredi*, 45. For some further comment on local recruitment in Galloway, see Stringer, 'Reform Monasticism and Celtic Scotland', 152–3

231 *Historians of York* iii, 146–8; A.A.M. Duncan, *The Acts of Robert I King of Scots 1306–29* (*Regesta Regum Scottorum*, Vol. V, Edinburgh, 1988), no. 275.

232 'Historical MacBeth', 131.

not only of the opposition faced by the Scottish kings of the period, but also hinting at connections and cooperation among the king's enemies. Yet, the implications of this concept have yet to be fully worked out for the history of medieval Scotland, despite its tremendous potential.

Setting aside the debate over the utility of the term 'feudalism' for the study of medieval history,[233] at one level the concept of an 'anti-feudal faction' in twelfth- and thirteenth-century Scotland is oversimplistic, since the motives behind the insurrections varied tremendously. Many were dynastically driven, especially those of the MacWilliams and probably also the MacHeths. Some were rooted in opportunism and xenophobia, like that in Galloway in 1174–75. Still others, like those of Somerled in 1164 and Harald Maddadsson in the 1190s, come close to appearing 'anti-feudal' in the sense that they were consequences of Scottish expansion and territorial aggrandisement, a process that was in turn closely connected to the spread of military feudalism with its symbols of knights, fiefs, and castles. Yet at the same time such generalisations can obscure as much as they clarify. Thus, it is important to realise that several members of the 'anti-feudal faction' appear to have embraced some aspects, at least, of the European civilisation that was penetrating Scotland in the twelfth and thirteenth centuries. Fergus of Galloway, for instance, was receptive to the reformed religious orders that were so popular throughout Europe and Britain in the twelfth century, and is known to have utilised charters to record grants of land; similarly, among the MacSorleys in the very next generation after Somerled, there is strong evidence that aspects of knighthood were becoming known in the Hebrides. Although it has been popular in the past to regard the kin-based Celtic society as fundamentally and diametrically opposed to European, 'feudal' societies, recent scholarship has highlighted the flaws in this view and has shown how members of the Gaelic or Scoto-Norse élite in the outer zones of the Scottish kingdom adapted certain aspects of European society to their own ends, thereby accommodating themselves to European impulses, creating in the process a new hybrid society.[234]

It is at the level of emphasising the connections among the leaders of opposition that the notion of 'anti-feudal faction' carries the most validity;

233 The debate is articulated in Brown, 'Tyranny of a Construct', 1063–88; see now Reynolds, *Fiefs and Vassals, passim.*

234 Bartlett, *Making of Europe*, and Davies, *Domination and Conquest*, are seminal in regard to themes of accommodation and acculturation. For a study specific to the peripheral regions of Scotland, see McDonald, 'Coming in from the margins', 179–98; see also Neville's study of the earldom of Strathearn under Gilbert: 'A Celtic Enclave', 75–92. On literacy in Gaelic society, see the important work of D. Broun, *The Charters of Gaelic Scotland and Ireland in the Early and Central Middle Ages* (Quiggin Pamphlets on the Sources of Mediaeval Gaelic History 2, Cambridge, 1995).

indeed, it is one of the striking aspects of resistance to the Scottish kings that most of the leaders were connected with one another through ties of kinship or matrimony. Marriage alliances and matrimonial politics were one mechanism that greatly assisted in blurring distinctions between dynastic and political opponents and connecting some of the various rivals of the Scottish kings. Perhaps the most obvious example of a marriage alliance between opponents of the Scottish kings is that between the dynasty of Somerled and the MacHeth kindred. In its discussion of the rising of Somerled and the MacHeths in 1153, the *Chronicle of Holyrood* calls the sons of Malcolm MacHeth Somerled's nephews.[235] This would indicate that a sister of Somerled had married Malcolm MacHeth, almost certainly before the latter's capture and incarceration in 1134. The alliance bore fruit in 1153, when Somerled allied with the sons of Malcolm against Malcolm IV. Harald Maddadsson of Orkney/Caithness was also connected to the MacHeth dynasty, for sometime around 1168 he had married a daughter of Malcolm named Hvarflod. This connection is particularly interesting since Harald's first wife was a daughter of Earl Duncan I of Fife, a member of the native Scottish nobility who nevertheless was a prominent supporter of the Canmore kings and possibly even a representative of a cadet branch of the royal kindred.[236] Since marriage alliances among the medieval nobility were always carefully calculated and crafted political schemes, in repudiating his first wife and taking instead a daughter of Malcolm MacHeth, Earl Harald was almost certainly 'consciously associating himself with the MacHeth faction'.[237] This contention is strengthened by the fact that the Scottish kings were clearly threatened by the connection: one condition of the prospective peace between Earl Harald and the king in 1196 was that the earl should dismiss MacHeth's daughter as his wife, which he refused to do.[238] Similarly, but moving in an opposite direction, marriages could also be used to draw potentially troublesome chieftains from the periphery closer to the core of Alba. Thus Ewen of Argyll, the great-grandson of Somerled, married his daughter to Malise, the earl of Strathearn, sometime about 1268; this marriage moved in an opposite direction to that of Earl Harald since Ewen's daughter's had previously been wedded to the Manx king, Magnus, who perished in 1265. This new marriage alliance to a member of the eastern nobility demonstrates how the winds of change were sweeping over the rulers of the west in the wake of the events of 1263–65. Marriages, therefore, could be and were used to forge alliances among the opponents of the Scottish kings, just as they could be used

---

235 *Chron Holyrood*, 125.
236 Earl Harald's marriage alliances are recorded in *OS*, ch. 109; Howden in *SAEC*, 318.
237 R.A. McDonald, 'Matrimonial politics and core-periphery interactions in twelfth-and early thirteenth-century Scotland', *JMH* xxi (1995), 243.
238 *Chronica* iv, 10–12; trans. in *SAEC*, 318.

to lever chieftains on the periphery and erstwhile enemies closer toward the camp of the Scottish kings themselves.[239]

It is clear that some of those who opposed the Scottish monarchs were connected by matrimony, while most were united by the forces of geography, if not by a common antipathy toward the Scottish royal house. On the other hand, it is also striking that the forces of reaction represented by individuals like Fergus, Somerled, Earl Harald, the MacHeths, and MacWilliams never united to make a common, overwhelming, cause against the Scottish kings. It is true that the rising of 1153–60 was a joint effort between Somerled and the MacHeths, and there is some evidence that Harald Maddadson was acting with the MacHeths in 1186 and with the MacWilliams later. It is not until 1215, however, that there is firm evidence of MacHeths and MacWilliams acting together, and by then it was too late: not only had the opponents of the Scottish kings been further marginalised by nearly a century of setback and defeat, but other members of the native Scottish nobility like Roland of Galloway and Ferchar of Ross, who might have made powerful allies, had instead moved firmly into the camp of the Scottish kings.

The best explanation of why those who resisted the Scottish kings at various times never united probably lies in a combination of geographical and political factors. It is all too easy to view things from the perspective of the expanding Scottish kingdom, which places rulers like Fergus, Somerled and Earl Harald on the periphery while highlighting developments in the core. If, however, the map is turned on its head, and expanded to encompass the maritime seaways that united the Atlantic zones of Scotland with Ireland, Man, and Scandinavia, then the relative positions of centre and periphery are reversed: Galloway, Argyll, Ross, Caithness and Orkney appear rather as the centre, while the Scottish kingdom itself becomes peripheral. This means, in turn, that many of those who resisted the Scottish kings – particularly those with comital or regnal status in their territories – had other interests to maintain, and it may well be that the Scottish kingdom itself, peripheral from this perspective, was of secondary importance in their considerations. Both Fergus and Somerled struggled to maintain extensive interests and connections within the Irish Sea region, and in particular with the Isle of Man, while Earl Harald, like many earls of Orkney/Caithness, possessed strong links to Scandinavia and walked a delicate tightrope between the expanding monarchies of Scotland on the one hand and Scandinavia on the other. As for the MacWilliams, their connections with Gaelic Ireland would have dictated that events there – and especially the ebb and flow of the English advance in the north – occupied a good deal of their attention as well. In the final analysis, it was because each essentially looked outward to the Atlantic rather than

---

239 See McDonald, 'Matrimonial politics', *passim*; *Kingdom of the Isles*, 46.

inward toward Scotland that the various rivals of the Scottish kings never united. The pull of the Atlantic was strong, and there were simply too many competing and overlapping spheres of influence to make a united stand against the territorially advantaged kings of Scots.

THREE

'THE PLUNDER OF STABLE ALBA'?
The Magnitude and Impact of Opposition

It's bad, what Mael Coluim's son has done,
dividing us from Alexander;
he causes, like each king's son before,
the plunder of stable Alba.

This verse refers to the tensions between King Alexander I and his brother when David claimed Lothian by threat of military force in 1113, and it represents the sentiments of the poet and others who were disadvantaged by the estrangement of the two sons of Malcolm III.[1] The image of 'the plunder of stable Alba' seems a fitting one to apply to the challenges of the twelfth and thirteenth centuries, not least because historians have generally tended to emphasise the internal stability and harmony of the kingdom of the Scots.[2] Yet some of the most striking images from the challenges are of destruction, and relate to their impact upon the Scottish landscape, people, and kingdom. The *Carmen de Morte Somerledi* paints a vivid picture of the Clyde valley ravaged and Glasgow nearly deserted in the face of Somerled's invasion of 1164. Roger of Howden describes in detail the expulsion of royal agents, the slaying of English and French, and the razing of castles in Galloway in 1174. Walter Bower relates the deadly game of cat and mouse between Guthred MacWilliam and the royal army sent to bring him to heel in 1211–12. The Melrose abbey chronicle tells of a Scottish army on the rampage in Galloway in 1235. But just how accurate are these images? What impact did opposition to the Scottish kings, and royal campaigns against rivals, have on the Scottish kingdom as a whole? How well equipped were the armies of the king's enemies? Why did the challenges mounted by the king's enemies ultimately end in failure? These are the questions for the present chapter.

1 'A Verse on David Son of Mael Coluim', trans. Clancy, *Triumph Tree*, 184; see also T.O. Clancy, 'A Gaelic polemic quatrain from the reign of Alexander I', *Scottish Gaelic Studies* xx (2000), 88–95.
2 See recently, for example, R. Frame, 'Conquest and Settlement', in *The Twelfth and Thirteenth Centuries*, 57–8, although in fairness, Frame does remark that 'The almost complete absence of chronicle evidence . . . may leave the impression that Scotland was freer from friction and violence than was the case'.

Battlefield Scotland?

At various times throughout the twelfth and early thirteenth centuries, many of the peripheral regions of Scotland were turned into battlefields, where armies raised by the likes of Wimund, Somerled or the MacWilliams slugged it out with royal armies intent on their destruction. Moreover, given the frequency with which uprisings occurred, at any given decade in our period the chances are good that a royal army was on the move somewhere in Scotland (Appendix 1). It is relatively simple to pinpoint the regions from which challenges were launched and against which royal campaigns were directed, but it is a more difficult task to be specific about the nature of the damage inflicted.

Without question the most devastated and war-torn regions of Scotland in the late twelfth and early thirteenth centuries were the large and imperfectly assimilated northern territories of Moray and Ross, which became, quite literally, battlegrounds between the kings of Scots and their rivals from the time of King Malcolm III until the reign of Alexander II nearly two centuries later. In 1058, the hapless Lulach, stepson and briefly successor of Macbeth, was slain at Essie in Strathbogie by Malcolm III. Twenty years later, in 1078, the *Anglo-Saxon Chronicle* records how 'King Malcolm captured Mael-slaehta's [Máelsnechtai's] mother . . . and all his best men, and all his treasures and his cattle . . .'[3] Given its outcome, King Malcolm's raid must have been directed at Moray; how else to explain the capture of Máelsnechtai's mother, men, and livestock? The battle of Stracathro in 1130 was fought in Angus, not in Moray; but a royal army pursued fugitives from the battle into the north and Orderic Vitalis detailed how David 'conquered the whole of that extensive duchy [i.e. Moray]'.[4] It may be that this Scottish conquest and subsequent colonisation of Moray underlies the cryptic entry in the Holyrood Abbey chronicle to the effect that 'King Malcolm moved the men of Moray' in 1163.[5] In 1187 Donald MacWilliam was slain and his army annihilated at the unknown site of Mam Garvia, probably Strath Garve west of Dingwall in Ross. MacWilliam's demise may have brought a temporary respite to the inhabitants of Moray and Ross, but within ten years Harald Maddadsson was on the rampage, and a nasty game of invasion and counter-invasion ensued in the far north. The *Chronicle of Melrose* states that a battle took place in Moray, near Inverness, between the forces of Harald and the king's men; afterwards, King William launched his own invasion of Caithness that resulted in the destruction of the earl's fortress at Thurso. Less than a decade later, Donald MacWilliam's son Guthred appeared on the scene in Ross in 1211. When Donald Bàn MacWilliam and Kenneth MacHeth landed in Scotland in 1215, they are said to have entered Moray, and the northern locus

3   *ASC*, 213 (1078).
4   *Ecclesiastical History of Orderic Vitalis* iv, 276–7.
5   *Chron Holyrood*, 142.

of this insurrection is reinforced by the fact that the two men were defeated and slain by Ferchar Maccintsacairt, a noble of Ross. Finally, Bower relates that in 1223 Gillescop MacWilliam appeared 'in the furthest limits of Scotland'.[6] Subsequent events demonstrate that Moray and Ross were meant, since in 1228 Gillescop fired defensive works in Moray, slew Thomas de Thirlestane in his castle – Thomas was lord of Abertarff at the south end of Loch Ness, so presumably this castle is meant[7] – burned part of Inverness, and plundered nearby royal lands.

If Moray and Ross headed the list of the peripheral regions at odds with the centre of the Scottish kingdom throughout the twelfth and early thirteenth centuries, and bore the brunt of military activities, other regions were certainly not immune. William of Newburgh, our chief source of information for the activities of Wimund, likened him to 'Nimrod, a mighty hunter before the Lord', and described his 'fierce ravages through the neighbouring lands'.[8] William's vague geographical descriptions notwithstanding, it seems a fair enough speculation that these 'neighbouring lands' were Cumbria, the Irish Sea and the Hebrides. Wimund's context was essentially an insular one – he was bishop of the Isles, with links to Man and the Hebrides, and there seems little doubt that his army was composed of Islesmen. It would appear that Cumbria bore the brunt of his military activity, since David I ultimately ceded part of it to the troublesome bishop. And if Newburgh's account of Wimund's battle with another bishop is correctly placed in Galloway, then it seems likely that many of the eastern shores of the Irish Sea had been drawn into the conflagration of this insurrection.

In similar fashion, the rising of Somerled and his nephews in 1153 was said by a Scottish chronicle to have 'perturbed and disquieted Scotland in great part'.[9] Once again the vague nature of the chronicle's geographical description is frustrating, but it seems logical to assume that Argyll, and quite likely the Clyde estuary, were intended. It may also be significant that Donald, the son of Malcolm associated with Somerled in 1153, was captured at Whithorn in Galloway in 1156 – although whether by treachery or military action is not stated. Whichever regions of Scotland were perturbed in the 1150s, there is no doubt that Somerled's invasion of 1164 brought devastation to the peasant farmers of the Clyde valley and fear to the inhabitants of Glasgow. Certainly the Clyde valley seems to have been the target of Scottish military activity in the campaigns of 1221 and/or 1222, when the burgh of Dumbarton was established. In 1197 the Scottish king erected a new castle between the Doon and the Ayr – a strategic location designed to help control the turbulent western seaways as much as the southwest. And, lending

---

6 *Scotichronicon* v, 117.

7 *Scotichronicon* iv, 631–2.

8 *Historia Rerum Anglicarum*, in *Chron Stephen* i, 74; trans. *SAEC*, 225.

9 *Chron Holyrood*, 124–5.

symmetry to over a century of military threats from the west, the skirmishes in 1263 were fought at Largs on the Ayrshire coast.

Galloway in the southwest also saw a good deal of military activity in the period 1160 to 1235. Not only did King Malcolm campaign there three times in 1160–61, ultimately removing Fergus, Lord of Galloway, but his sons, Uhtred and Gilbert, unleashed their own reign of terror in 1174–75. The death of Gilbert of Galloway in early 1185 seems to have done little to stabilise the situation, since Roland, Uhtred's son and heir, sought to recover and consolidate his father's territories. The *Chronicle of Melrose* records that in 1185 'There was a battle in Galloway between Roland and Gillepatric . . . and in it more men fell on the side of Gillepatric: and he himself perished, with many others'. A few months later, 'Roland fought a battle against Gillecoluim; and in it Roland's brother fell, and Gillecoluim perished'.[10] Quite apart from Roland's efforts to annihilate those who had sided with his father's killer, there is also evidence of royal campaigns in the southwest during the same period. King William was probably responsible for the construction of a castle at Dumfries in the late 1170s. But perhaps no events were more destructive in the southwest than those following the death of Alan, when the proposed partition of the lordship by Alexander II sparked a spontaneous uprising that had to be harshly suppressed.

Insurrection, then, was closely linked with the outer Atlantic zones of the Scottish kingdom in the twelfth and thirteenth centuries. Characterised by their geographical remoteness from the centre of the Scottish kingdom, and their rugged terrain, these regions possessed, in many cases, strong identities of their own, sometimes bound up with regnal traditions distinct from those of the expanding kingdom of Alba. They were, moreover, regions that were only imperfectly assimilated within the Scottish kingdom. Little wonder, then, that these were the regions where the enemies of the Scottish kings found both support and shelter. Yet what is even more striking than the geographical nexus of insurrection is the fact that, from time to time in the course of our period, these outer zones intruded, often violently, into the very heartland of the Scottish kingdom.[11] Sometime in the 1110s, probably 1116, the Moravians ambushed King Alexander at Invergowrie near Dundee; it is said that Alexander was staying on one of his royal estates when he was attacked. The ensuing campaign carried Alexander and his army all the way 'oure the Mownth' to the 'Stokfurd into Ross'[12] – possibly the cattle ford over the Beauly River – and while the geographical setting of the final campaign is illustrative of the role of Moray

---

10 *Chron Melrose*, 45; *ES* ii, 309–10.
11 Outwith the present scope but nonetheless significant is the fact that Aberdeen was plundered by a Scandinavian fleet in the early 1150s: *Morkinskinna: The Earliest Icelandic Chronicle of the Norwegian Kings (1030–1157)*, trans. T.M. Andersson and K.E. Gade (Ithaca and London, 2000), 391; also in *ES* ii, 215–6.
12 *Orygynale Cronykle* iii, 174–5; Bower, *Scotichronicon* iii, 104–7.

and Ross in these insurrections, the fact that a king of Scots could be ambushed a few miles from Dundee, in the heartland of the Scottish monarchy, is startling. The events of 1116 may be problematic, of course, but they are not isolated. Less than twenty years later, in 1130, Angus of Moray and Malcolm MacHeth are said to have 'entered Scotland' where they were met and defeated by Edward son of Siward, the constable of Kings Alexander and David. Once again there can be no doubt of the role of Moray in the insurrection – the shattered Moravian army was pursued 'into the territory of Moray' which was subsequently annexed to the Crown. Yet, as with the events of the 1110s, it is striking that an army could penetrate deep into the Scottish kingdom itself: its defeat took place at Stracathro in Angus. Exactly thirty years after Stracathro, and mid-way through the reign of Malcolm IV, there occurred the so-called 'revolt of the earls.' Although the nature of this event remains uncertain, there is no doubt at all about the geographical framework: when King Malcolm returned from France, his outraged earls besieged him at Perth – one of the four great towns of medieval Scotland and a centre with strong royal associations in the twelfth century.[13] Four years later, in 1164, Somerled sailed up the Clyde as far as Renfrew, where he was met and defeated in battle. Although Renfrew represented one of the most westerly penetrations of Scottish royal authority in the period, its proximity to Glasgow, with its important economic and religious centres, was striking: indeed, the author of the *Carmen de Morte Sumerledi* implies that the citizens of Glasgow fled in the face of the onslaught, and paints a vivid picture of the cathedral being all but abandoned by its clergy. Even as late as 1186, and probably related to the MacWilliam insurrection of 1181–87, a warband of about sixty men led by Adam the son of Donald was able to penetrate as far south as Coupar Angus abbey, a dozen or so miles from Perth, where Adam was seized, his nephew beheaded, and the remainder burned alive. Later insurrections and military activities were notably confined to the remoter territories of the kingdom, but it is appropriate that the final act of the MacWilliam insurrections was played out at Forfar, where a little girl, the last of that kindred, was cruelly executed in 1230. The curtain thus fell on the MacWilliams only a short distance from Stracathro, where, a century earlier, it had risen on one of the opening acts in the story of challenges to the Scottish kings, as the constable of David I defeated Angus of Moray and Malcolm.

As is the case with their geographical descriptions, the various chronicles, annals, sagas, and other sources for these insurrections are frustratingly vague about the extent and nature of the damage they caused. Wimund's army, for

---

13 Perth appears thirteen times as a place-date in the charters of Malcolm IV, for example, and its significance is highlighted by the fact that these charters are spaced out chronologically through the reign: see Barrow, *Acts of Malcolm IV*, 27.

example, was said to have 'made incursions into the provinces of Scotland, harrying everything with fire and slaughter'. In similar fashion, the rising of Somerled and the sons of Malcolm MacHeth in 1153 is said to have 'perturbed and disquieted Scotland in great part'. Describing Donald MacWilliam's incursion of 1181, Roger of Howden notes his arrival in Scotland, 'wasting and burning as much of the land as he reached; and he put the folk to flight, and slew all whom he could take'. *Gesta Annalia*, meanwhile, described how MacWilliam had 'seized the greater part of the kingdom, with fire and slaughter . . .' Stock images of fire and slaughter aside, then, there appears to be little real detail that can be recovered relating to the impact of these insurrections on the Scottish land, people, and kingdom.

Nevertheless, several texts move beyond the vague, generalised images of fire and slaughter and illuminate the real extent of the damage caused by twelfth- and thirteenth -century revolts. The document known as the *Carmen de Morte Sumerledi* relates details of Somerled's 1164 invasion of the Clyde estuary and his subsequent defeat at Renfrew. Its author was William, apparently a Glaswegian clergyman, who claimed to be an eyewitness to the events that he described. 'All that he saw and heard, William has written down,' he tells us at the conclusion of the poem.[14] Described by its most recent editor and translator as 'fantastical', no doubt because it attributes the victory over Somerled to supernatural elements, the poem nevertheless has all the value of an eyewitness account and provides remarkable and vivid images of the devastation wrought by – and eventually upon – Somerled's invading army. Although the first stanza contains the usual stock references to fire and slaughter, the account becomes more detailed in the second, when the plight of both the peasant farmers of the Clyde valley as well as the citizens of Glasgow is outlined. 'Gardens, fields and plough-lands were laid waste and destroyed; the gentle, menaced by barbarous hands, were overwhelmed,' William says, in a description that sounds remarkably like those from some three centuries earlier relating the onslaught of the Norsemen. The plight of the citizens of Glasgow is also revealed: 'Wounded, Glasgow's people fled the blows of two-edged swords'. Although there is no other evidence that Somerled's army penetrated further than Renfrew, it is not beyond the bounds of possibility that raiding parties reached Glasgow, just as it seems likely that many of Glasgow's inhabitants might have fled in anticipation of the onslaught of the Islesmen. Among those who fled were most of the clergy of the cathedral, since we are told that 'Mark, of all the scattered clergy, murmuring remained within the church's hard high walls, bearing his harsh fate, weeping and lamenting the prosperous days of old'. Some of the most vivid imagery, however, is reserved for describing the fate of Somerled and many of his soldiers:

14 'Carmen de Morte Sumerledi', in Symeon of Durham, *Symeonis Monachi Opera Omnia* ii, 386–88; trans. Clancy, *Triumph Tree*, 212–4.

Their savage leader now laid low, the wicked turned and ran,
But many of them were butchered in the sea as on dry land.
They sought to clamber from the blood-red waves into their ships
But were drowned, each and all, in the surging tide.
Such was the slaughter, such destruction of the treacherous thousands.

Another account that moves beyond stock imagery is Roger of Howden's of the Gallovidian insurrection of 1174. Howden was not only a contemporary but had played a personal role in the events of the mid-1170s in Galloway: he was a royal clerk and had acted as a diplomatic envoy for King Henry II in his dealings with Gilbert of Galloway. He had also made several subsequent visits to Scotland.[15] Roger was therefore well informed on Scottish events, and this is abundantly clear in his account of the devastation wrought by Gilbert and Uhtred in 1174. Howden describes how, when the news that King William had been captured at Alnwick reached Gilbert and Uhtred in the summer of 1174, they

> at once expelled from Galloway all the bailiffs and guards whom the king of Scotland had set over them; and all the English and French whom they could seize they slew; and all the defences which the king of Scotland had established in their land they besieged, captured and destroyed, and slew all whom they took with them.[16]

Here is a very specific catalogue of devastation, similar to that provided by William of Glasgow. No doubt Howden had first-hand knowledge of the events that he described, since he tells us that he met with Gilbert not long afterward, and although the site of the meeting is unknown, it is possible that it had taken place in Galloway, in which case the chronicler might even have witnessed some of the devastation for himself. Whatever the case may be, archaeology seems to corroborate this version of events. Tantalisingly, excavations at the motte of Urr, one of the most extensive in all of Scotland constructed by Walter de Berkeley, lord of Urr, in about 1160, have revealed that the timber buildings there were destroyed by fire in the late twelfth century, almost certainly in the events of the mid-1170s.[17] It is also perhaps telling that the height of the motte was increased after this destruction.[18] Similarly, excavations at Whithorn revealed the destruction of some buildings there by fire in the late twelfth

---

15 See the discussion in Ch. 2, p. 72 with references.
16 *Gesta Henrici Secundi* i, 67–8.
17 Brooke, *Wild Men and Holy Places*, 104; C. Tabraham, *Scotland's Castles* (London, 1997), 132.
18 G. Stell, *Exploring Scotland's Heritage: Dumfries and Galloway* (Edinburgh, 1986), 115; see also J. Gifford, *Dumfries and Galloway: The Buildings of Scotland* (London, 1996), 338.

century, though whether by accident or as the result of conflict cannot be ascertained.[19]

Turning from Galloway to the far north, there is also detailed evidence for the MacWilliam insurrections of 1211/12 and the 1220s, led by Guthred and Gillescop respectively. Walter Bower, the abbot of Inchcolm whose massive *Scotichronicon* was composed in the 1440s, provided very detailed accounts of the campaigns of the king against Guthred in 1211–12 and the activities of Gillescop in the late 1220s. We learn, for instance, that Guthred landed in Scotland from Ireland, laid ambushes for the royal army sent against him, and drove off booty from the king's land. Very specific details are provided about the size and leaders of the royal army sent against him, and it is said that he managed to besiege and capture one of the castles built by the king in Ross. There follows an account of Guthred's betrayal by his own men, his deliverance to the earl of Buchan, and his execution at Kincardine.[20] Bower concludes his discussion with the remark that Guthred 'trod underfoot everything he encountered and plagued many parts of the kingdom of Scotland'. In similar fashion, Bower's account of Gillescop's insurrection in the late 1220s is also unusually detailed, particularly in relation to geographical details. He relates how

In 1228 a certain Scot called Gillescop set fire to some wooden defensive works in Moray and killed a certain thief called Thomas de Thirlestane after attacking his castle unexpectedly during the night. Afterwards he burned a large part of Inverness, and about [the time of the feast of] the Nativity of the Blessed Mary [8 September] he plundered some lands belonging to the lord king.[21]

These accounts share descriptions of castles being captured and attacked as well as plundering and the driving off of booty, and taken together with the accounts of Howden and William of Glasgow, they provide a much more detailed picture of the devastation that could be wrought by the king's enemies.

Although it might be objected that Bower was writing some two centuries after the events that he described, the detail in these accounts is not likely to have been invented, and requires explanation. Bower's account of the Mac-William insurrection of 1211/12 is based upon an otherwise untraced document, one that provides much more information than that which Bower had available in the *Gesta Annalia*. This source constituted an 'unusually detailed record from the Scottish side of the movements and discussions of the time', which Professor Duncan has regarded as part of a detailed itinerary of William

19 Hill, *Whithorn and St Ninian*, 22, 211–16.
20 *Scotichronicon* iv, 464–7.
21 *Scotichronicon* v, 142–3.

and his brother for the period 1209 to 1212 or 1214.[22] There can be little doubt that it was written up very soon after the events that it described, and that its author was either someone close to the scene, or else someone with a well-positioned informant. Candidates for authorship include the bishops of St Andrews or Glasgow, the abbot of Melrose, or William del Bois, a royal clerk who became chancellor in 1211.[23] As for the account of events in 1228, no source is known for the majority of events detailed in this chapter, and it has been suggested that Bower was relying here on a lost chronicle.[24] Thus, although Bower was writing some two centuries after the events that he was describing in these passages, there is every indication that he was drawing upon earlier, contemporary, and well-informed documents that are now lost, and his account should be regarded as providing important insight into the MacWilliam challenges of the early thirteenth century.

Lands laid waste; cities and cathedrals all but abandoned; castles destroyed; royal officials slain: from the well-informed accounts of William of Glasgow, Roger of Howden, and Walter Bower there emerge stark and frightening images of the devastation that might be wrought by the king's enemies. These accounts emphasise the impact of the insurrections of the twelfth and thirteenth centuries on both people and landscape, and flesh out the less substantial chronicle accounts that rely upon stock images of fire and slaughter to sum up the damage caused by the various insurrections.

There is another side to the issue, however. Bower's discussion of the campaigns against Guthred MacWilliam and his eventual demise provides a potent reminder that the enemies of the Scottish kings did not always bear sole responsibility for devastating a region. Describing King William's campaign against Guthred in 1211, Bower states that the king 'laid waste pretty well all of Ross'. This was not an isolated incident. About fifty years later, in 1262, a royal expedition led by the earl of Ross attacked the Isle of Skye, 'and burned a town and churches, and slew very many men and women'. A Scandinavian saga account recalled how 'the Scots had taken the little children, and laid them on their spear-points, and shook their spears until they brought the children down to their hands, and so threw them away, dead'.[25] This reads like the account of a Viking raid of the ninth century, and, indeed, the practice of impaling children on spears, known as *gallcerd*, was originally Scandinavian.[26]

But just how are these references to be explained? Even allowing, as we surely must, for a certain amount of hyperbole on the part of the chroniclers, it is difficult

---

22 *Scotichronicon* iv, notes on 616 and 631–2; ix, 247–7; Duncan, *Scotland*, 243–7.

23 *Scotichronicon* iv, notes on 616.

24 *Scotichronicon* v, notes on 256.

25 *ES* ii, 601–2.

26 Cowan, 'Hakon IV and Alexander III', 130 n. 70.

to avoid the conclusion that King William's activities in Ross in 1211 look like a deliberate attempt to ruin the population of this troublesome district with a policy of harrying, the object of which was, of course, to prevent further disturbances and to deprive enemies of resources. This calls to mind the infamous devastation of the north of England by William the Conqueror in 1069–70, when Yorkshire, Cheshire, Shropshire, Staffordshire and Derbyshire were so completely devastated that large areas were still derelict seventeen years later, when the Domesday survey was undertaken.[27] The Anglo-Norman chronicler Orderic Vitalis provides a graphic description of William the Conqueror's campaign in the north of England that may shed some light on what his Scottish namesake perpetrated upon the population of Ross: 'In the fullness of his wrath he ordered the corn and the cattle, with the implements of husbandry and every sort of provisions, to be collected in heaps and set on fire until the whole was consumed, and thus destroyed at once all that could serve for the support of life in the whole country lying beyond the Humber'.[28] Exactly what such tactics might achieve is further illuminated by a campaign of King William II of England against Gruffudd ap Cynan of Gwynedd (d. 1137) when the English king is said to have intended 'to cut down all the woods and groves, so that there would not be shelter or protection for the people of Gwynedd from then on'.[29] This statement should provide important insight into what the Scottish king might have hoped to accomplish in Ross in 1211, for this area was heavily wooded.[30] It is also noteworthy that Robert I employed similar tactics a century later in the infamous 'herschip of Buchan' of 1308, in which the earldom of Buchan was devastated from end to end, supporters of John Comyn, Bruce's rival, were killed, livestock was slaughtered, and stores of grain destroyed.[31] A famous passage from John Barbour's epic poem *The Bruce* (c. 1375) describes this event:

Now ga we to the king agayne
That off his victory wes rycht fayn
And gert his men bryn all Bowchane
Fra end till end and sparyt nane,
And heryit thaim on sic maner
That eftre weile fifty yer
Men menyt the herschip off Bouchane.[32]

27 See F.M. Stenton, *Anglo-Saxon England* (3rd ed., Oxford, 1971; pb. ed. 1989), 601–5.
28 *Ecclesiastical History of Orderic Vitalis* ii, 232.
29 *A Mediaeval Prince of Wales: The Life of Gruffudd ap Cynan*, ed. and trans. D. Simon Evans (Lampeter, 1990), 43, 74.
30 See note 117 below.
31 See Barrow, *Robert Bruce*, 176–7.
32 John Barbour, *The Bruce*, trans. A.A.M. Duncan (Edinburgh, 1997), Bk ix, ll. 295–300.

The examples of William the Conqueror's harrying of the north of England and Robert Bruce's 'herschip' of Buchan simply provide parallels for what might have happened in Ross in 1211 (or Skye in 1262); they do not, of course, prove that this is what happened. But just as the north of England had been a troublesome district for the Conqueror to subdue, and just as Buchan was home to one of Robert Bruce's most implacable foes, so too, by 1211, must Ross have appeared much the same to the Scottish kings, given its thirty-year association with some of the king's most formidable rivals. A 'herschip' of Ross in 1211 is not beyond the bounds of possibility, and might provide a fitting explanation for Bower's imagery. That such devastation need not necessarily be inflicted only by invaders is illustrated by Matthew Paris's account of events in Galloway in 1235. He tells how, in the course of their insurrection, the Gallovidians 'burned their own and their neighbours' houses'. This was undertaken, he explained, 'that the king when he arrived with his army might not find lodging or food',[33] surely an apt description of a scorched-earth policy designed to prevent invaders from obtaining supplies.

'Soldiers Most Unfortunate': Victors and Vanquished
The human cost of these battles, skirmishes, ambushes, sieges and harryings will never be known and is impossible to calculate on the basis of the scanty evidence at our disposal. The chronicles contain many references to slaughters and devastation but provide no precise information on casualties. It is true that the *Annals of Ulster* state that four thousand Moravians perished at Stracathro in 1130, but this should probably not be taken literally. The *Carmen de Morte Somerledi* says that Somerled's forces were overwhelmed and largely annihilated by a smaller army that suffered few losses: 'Such was the slaughter, such destruction of the treacherous thousands/ but not one of those who fought them was wounded here or died'.[34] Such literary descriptions are hardly conducive to the analysis of casualty rates, and it has to be admitted that there is no way of knowing the precise number of those who fell on either side in any of these encounters. Most chroniclers were content to record the outcomes of these clashes in general terms. Thus, the *Annals of Inisfallen* laconically but powerfully note the 'slaughter of the men of Moray' in 1130.[35] The *Annals of Ulster*, recording the defeat of Somerled in 1164, note that 'slaughter was made of the men of Argyle and of Kintyre, and of the men of the Hebrides, and the Foreigners of Dublin'.[36] Roger of Howden states that Roland's contingent slew 'many of [MacWilliam's] army' in 1187, and Walter Bower wrote that, in the

---

33 *Chron Majora* iii, 364–6; trans. *SAEC*, 342.
34 'Carmen de Morte Sumerledi', trans. Clancy, *Triumph Tree*, 214.
35 *AI*, 292–3.
36 *AU* (Hennessy), ii, 144.

encounter between Guthred MacWilliam and the royal army in 1211, 'Many were killed on both sides, but more from among the rebels'.[37] In 1235 many of Thomas of Galloway's Irish levies were caught near Glasgow, where the citizens 'went out in a body; and they cut off the heads of as many as they found, and caused them to give up the ghost'. Was this revenge for the devastation wrought by Somerled's Hebridean and Irish levies seventy years earlier? Two of the 'older men' among the levies (captains, perhaps?) were taken to Edinburgh where they were 'torn asunder by horses'.[38] Orderic Vitalis tells how, in a passage not related by any other source, a Norwegian priest who disembowelled David I's infant son with his prosthetic fingers also endured this fate.[39]

More can be said of the fates of the leaders of opposition (summarised in Appendix 2). Angus of Moray fell at Stracathro in 1130. Somerled of Argyll perished at Renfrew in 1164 and, according to the *Carmen*, 'A cleric hacked off the head of the wretched leader Somerled/ and placed it into bishop Herbert's outstretched hands/ He said 'The Scottish saints are surely to be praised!" In 1186 Adam, the son of Donald, who may or may not have been a relative of Donald MacWilliam, was seized at Coupar Angus abbey by the earl of Atholl; his unnamed nephew was beheaded before the altar and the rest of his followers burned alive. Donald MacWilliam himself fell at Mam Garvia, and his head was presented to king William. Guthred MacWilliam was captured, beheaded, dragged by the feet and strung up, although an English chronicle relates that he was hanged on the gallows. Bower stated that 'He was already very close to death, for he had refused food ever since his capture', a detail that has the ring of authenticity to it.[40] A few years later, in 1215, Ferchar Maccintsacairt cut off the heads of Donald Bàn MacWilliam and his allies, 'and presented them as new gifts to the new king [Alexander II].'[41] Bower says that in 1229 Gillescop and his two sons suffered the same fate, while the English *Chronicle of Lanercost* graphically recorded the demise of the last MacWilliam in 1230:

> And after the enemy had been successfully overcome, a somewhat too cruel vengeance was taken for the blood of the slain: the same MacWilliam's daughter, who had not long left her mother's womb, innocent as she was, was put to death, in the burgh of Forfar, in view of the market-place, after a proclamation by the public crier: her head was struck against the column of the [market] cross, and her brains dashed out.

---

37 *Gesta Regis Henrici* ii, 7–9; *Scotichronicon* iv, 464–5.
38 *Chron Melrose*, 84–5 (1235); *ES* ii, 498.
39 *Ecclesiastical History of Orderic Vitalis* iv, 274–7.
40 *Scotichronicon* iv, 466–7.
41 *Chron Melrose*, 59–60.

The chronicler was, however, clearly uneasy about the murder of an infant girl, since he appended to this account a scriptural citation that 'Sons shall not be slain for their fathers'.[42] It has been suggested that the lack of conflict among the Scottish royal family in the second half of the twelfth century meant that the house of Canmore formed a notable exception to the brutality that characterised dynastic politics in many parts of contemporary Europe.[43] But such a view depends upon a relatively narrow definition of the royal kindred concerned, and if that view is broadened to include cast-off segments of the royal kindred like the MacWilliams, then it becomes more difficult to maintain.

While the Scottish kings had, by the 1230s, acquired a grisly but substantial collection of MacWilliam heads, it is noteworthy that this was not the universal fate of all of their rivals, and that some of the king's enemies managed to escape with their lives. Some were forced to enter monasteries. One such might have been Máelsnechtai, the son of Lulach. Malcolm III had campaigned against him in 1078, and then in 1085 Irish annals recorded that he 'happily ended his life' together with a number of others. Since all the others named in the entry were ecclesiastics, and the phrase 'happily ended his life' is taken to mean that an individual died in religion, it is tempting to suppose that Malcolm III forced Máelsnechtai to become a monk or canon. It may be significant that his name appeared in the Gaelic notes of the *Book of Deer* as a donor to the old Celtic monastery there: 'Mal-Snechta son of Lulach gave Pett Malduib [the estate of Meldub] to Drostán [the patron saint of Old Deer]'.[44] Perhaps he was forced to retire to the religious community there, although this is speculation.[45] The fate of Fergus, Lord of Galloway, however, is clear. The *Chronicle of Holyrood* tells how Malcolm, king of Scots, led three campaigns against the Gallovidians in 1160 'and made a treaty with peace; and he returned without loss'. The chronicle continues: 'Fergus, the prince of Galloway, received the habit of a canon in the church of Holyrood at Edinburgh'. It is difficult to believe that there was no connection between the two events, and that Fergus's retirement to Holyrood, where he died in 1161, was not a direct consequence of the military campaigns of 1160.[46] Most probably, this was a forced retirement; there is no evidence to support the view that, following his defeat, Fergus requested that he be allowed to retire to a monastery of Malcolm's choosing.[47] Holyrood,

---

42 *Chron Lanercost*, 40–1; *ES* ii, 471 and n. 3. The chronicler is citing Deuteronomy XXIV, 16 and other passages.

43 G.W.S. Barrow, *Feudal Britain* (London, 1956), 241.

44 Jackson, *Gaelic Notes in the Book of Deer*, 33–3 (text), 42, 52–3 (notes).

45 R. Ellsworth and P.B. Ellis, *The Book of Deer* (London, 1994), 15. The impending publication of *Studies in the Book of Deer*, ed. K. Forsythe (Dublin, forthcoming), will no doubt shed further light on the problems referred to here.

46 *Chron Holyrood*, 137.

47 Brooke, *Wild Men and Holy Places*, 95.

founded for Augustinian canons by David I in 1128, was an ideal choice – it had strong royal connections, and to force Fergus to retire here, rather than to his own foundation of Dundrennan, for instance, merely reinforced the humiliating nature of his defeat and submission.

Retirement to a monastery was one way of dealing with rivals; straightforward incarceration was another. Malcolm, who was associated with Angus of Moray in the 1124 and 1130 uprisings, provides a good example. He was captured in 1134 and imprisoned in Roxburgh castle, and, as we have seen, it is a matter of some debate as to whether he was the same Malcolm who was reconciled with the king in 1157. If this is the case, then he spent twenty-three years in captivity; if, on the other hand, we need to distinguish between two Malcolms in this period, then his fate remains unknown and he probably died in captivity. Either way, the incarceration of Malcolm calls to mind the treatment of Robert Curthose at the hands of his brother, Henry I, after his capture at Tinchebrai in 1106. Confined in turn at Wareham, Devizes, Bristol, and Cardiff, Robert spent nearly twenty-eight years in captivity before dying in 1134 at the age of eighty.[48] Malcolm's son, Donald, captured at Whithorn in 1156, was also sent to Roxburgh; his fate is unknown, and it is not beyond the realm of possibility that he, too, perished as a prisoner of the Scottish king. About forty years later, the mighty earl of Orkney/Caithness, Harald Maddadsson, endured incarceration at the orders of King William when he failed to produce his son Thorfinn as a hostage for good behaviour. Roger of Howden says that Harald was imprisoned until his son was turned over to the authorities, at which point Harald was released. Thorfinn was then taken to the 'castle of the Maidens' – a fanciful twelfth-century name for Edinburgh castle[49] – but the *Chronicle of Melrose* states that he was imprisoned at Roxburgh. If the Melrose chronicler is correct on this point, then Roxburgh castle was a veritable Scottish 'Tower of London', housing some of the most formidable opponents of the Canmores in the twelfth century: given the premier status of its burgh, and a castle already on record as early as about 1128, this should hardly prove surprising.[50]

But without question the record for incarceration in a Scottish, if not a British, context belongs to Thomas, the illegitimate son of Alan of Galloway, who rose against Alexander II in 1234/35 with Irish help. After the collapse of his insurrection, the *Chronicle of Melrose* says that 'The bastard [Thomas], being thus deprived of counsel and support, was compelled to seek the king's peace. And the king detained him for a short time in Maidens' castle; and afterwards

---

48 See A.L. Poole, *Domesday Book to Magna Carta* (2nd ed, Oxford, 1955; pb. ed. 1993),120–1.
49 Barrow, *Acts of Malcolm IV*, 80 for discussion.
50 Royal Commission on the Ancient and Historic Monuments of Scotland, *An Inventory of the Ancient and Historical Monuments of Roxburghshire* (2 vols., Edinburgh 1956), i, no. 521, pp. 252–4 (burgh), and no. 905, pp. 407–11 (castle).

allowed him to go away'. In fact, Thomas was delivered into the custody of John de Balliol, who had married Thomas's half-sister, Lady Dervorgilla; the English *Chronicle of Lanercost* relates how 'he remained, till decrepit old age, shut up in the interior of Barnard Castle'. This was no exaggeration: Thomas remained in captivity for over sixty years, and on the day that King Alexander III died in 1286, his council was discussing Thomas's possible release. The death of the king postponed his release for another ten years, until, at the age of eighty-eight, he was liberated, shaved, given clean clothes and restored to his lands in Galloway by Edward I.[51] He never made it, however, being taken back into custody later in 1296: this is our final glimpse of this pathetic figure, the last of the enemies of the Canmore kings.

Mutilation was also practised. In 1097 Donald Bàn, the brother of Malcolm III who reigned briefly in 1093–94 and again from 1094–97, was captured and had his eyes put out. According to William of Newburgh, the unfortunate Wimund, bishop of the Isles, was betrayed by his own men, who 'seized and bound him, and put out each of his eyes – since each was wicked – and with mutilation emasculated him, for the peace of the kingdom of Scots, not for the sake of the kingdom of Heaven'. Wimund survived, and 'afterwards he came to our [abbey of] Byland, and there lived quietly for very many years, until his death',[52] thus combining mutilation with a forced monastic retirement. Another victim of mutilation was Thorfinn, son and heir of Earl Harald of Orkney/Caithness. The *Orkneyinga Saga* says that 'During the war, Thorfinn, Earl Harald's son, who had been taken a hostage by the King of Scots, had been blinded'.[53] *Gesta Annalia* has an even more graphic description of his fate: 'the son was deprived of his eyes and genitals, and died in the aforesaid dungeon [at Roxburgh]'.[54] Twenty years later, and also in a northern context, the Scottish king took a harsh vengeance upon those who had participated in the burning of Bishop Adam of Caithness in 1222: the Icelandic annals record that 'the king of the Scots caused eighty men who had been present at the burning to have their hands and feet cut off, and many of them died'.[55] It is certainly not going too far to say, as John Gillingham has done, that 'It was by killing and mutilating rivals that the line of David secured its hold on the throne of Scotland in the twelfth and thirteenth centuries'.[56]

Of course, the enemies of the Scottish kings could dish it out as well as take it. Uhtred, the son of Fergus of Galloway, had his eyes and tongue cut out, and was

51 *Chron Lanercost*, 116–7, 177; *CDS* ii, nos. 728–9.
52 *Historia Rerum Anglicarum*, in *Chron Stephen* i, 75–6; trans. *SAEC*, 226.
53 *OS*, Ch. 112.
54 *Chron Fordun* i, 275; ii, 270.
55 *ES* ii, 451–52.
56 Gillingham, '1066 and the Introduction of Chivalry into England', in *The English in the Twelfth Century*, 225.

also castrated and left half-dead, after an assault by his brother, Gilbert, in 1174. Not surprisingly, Roger of Howden says he died shortly thereafter. Similarly, Bishop John of Caithness had his eyes and tongue put out at the orders of the earl of Orkney/Caithness in 1201. *Gesta Annalia*, however, relates that 'it turned out otherwise, for the use of his tongue and of one eye was, in some measure, left him'.[57]

The treatment of their enemies by the Scottish kings may better be understood when placed in the larger context of the killing and maiming of high-ranking political rivals by western European rulers in this era. Although by the twelfth century the convention on the Continent and in England was to spare the life and limb of defeated high-status opponents, this convention moved only gradually into the Celtic lands of the British Isles. A glance at the contemporary Irish or Welsh annals confirms this, and Gerald of Wales observed the outcome of succession disputes among the Welsh: 'Quarrels and lawsuits result, murders and arson, not to mention frequent fratricides'. He goes on to say that after the death of a prince, 'The most frightening disturbances occur in their territories as a result, people being murdered, brothers killing each other and even putting each other's eyes out, for as everyone knows from experience it is very difficult to settle disputes of this sort'.[58] John Gillingham suggests that 'Scottish political *mores* were very like those of Ireland and Wales' in this period, and argues that it was only in the middle of the thirteenth century that political struggles in Scotland came to be treated in 'English' fashion. He goes on to state that 'It is noticeable that those high-status enemies whom William I and Alexander II killed or mutilated were all of Gaelic or Scandinavian affiliation'.[59]

Certainly the treatment of the MacWilliams by the Scottish monarchs bears this out. Even though it is not absolutely clear from the words of the chroniclers whether Donald MacWilliam in 1187, Donald Bàn MacWilliam in 1215, and Gillescop in 1229 fell in battle or were executed, there is no doubt at all about the treatment meted out to the nephew of Adam son of Donald in 1186, to Guthred in 1212, and to the infant MacWilliam in 1230. Similarly, Wimund appears to have been mutilated by his own men rather than by royal order, but Thorfinn the son of Harald Maddadsson was almost certainly mutilated on the orders of King William. Even so, we are left to explain the imprisonment as opposed to the execution of Malcolm in 1134, and of Fergus in 1160. It might be, of course, that, as Gillingham suggested, 'in the middle decades of the

---

57 *Chron Fordun* i, 276; ii, 271–72.
58 Gerald of Wales (Giraldus Cambrensis), *The Journey Through Wales/ The Description of Wales*, trans. L. Thorpe (London, 1978), 261.
59 J. Gillingham, 'Killing and mutilating political enemies in the British Isles from the late twelfth to the early fourteenth century: a comparative study', in *Britain and Ireland 900–1300*, 124.

century David I had presided over a relatively 'civilized' period of Scottish politics',[60] in which case Malcolm, at least, might have been one of its beneficiaries. On the other hand, if this Malcolm was indeed an illegitimate son of Alexander I, then his imprisonment at Roxburgh might be more easily explained: presumably David had no desire to execute his nephew, and Malcolm's circumstances after 1134 were akin to those of Robert Curthose after his defeat at Tinchebrai in 1106. The case of Fergus, however, is more problematic. According to Gillingham's model, he ought to have been executed, for his Gaelic affiliations are clear enough. But there were several extenuating circumstances that might have saved Fergus's life. In the first place, there was the closeness of the Gallovidian dynasty to the English royal house: Fergus had married a daughter of Henry I, and it is clear that Henry II regarded himself as a kinsman of the Galloways. Given the relatively junior position of King Malcolm IV vis-à-vis Henry II, it may be that Henry's influence – or fear of his reprisals – spared the ruler of Galloway. Another explanation is that Malcolm was 'magnanimous' toward his defeated enemy.[61] Certainly Malcolm IV was an ardent devotee of the cult of knighthood: in 1159 he followed King Henry II to Toulouse in hopes of being made a knight at his hands, and this, it seems, was achieved in 1160. Perhaps, then, it was Malcolm's attachment to contemporary chivalric ideals that spared Fergus's life. Whatever the case, it is difficult to avoid the conclusion that Fergus represented the exception rather than the rule, and that the road to success for the Canmore kings was littered with the corpses of their enemies.

'Warlike Figures'
One of the most difficult problems surrounding the armies raised by the likes of Malcolm MacHeth, Somerled, and Donald MacWilliam against the Scottish kings is how well they were equipped. Specific evidence is sparse: no chronicler, annalist or poet who recorded episodes of opposition took the time to record military details. One way to approach the problem is to consider the arms, armour, and military capabilities of the other Celtic peoples of the British Isles, the Welsh and the Irish. One of the things that immediately struck contemporary English observers about their Celtic neighbours was the lightly armed nature of the Welsh, Irish and Scots. Thus, Gerald of Wales remarked of the Welsh (as well as the Irish) that 'They are lightly armed and they rely more on their agility than on brute strength. It follows that they cannot meet the enemy on equal terms, or fight violently for very long, or strive hand-to-hand for victory . . .'[62] Closer to home, at the battle of the Standard between the English

---

60 Gillingham, 'Killing and mutilating political enemies', 117.
61 Brooke, *Wild Men and Holy Places*, 95.
62 Gerald, *Journey/Description*, 260.

and the Scots in 1138, some contingents of the Scottish army were equipped in similar fashion. The famous speech that Ailred of Rievaulx put in the mouth of Robert de Brus just before the battle recounts the triumphs of the conquering Normans and heaps scorn upon the backward Scots, mocking their arms and armour (or lack thereof): 'they oppose their naked hide to our lances, our swords, and our arrows, using a calf-skin for a shield, inspired by contempt of death rather than by strength'. Later Ailred has de Brus remark: 'Who would not laugh rather than fear, when to fight against such men [the Normans] runs the worthless Scot with half-bare buttocks?'[63] All of this stood in stark contrast, of course, to the heavily armoured and mounted warrior of the middle ages, the knight with his characteristic mail armour, lance, sword, shield and, crucially, his horse.[64] One possible interpretation of the confrontations between the royal armies and those of the MacWilliams, MacHeths and others, then, is that armies of knights, the shock troops of medieval Europe, trampled hordes of half-naked Gaelic and Scoto-Norse barbarians. R.L.G. Ritchie, for instance, considered that Alexander's triumph over the Moravians in about 1116 was essentially a victory of mounted knights over infantry, even remarking that 'few [of the Moravians] can even have had horses, and sorry nags they must have been, compared with the Norman chargers'. Firm evidence for this view is, however, lacking. It is true that Alexander had campaigned with Henry I in Wales only a few years earlier, in 1114, and that he must have possessed some knowledge of 'horse-craft and cavalry tactics' as Ritchie put it.[65] But neither Bower nor Wyntoun, the chief sources for the episode at Invergowrie, specifically refers to a cavalry force led by the king, although both accounts suggest fast-paced action, which might, in turn, indicate that horsemen were involved. In sum, it is almost certainly going too far to construct from these accounts the triumph of mounted knights over poorly-equipped opponents: Professor Duncan has doubted that Alexander introduced any Frenchmen or Anglo-Normans to Scotland at all.[66]

Apart from the fact that these descriptions come from English chroniclers who were shocked by the behaviour of their opponents and who sought to disparage them as barbarians, there are other reasons for believing that such an impression is inaccurate. In the first instance, it is not at all clear that the Scottish army included large numbers of mounted troops. Among scholars who have examined the question of the Scottish host in the twelfth and thirteenth

63 *De Standardo* ii, 185–7; trans. *SAEC*, 197–98.
64 There is an enormous amount of literature on the medieval knight. A good introduction is R. Barber, *The Knight and Chivalry* (Woodbridge, 1970), and there is much of value in P. Coss, *The Knight in Medieval England 1000–1400* (Stroud, 1993). Knighthood in Scotland lacks a comprehensive study.
65 Ritchie, *Normans in Scotland*, 131.
66 Duncan, *Scotland*, 128. Professor Barrow is also sceptical: see 'Beginnings of Military Feudalism', esp. 279–81.

centuries, several salient points emerge. The first is its essential duality: from the early twelfth century until the later thirteenth, the Scottish army consisted of two components, unequal in size. These have been characterised by Matthew Strickland, describing the Scottish armies of 1138 and 1173/74, as 'an indigenous native levy, itself composed of a multiplicity of tribal elements, and an Anglo-Norman or 'Frankish' element consisting of the royal *familia*, Franco-Norman feudal settlers and other external mercenary units'.[67] The former group, and especially the Gallovidian levies, seem to have been the larger, although poorly equipped,[68] and it was this element of the Scottish army that Robert de Brus mocked in the speech attributed to him by Ailred of Rievaulx cited above. A second important point about the Scottish military of this period concerns its limitations. There were several, but none was more significant than the lack of a powerful cavalry wing.[69] Even though the kings of Scots from the time of David I had begun a policy of enfeoffment in order to provide a nucleus of heavy cavalry with which to supplement the native levy, the number of knights that could be raised was actually very small, particularly when compared to England.[70] An English chronicler reported that the Scots fielded a mere two hundred knights at the battle of the Standard, while Professor Barrow's careful study of knight's fees suggests that only around one hundred knights could be provided by the late twelfth century.[71] If two hundred knights were indeed raised for the battle of the Standard in 1138, then it seems highly unlikely that anywhere close to this number were ever mobilised for action against the king's enemies; on the other hand, as Barrow suggests, the feudal host was 'doubtless useful to deal with rebellion in the remote and ungovernable parts of the kingdom, in the far north and west'.[72] Even so, as late 1212 King William found it necessary, or prudent, to utilise mercenaries to supplement the army sent against Guthred MacWilliam in Ross.[73]

67 M. Strickland, 'Securing the North: Invasion and the Strategy of Defence in Twelfth-Century Anglo-Scottish Warfare', in *Anglo-Norman Warfare. Studies in Late Anglo-Saxon and Anglo-Norman Military Organization and Warfare*, ed. M. Strickland (Woodbridge, 1992), 208–229, quotation at 222. See also the contribution of J. Bradbury, 'Battles in England and Normandy, 1066–1154', especially 190–91, and the remarks on military service in Barrow, *Acts of William I*, 55–57.

68 Strickland, 'Securing the North', 222–24.

69 Strickland, 'Securing the North', 224.

70 Strickland, 'Securing the North', 224–25; Barrow, 'Beginnings of military feudalism', *passim*; and the pertinent comments in 'The Army of Alexander III's Scotland', in *Scotland in the Reign of Alexander III*, 132–47 and especially 133.

71 John of Worcester, in Florence of Worcester, *Chronicon ex chronicis*, ed. B. Thorpe (2 vols., London, 1848–49), ii, 111–2; trans. *SAEC*, 207–08; see Barrow, 'Beginnings of Military Feudalism', *passim* and especially Table 1.

72 'Beginnings of military feudalism', 286.

73 Barrow, 'Beginnings of military feudalism', 286.

Secondly, it is by no means certain that the Celtic warrior of the twelfth century was actually as lightly armed as some chroniclers and modern historians would have us believe. Even Gerald of Wales, whose passage on the lightly-armed appearance of Celtic soldiers was quoted above, provides another more detailed, if contradictory, description of Welsh warriors: 'They use light weapons which do not impede their quick movements, small leather corselets, handfuls of arrows, long spears and round shields. They wear helmets and sometimes iron greaves. Their leaders ride into battle on swift mettlesome horses . . .'[74] There are other indications that the Welsh military élite were less primitive than is sometimes suggested. In 1075, for instance, at the bloody battle of Bron-yr-erw near Clynnog Fawr, Gruffudd ap Cynan fought on horseback against an alliance of Welsh princes, by whom he was ultimately defeated. A near-contemporary history of Gruffudd provides details of the battle: 'King Gruffudd . . . was seated on his horse in the midst of his army, with his flashing sword mowing down both his traitors and enemies'.[75] On the periphery of the Scottish kingdom itself, Gerald of Wales remarks of the Scandinavians and Islesmen who attacked Dublin in 1171 that

> They were warlike figures, clad in mail in every part of their body after the Danish manner. Some wore long coats of mail, others iron plates skilfully knitted together, and they had round, red shields protected by iron round the edge. These men, whose iron will matched their armour, drew up their ranks and made an attack on the walls at the eastern gate.[76]

These descriptions of Welsh, Scandinavian, and Hebridean warriors of the twelfth century do not, of course, prove that the armies raised by the opponents of the Scottish kings were similarly armed and equipped. They merely demonstrate what was possible in a similar cultural milieu, and they do accord well with accounts of the Gallovidian contingent of the Scottish army that invaded England in 1173. Ralph de Diceto, the late twelfth-century dean of St. Paul's, London, provided a brief description of these warriors:

> . . . men agile, unclothed, remarkable for much baldness; arming their left side wide knives formidable to any armed men, having a hand most skilful at throwing spears, and at directing them from a distance; raising their lance as a standard when they advance to battle.[77]

---

74 Gerald of Wales, *Description/ Journey*, 234.
75 *A Mediaeval Prince of Wales*, 13–14, 31–32, 62–63. On Gruffudd, see also K. Maund, *The Welsh Kings: The Medieval Rulers of Wales* (Stroud, 2000), 74–77 and *passim*, and *Gruffudd ap Cynan: A Collaborative Biography*, ed. K.L. Maund (Woodbridge, 1996).
76 Gerald of Wales (Giraldus Cambrensis), *Expugnatio Hibernica. The Conquest of Ireland*, ed. and trans. A.B. Scott and F.X. Martin (Dublin, 1978), 77.
77 *The Historical Works of Master Ralph de Diceto*, ed. W. Stubbs (Rolls Series, 1876), i, 376; trans. *SAEC*, 247.

Certainly contemporaries, even those who regarded the Gallovidians as barbarians, were forced to admire their ferocity in battle. Ailred of Rievaulx provided a famous description of the Gallovidian warriors who formed part of a Scottish army of 1138: 'Like a hedgehog with its quills, so would you see a Galwegian bristling all round with arrows, and none the less brandishing his sword and in blind madness rushing forward now smite a foe, now lash the air with useless strokes'.[78]

One of the more important lessons to emerge from recent studies of Irish and Welsh warfare in the eleventh to thirteenth centuries is that these societies were far more sophisticated militarily than is often allowed, and once the biased accounts of writers like Gerald of Wales are placed in their proper perspective, it is apparent that warfare in both societies extended beyond mere cattle-raiding and plundering.[79] Similarly, few would now argue that there was a substantial difference in equipment between the Normans and Saxons at Hastings in 1066.[80] This means that it is almost certainly wrong to suppose that the armies raised by the likes of Wimund, Somerled, or the MacWilliams were simply lightly armed and undisciplined barbarian hordes who preferred to fight without benefit of armour.

Evidence for modernity in military terms among native Scottish potentates is at hand in their portrayal of themselves on their seals as mounted equestrians with armour, sword, and shield. It is of course true that not every noble who depicted himself in this manner was necessarily knighted, although it is likely; what is significant is that the depiction of native Scots nobles as knights indicates a willingness to show themselves to be fully up-to-date magnates.[81] In Scotland knighthood was penetrating the ranks of the native aristocracy by the second half of the twelfth century. By then, great magnates like the earls of Fife, including Duncan II (d. 1204) and Malcolm I (d. c. 1228), were portraying themselves as equestrians; one of Malcolm's seals shows him wearing armour and a helmet, holding a drawn sword in his right hand and carrying a shield in his left. So much is to be expected, given that the earls of Fife moved in what might be considered an Anglo-French cultural milieu at the heart of the

---

78 *De Standardo*, in *Chron Stephen* iii, 196; *SAEC*, 202–03.

79 See, e.g., M.T. Flanagan, 'Irish and Anglo-Norman warfare in twelfth-century Ireland', in *A Military History of Ireland*, ed. T. Bartlett and K. Jeffery (Cambridge, 1996), 52–99; K. Simms, 'Gaelic warfare in the Middle Ages', in *idem*, 99–115; D. Crouch, *The Image of Aristocracy in Britain 1000–1300* (London and New York, 1992), 155–63.

80 Gillingham, 'The Introduction of Knight Service into England', in *The English in the Twelfth Century*, 187.

81 See the discussion in Crouch, *Image of Aristocracy*, 153–63; there are some apposite comments on the subject (mostly in an English context) in R. Bartlett, *England Under the Norman and Angevin Kings 1075–1225* (Oxford, 2000), 232–49.

kingdom and were frequently associated with the kings (themselves great devotees of chivalry). But by the late twelfth and early thirteenth centuries even native lords like the earls of Strathearn, who had traditionally been less active at court, also began adopting the convention: Earl Gilbert of Strathearn's (1171– 1223) great charter to Inchaffray Abbey of 1200 bears a seal depicting its owner as an equestrian.[82] Of more relevance in the present context is the evidence for knighthood among potentates in the outer zones of the Scottish kingdom. Even here, however, by 1200 the conventions of knighthood were becoming known. Ranald son of Somerled possessed a double-sided seal which depicted its owner on one side as a knight with a drawn sword and on the other displayed a highland galley (a nice encapsulation of the cultural synthesis taking place in the thirteenth-century Hebrides), while among the Lords of Galloway Alan possessed a seal depicting him as an armoured equestrian.[83] And then there is the famous example of Ferchar Maccintsacairt, knighted by the king as a reward for his role in quashing the 1215 MacHeth/MacWilliam insurrection. Finally, it is also worthwhile noting that the kings of England had knighted some of the thirteenth-century Manx rulers.[84] None of this, of course, proves that Guthred was knighted or had access to mounted troops. What it does suggest, however, is that the confrontations between the Scottish kings and their enemies in the twelfth and thirteenth centuries are unlikely to have been lopsided contests between mounted shock troops on one hand and naked, lightly armed barbarian hordes on the other. It is clear that Celtic, Norse, and Celtic-Norse warlords on the peripheral regions of the British Isles were able to adapt to changing conventions of warfare in the twelfth and thirteenth centuries, and there is no reason to suppose that Guthred MacWilliam and his ilk were any less able to adapt than their contemporaries elsewhere in Scotland, Ireland, Wales or Man.

If there was little discrepancy in terms of arms and armour between the forces commanded by figures like Donald MacWilliam and the royal armies that they faced down, there is little doubt that a major imbalance existed in numerical terms. Indeed, perhaps the most difficult problem of all when assessing the military aspects of these insurrections involves the size of the

---

82 J. H. Stevenson and M. Wood, *Scottish Heraldic Seals* (Glasgow, 1910), ii, 354 for Duncan and Malcolm of Fife; *Charters, Bulls, and Other Documents Relating to the Abbey of Inchaffray*, ed. W.A. Lindsay *et al* (Edinburgh, 1908), Facsimile 4; see also facsimile 1, for Gilbert of Strathearn.

83 For Ranald: *Registrum Monasterii de Passelet*, ed. C. Innes (Edinburgh, 1832), 125, 148, discussed in R.A. McDonald, 'Images of Hebridean Lordship in the Late Twelfth and Early Thirteenth Centuries: The Seal of Raonall MacSorley', *SHR* lxxiv (1995), 129–43; and *idem*, 'Coming in from the margins', 191–95; for Alan, see Stringer, 'Acts of Lordship', 211, and 'Periphery and Core', 108–09 (with illustration).

84 King Henry III of England knighted Olaf of Man; Olaf's sons Harald and Magnus were knighted in 1247 and 1256 respectively: *Chron Man*, f. 46r and 49r – 49v.

armies involved, especially those of the king's enemies – although this is a common difficulty where medieval armies are concerned. Apart from general-isations like that of Roger of Howden, who stated that Donald MacWilliam landed in Scotland with an 'innumerable armed host' in 1181, there are several more specific statements on the size of the armies led by the rivals of the Canmores. Orderic Vitalis says of the force raised by Malcolm and Angus in 1130 that it numbered five thousand men, and the entry in the *Annals of Ulster* that records their defeat says that four thousand of the men of Moray perished in the fray. If these numbers are taken literally, then some four-fifths of the Moravian host was annihilated in 1130. While this is not impossible, it is more likely that these numbers are not to be taken literally. Medieval chroniclers are notoriously unreliable where numbers and sizes of armies are concerned, and it is more likely that these precise-looking figures should be read simply to signify Howden's 'innumerable armed host'. Similar problems surround the passage in the *Carmen de Morte Sumerledi* to the effect that 'Somerled stood with a thousand of our enemies/ ready to make war against a mere one hundred innocents'.[85] This certainly has the ring of poetic licence about it, and was no doubt designed to highlight the message of the poem, namely, that a smaller force defeated Somerled and his army with supernatural aid from St Kentigern himself.

Such limitations notwithstanding, it may still prove possible to set some idea, at least, of the scale of these armies. The thirteenth-century *Chronicle of the Kings of Man*, which is, at best, a difficult and unreliable source, states that Somerled's fleet in 1164 numbered 160 galleys; in a naval battle of 1156, he is said to have commanded eighty ships, and at another in 1158, fifty-three.[86] If these figures are reliable (most other sources spoke only of a 'large fleet' or 'large army'), then it might prove possible to estimate the size of Somerled's army. How many men might a twelfth-century galley hold? The *Annals of Ulster* record how, in 1098, 'three of the ships of the foreigners of the Isles were plundered by the Ulaid and their crews were killed, i.e. a hundred and twenty or a little more'.[87] This suggests that a galley might hold about forty warriors, while modern scholars place their estimate at around fifty.[88] Assuming a certain similarity between the vessels attacked by the men of Ulster in 1098 and those that sailed up the Clyde in 1164, Somerled's army could have numbered somewhere between 6400 and 8000 warriors, provided – and it is a rather large assumption – that the figures given in the chronicles relating the size of Somerled's fleet are to be believed.

85 'Carmen de Morte Sumerledi', in Clancy, *Triumph Tree*, 213.

86 *Chron Man*, f.37v, f. 39r.

87 *AU* (MacAirt), 533.

88 E. Roesdahl, *The Vikings*, trans. S. M. Margeson and K. Williams, 2nd ed. (London, 1998), 192.

Such a figure tallies well, however, with an army raised by Earl Harald of Orkney/Caithness in 1201: the author of *Orkneyinga Saga* states that 'people say that he raised about six thousand men'.[89] Whether or not these precise figures are accepted – and there are certainly grounds for taking them with a grain of salt – what is clear is that war-leaders like Somerled and Earl Harald, and in all probability the MacHeths and MacWilliams too, had the potential to raise formidable armies with which to strike at the Scottish kings.

A better understanding of the scale of forces available to rulers on the margins of the Scottish kingdom in this period can be obtained by considering the case of Alan, Lord of Galloway and Constable of Scotland, who died in 1234. Alan's military forces were formidable. Sturla Thordarsson, the author of *Hakon's Saga*, placed his strength at between 150 and two hundred ships, indicating an army of potentially between two and three thousand men.[90] Certainly in 1212 Alan was able to provide a force of one thousand hand-picked Gallovidian warriors which joined the English army for a campaign against the Welsh.[91] Alan is even known to have referred to the common army of Galloway as 'exercitus noster',[92] thereby emphasising its potential as a private fighting force. Keith Stringer is certainly justified, therefore, in concluding that 'few magnates in Britain, let alone Scotland, could command such resources'[93] – a comment which should probably be extended, by analogy, to the likes of Somerled, Harald Maddadsson, and Donald MacWilliam as well.

On the other side of the equation, since even the size of the fairly well-documented Scottish armies that invaded England in 1138 and 1173/74 remains uncertain, there can be little hope of estimating figures for the royal armies that brought the king's enemies to heel in Ross, Moray, Galloway, and Argyll. It is true that the chroniclers provide some exact statistics. Roger of Howden relates that Roland of Galloway led three thousand 'warlike youths' [juvenes bellicosos], including his own 'household' [familia] – echoing, no doubt, his son's 'exercitus noster' – against Donald MacWilliam in 1187, and Walter Bower states that a contingent of four thousand warriors was selected to seek out Guthred.[94] In both cases it is clear that these forces represented only detachments from the royal army, which was presumably substantially larger, but even though Howden and Bower are well-informed on these events, it is still difficult to know whether to treat these figures as precise records of the

89 *OS*, Ch. 112.
90 *ES* ii, 476, and n. 12; Stringer, 'Periphery and Core', 84. This estimate might be on the low side, as it would mean there were only approximately thirteen to fifteen warriors per vessel.
91 *CDS* i, no. 529; Stringer, 'Periphery and Core', 84, 88.
92 Stringer, 'Periphery and Core', 84.
93 Ibid., 84.
94 *Gesta Regis Henrici* ii, 7–9; *Scotichronicon* iv, 466–7.

numbers involved. A similar figure of three thousand soldiers is said by Jordan Fantosme to have been provided by the earl of Buchan for the royal army that invaded England in 1173.[95] Another telling comment is provided by the author of the *Orkneyinga Saga*, who related how, in 1201, an angry King William 'sent word to all the chieftains in his kingdom and raised a great force from every part of the land, leading all these troops north to Caithness against Earl Harald'. The sagaman goes on to state that 'It was a truly massive army that the king of Scots led. He marched ahead to Ausdale near the boundary between Caithness and Sutherland, and there his camp extended from one end of the valley to the other, quite a distance'.[96] Little wonder that Earl Harald was reluctant to join battle! In the final analysis this is a telling remark about the military capacity of the Scottish kings in the twelfth century, and it adds weight to the suggestion that the Scottish army of the period was no doubt sufficient to deal with disturbances in the remoter regions of the realm, even if it was weak by comparison with its southern counterpart.

A compelling piece of evidence for the relative inferiority of the armies of the king's enemies vis-à-vis the royal armies that faced them down is the behaviour of their leaders, who, in common with most military commanders of the age, generally eschewed pitched battles.[97] Earl Harald of Orkney/Caithness, for instance, seems to have been a shrewd enough military commander to know when discretion was the better part of valour. In 1196, when King William sent a royal army against the earl, 'before the king entered Caithness Harald fled to his ships, refusing to enter into battle against the king'.[98] Since Harald does not have a reputation for being gun-shy, there must have been some compelling reasons for his actions. Later still, in 1201, Earl Harald was said to have been able to raise an army of about six thousand men – but, the saga man added, 'even so he was far from strong enough to fight the king of Scots'.[99]

It has been noted of twelfth-century Irish warfare that 'Forays, raids, skirmishes and burnings and the capture of fortified positions were far more common occurrences than pitched battles'.[100] This statement holds equally true for the opposition to the Scottish kings, and in the long history of challenges there were only three battles that may or may not prove worthy of the designation: Stracathro, Renfrew, and Mam Garvia. The admittedly imperfect impression we have of Stracathro in 1130 is that it was a set-piece battle, and the battle of Renfrew in 1164 seems to have represented the victory of a local

---

95 *Jordan Fantosme's Chronicle*, ed. with introduction, translation and notes by R.C. Johnston [Fantosme] (Oxford, 1981), Chs. 46–47.

96 *OS*, Ch. 112.

97 Bradbury, 'Battles in England and Normandy 1066–1154', 182–84.

98 Roger of Howden, *Chronica* iv, 10; trans. *SAEC*, 316.

99 *OS*, Ch. 112.

100 Flanagan, 'Irish and Anglo-Norman warfare', 69.

defence force over Somerled's army. But for the most part events like these are rare, and the story of the uprisings is largely a story of raids, forays, and skirmishes.

Some of the best evidence of this style of warfare comes from William of Newburgh's account of Wimund's insurrection. William relates that:

> He made incursions into the provinces of Scotland, harrying everything with rapine and slaughter. And when the royal army was sent against him he retired into remoter passes, or fled back to the ocean, and escaped all the preparation of war; and when the army had returned broke out again from his hiding places to molest the provinces.[101]

Guthred MacWilliam, too, used the landscape to his advantage. Bower notes that 'Guthred himself always avoided the king's army, meanwhile laying ambushes for it wherever he could by night or day, and driving off booty from the lord king's land.'[102] These same sorts of tactics are seen in Howden's account of Donald MacWilliam's invasion and subsequent defeat. Howden relates how Donald had landed with a large army in 1181, 'wasting and burning as much of the land as he reached; and he put the folk to flight, and slew all whom he could take'. This sounds like a scorched-earth policy, and Howden's description of MacWilliam's defeat in 1187 makes it clear that Donald was defeated not in a set-piece battle but rather in a surprise skirmish. Howden explains that the leaders of the army quarrelled over their loyalty to William and debated the best course of action. He says that 'they agreed that the chiefs of the army should remain, and should forward scouts to seize food'. Three thousand youths, headed by Roland, were chosen for the task, and it was this detachment that defeated and slew MacWilliam: 'when they approached the army of the aforesaid [Mac]William, they made an attack upon them, and slew [Mac]William himself, and many of his army . . .'[103] Donald's forces seem to have been surprised and defeated in a chance encounter with a foraging party led by Roland. This is precisely the scenario described by the author of the *Gesta Annalia*, who says that:

> . . . it fell out, one day, that some of his [the king's] men, whom he had as usual sent out, to the number of two thousand, throughout the woods and country to plunder and reconnoitre . . . all of a sudden, stumbled unawares upon MacWilliam and his troops lurking in a moor . . . MacWilliam, seeing that those of the king's army were few in comparison with his own men, engaged them at once . . .[104]

---

101 *Historia Rerum Anglicarum*, in *Chron Stephen*, i, 74; trans. *SAEC*, 226.
102 *Scotichronicon* iv, 464–5.
103 *Gesta Regis Henrici* ii, 7–9.
104 *Chron Fordun* i, 268; ii, 263–4.

Like Howden, this account reinforces the fact that it was only a contingent of
the royal army that defeated Donald MacWilliam, and it also emphasises the
element of surprise. It is, therefore, difficult to disagree with E.W. Robertson,
who judged that 'the fate of Scotland was decided by an accident'[105] at Mam
Garvia in 1187.

The ambush was stock-in-trade of the enemies of the Scottish kings. The
fifteenth-century chronicler Andrew of Wyntoun, describing the attack on
King Alexander I at Invergowrie in about 1116, leaves little doubt as to its
nature:

> Swa, suddanly apon hym then
> A multitude off Scottys men
> [Come] in entent to sla the kyng.[106]

Similarly, Walter Bower states explicitly that Guthred MacWilliam laid
ambushes for the royal forces that pursued him in Ross in1211/12. When
Guthred's (presumed) kinsman Gillescop attacked Thomas of Thirlestane's
castle of Abertarff at the south end of Loch Ness in 1228, he did so
'unexpectedly during the night'.[107] And in 1235 the Gallovidians, who had
been hiding in the mountains, attacked a royal army that had become bogged
down in marshy ground. But for the intervention of Ferchar Maccintsacairt, the
day might have ended differently for the Scottish king.

Such hit-and-run tactics were certainly not unknown in the contemporary
Celtic world. Gerald of Wales, writing in the late twelfth century, included in
his *Description of Wales* some observations about Welsh battle tactics. He
remarked that:

> They may not shine in open combat and in fixed formation, but they harass
> the enemy by their ambushes and their night-attacks. In a single battle they
> are easily beaten, but they are difficult to conquer in a long war, for they are
> not troubled by hunger or cold, fighting does not seem to tire them, they do
> not lose heart when things go wrong, and after one defeat they are ready to
> fight again and to face once more the hazards of war.[108]

That the Welsh were experts at guerrilla tactics is evident from the example of
Gruffudd ap Cynan: when King William II led an expedition against him,
Gruffudd 'marched against him, in order to prepare ambushes for him, in
narrow places when he should come down the mountain'. Gruffudd's biographer also relates how

---

105 Robertson, *Early Kings* i, 393.
106 *Chron Wyntoun* iii, p. 174.
107 *Scotichronicon* v, 143.
108 Gerald of Wales, *Description/Journey*, 260.

throughout that time, Gruffudd constantly engaged them [the English], sometimes in front, sometimes behind, sometimes to the right, sometimes to the left of them, lest they should cause any kind of loss in the territory. And had Gruffudd allowed his men to mingle with them in the woods, that would have been the last day for the king of England and his Frenchmen.[109]

Perhaps like the Welsh, the enemies of the Scottish kings also realised that their best hope for success lay in avoiding open combat. Certainly, the terrain in the marginal regions of the Scottish kingdom – the very regions that were flashpoints for insurrections and that provided havens for the enemies of the Scottish kings – favoured such tactics. The northern highlands of Scotland, with their steep, rugged mountains, heavy forest, and peat bogs, were among the most inaccessible regions of the country throughout the entire medieval period. These physical characteristics made the highland regions an ideal base from which to operate, giving the king's enemies the ability to disappear into the wilderness, or even, via the Great Glen, to the Isles or to Ireland. Moreover, the landscape of northern Scotland, like that of Ireland and Wales, had the added advantage of making it difficult for large groups of mounted horsemen to operate in preferred Norman or Anglo-French style. Gerald of Wales remarked that 'the tactics of French troops are no good at all in Ireland or Wales. They are used to fighting on the level, whereas here the terrain is rough; their battles take place in the open fields, but here the country is heavily wooded'.[110] For Scotland, Walter Bower preserves some lines from an unknown source that describe Robert I's famous guerrilla warfare of the early fourteenth century:

> Let Scotland's warcraft be this: footsoldiers, mountain and marshy ground;
> and let her woods, her bow and spear serve for barricades.
> Let menace lurk in all her narrow places among her warrior bands,
> and let her plains so burn with fire that enemies flee away.
> Crying out in the night, let her men be on their guard,
> and her enemies in confusion will flee from hunger's sword.
> Surely it will be so, as we're guided by Robert, our lord.[111]

All in all, then, there is evidence to suggest that, by avoiding direct confrontation with what must have been vastly superior royal forces, and by utilising the natural advantages of the terrain to opt instead for guerrilla-style warfare, raids and forays, Donald MacWilliam, Guthred, Wimund and perhaps others fore-

---

109 *Mediaeval Prince of Wales*, 43–44, 74–75.
110 Gerald of Wales, *Description/Journey*, 269.
111 'Scotland's Strategy of Guerrilla Warfare', in Clancy, *Triumph Tree*, 300; *Scotichronicon* vi, 320.

shadowed a strategy that Robert Bruce would find particularly successful against the English in the early fourteenth century.

The armies raised by the rivals of the kings of Scots might have been relatively small, and their resources limited, but it does not necessarily follow that they posed little or no serious threat. To begin, we may return to the events of 1124–34, when Malcolm and (until 1130) Angus of Moray launched a series of challenges against David I. We have already seen how Angus was slain at the battle of Stracathro in 1130, and how Malcolm escaped and remained at large until 1134, when he was incarcerated at Roxburgh castle. The *Chronicle of Holyrood*, which is our major source for Malcolm's incarceration, does not provide any details on the course of events that led up to his capture. But a speech that the English chronicler Ailred of Rievaulx put in the mouth of Robert de Brus at the battle of the Standard in 1138 fills in some of the gaps in our knowledge. Ailred has Robert describe the aid that David I received in his campaigns against Malcolm from the likes of Robert and other Anglo-Normans; in the course of this, Ailred unwittingly fills in details that the Holyrood Chronicler might have deliberately omitted, perhaps in a bid to downplay the danger posed by Malcolm. The English knights met David I at Carlisle, and de Brus also mentions that ships were employed, possibly sailing from the Tees or the Tyne.[112] This suggests a combined land-based and naval campaign, and the reference to the Anglo-Scottish forces having to make defence suggests also that resistance was encountered, possibly even that a series of engagements was fought. Ultimately, of course, many details are left wanting – critically, the geographical setting of the campaign. In the end, however, there remain enough clues to surmise that, despite Brus' boast that fear of the Anglo-Normans would paralyse potential foes, the capture of Malcolm in 1134 was no easy feat. This in turn reinforces the notion that the first decade of David's reign was a time of much greater instability than has hitherto been recognised.

Similarly, several points about the challenges orchestrated by the MacWilliams need to be highlighted. Neither Donald MacWilliam in 1187 nor his son Guthred in 1212 was easily brought to heel. In 1187 the king led an army north to Inverness, then stayed there while the royal forces scoured the countryside for Donald. Moreover, there was considerable dissent within the ranks of the army itself: Roger of Howden says that certain of the leaders held no love for the king. Although Howden's description of the defeat of Donald in 1187 is not unambiguous on the point, as we have seen above, it is quite likely that Donald's forces were taken by surprise and routed rather than being defeated in open battle. Donald's son Guthred proved even harder to eliminate. The first royal

112 Ritchie, *Normans in Scotland*, 232.

campaign against Guthred, in the 1211 season, assaulted his island stronghold, killed some of his soldiers, and scattered his forces, but it did not succeed in liquidating him or driving him from the land, and Guthred remained at large. The second campaign, which, significantly, included mercenaries provided by the English king, was well underway when Guthred was betrayed and handed over to the justiciar. What seems clear is that the suppression of the various challenges of the twelfth and thirteenth centuries was a serious endeavour that consumed substantial resources. Even so, it is certainly worthwhile reflecting upon how long Guthred might have been able to hold out had he not been betrayed – and the same question might also be asked of Wimund who, like Guthred, fell foul of his own people long before he was subdued by royal forces.

Another important and often overlooked point about the armies raised by the king's enemies is highlighted by Guthred's activities in 1211–12. According to Bower, in the course of the royal progress to subdue Guthred, King William built two castles in Ross. The account continues:

> But no sooner had the king departed than the said Guthred besieged one of the castles built by the king in Ross just a little earlier. He had made ready his siege engines and was just on the point of capturing it, when the garrison within lost their nerve and surrendered it of their own accord to save their lives, if nothing else. This Guthred granted them, and setting fire to the castle burned it down.[113]

This passage, with its reference to siege engines and to the capture and destruction of a royal castle, raises some important points that shed light on the question of the capabilities and sophistication of the armies led by the king's enemies. For instance, it would be illuminating to know what types of siege engines Guthred had at his disposal. Unfortunately, Bower's language, like that of most medieval chroniclers when describing siege weapons, is vague, and makes it difficult to know what is meant – terms like 'engine' or 'machine' were used indiscriminately and cover a wide range of weapons. The more common types of siege engine ranged from simple battering rams to siege towers or belfries (large, multi-storeyed wooden towers that could be wheeled up to walls), as well as a wide variety of missile-throwing engines like the ballista (a sort of giant crossbow), mangonel (a stone-throwing engine), and the formidable trebuchet. Bower's language prevents a detailed understanding of what sorts of weapons Guthred had at his disposal, but since siege towers were expensive and were generally built only by the wealthiest leaders, it seems unlikely that they were intended; trebuchets can probably also be ruled out, for similar reasons. That would leave smaller and less costly engines like ballistas or mangonels, neither of which needed to be very large but both of which packed a

113 *Scotichronicon* iv, 466–7.

considerable punch; such machines were well known in Europe by the thirteenth century, and it is not impossible that they could have been employed by an army in the north of Scotland.[114] Certainly the Scots themselves were familiar with siege weapons and warfare. Jordan Fantosme described King William's attack on Wark in 1174:

> . . . the king of Scotland grew very angry when he saw his sergeants dying and meeting with no success; and seeing that he was gaining nothing his heart was sorrowful within him, and he said to his knights in his great grief: 'Bring up your catapult without delay! If the engineer speaks truly, it will batter down the gate and we shall take the bailey in no time at all.'[115]

In his comprehensive study of medieval siege warfare, Jim Bradbury makes the interesting observation that substantial quantities of wood were required for the construction of large siege machines, and he also notes that sailors were often considered invaluable in the building and operation of siege weapons because of their experience with woodworking.[116] It may be noted in passing that an army operating in Ross with access to Ireland would presumably be able to secure both resources in abundance. Ross was more heavily forested in the medieval period than is the case today, and one of the reasons that the Orkney jarls sought to control the region was for its valuable timber resources: 'when the earls were looking for good ship-building timber . . . they needed to look no further than the Firthlands of easter Ross and south-east Sutherland'.[117] No doubt timber that was suitable for building longships was also suitable for constructing siege machines; it is interesting that Bower makes specific reference to the forests of Ross in his account of Guthred's activities there. Moreover, since the connections with Gaelic Ireland that the MacWilliams

114 For siege weapons and warfare, see J. Bradbury, *The Medieval Siege* (Woodbridge, 1992), esp. Ch 9; M. Prestwich, *Armies and Warfare in the Middle Ages. The English Experience* (New Haven and London, 1996), Ch. 12; and J. France, *Western Warfare in the Age of the Crusades 1000–1300* (Ithaca, N.Y., 1999), Ch. 9.
115 Fantosme, Ch. 127; see also Ch. 121. Fantosme relates what happened next, in a passage that lays bare the perils of operating such equipment:
> Now, my lords, hear how the first stone that it ever hurled for them left the catapult: the stone barely tumbled out of the sling and it knocked one of their own knights to the ground. Had it not been for his armour and the shield he was carrying he would never have returned to any of his relatives. He has good cause to hate the engineer who conjured up this thing for them, and so has the king of Scotland, who was the great loser by it [Ch. 128].
After this incident King William ordered a second siege machine to be brought up: Ch. 131.
116 Bradbury, *Medieval Siege*, 244, 245, 254.
117 B. Crawford, *Earl & Mormaer: Norse-Pictish relationships in Northern Scotland* (Rosemarkie, 1995), 11–17; quotation at 12.

almost certainly enjoyed (see below) would have required seaborne transport, it does not require a stretch of the imagination to suggest that they might have been able to call upon sailors to double as siege engineers. In the final analysis, it is no doubt easy to make Guthred out to have been better equipped than he actually was, and any discussion based on such generic (however tantalising) evidence is bound quickly to move into the realm of speculation. Whatever the nature of Guthred's siege machinery, two inescapable conclusions remain: first, that his army possessed siege engines of some sort; and second, that he did succeed in frightening the garrison of a royal castle in the north into submission in 1211.[118]

As a Celtic warlord with siege weapons at his disposal, Guthred was by no means unique. Thus, for instance, in 1193 Maelgwn ap Rhys of Deheubarth and his warband 'came with catapults to breach the castle of Ystraid Meurig [in Ceredigion] and they demolished the castle'. Three years later, Maelgwn laid siege to Paincastle 'with catapults and engines and forced it to surrender'.[119] In contemporary Ireland, which may have more relevance for the case of Guthred given the Irish connections of his kindred, siege warfare was not unknown before the arrival of the Anglo-Normans, and it was certainly a common enough activity in the later twelfth century.[120] In 1174, for instance, an expedition sent by Ruaidrí Ua Conchobair into Mide forced Hugh Tyrell to abandon an Anglo-Norman earthwork at Trim; Ruaidrí destroyed the site so that nothing remained. Two years later Slane castle was destroyed by the king of Cenél nEógain, after which three other castles in the vicinity were immediately abandoned out of fear.[121] If it is now becoming clear that 'there were more elaborate forms of warfare in use than simply cattle-raiding in twelfth-century Ireland',[122] the same must also be said for the activities of Guthred and his ilk.

'Those Who Stood With MacWilliam'

On the one hand, the king's enemies, lacking the resources and landed base of the Scottish kings, commanded relatively small armies and employed guerrilla-style tactics to offset their disadvantage. On the other hand, as Guthred's use of siege engines demonstrates, they were not entirely without resources, and it is surprising just how much time and effort the Scottish kings were forced to

---

118 Exactly which castle was captured is unclear. Bower states that the castle had been recently constructed, but since King William had built castles at Dunskeath and Redcastle in 1179, it is possible that one of these is meant.

119 *Brut Y Tywysogyon or The Chronicle of the Princes. Red Book of Hergest Version*, ed. T. Jones (Cardiff, 1955), 174–5, 176–7.

120 Flanagan, 'Irish and Anglo-Norman warfare', 66–7.

121 Flanagan, 'Irish and Anglo-Norman warfare', 67.

122 Flanagan, 'Irish and Anglo-Norman warfare', 66.

commit to the suppression of their challenges. This, in turn, suggests a more deeply-rooted resistance operating at the local level than is usually supposed. In fact, medieval chronicles talk of widespread support for some of the MacWilliam risings. Writing of Donald's invasion in 1181, Howden states that it was accomplished 'by a mandate of certain powerful men of the kingdom of Scotland' – although the lack of specific names is to be regretted. Later, describing Donald's activities in 1187, the same chronicler reiterates that Donald 'often did many and harmful things to William, king of Scotland, through consent and council of the earls and barons of the kingdom of Scotland'.[123] While there is little evidence of as much widespread dissent among the Scottish nobles as Howden suggests, it is worthwhile noting that some, at least, of the leaders of the royal army sent against MacWilliam in 1187 were, if not sympathetic to the MacWilliam cause, then at least unenthusiastic supporters of the Scottish king. Howden says that 'when they [the army] had set out, treason arose among the chiefs; for certain of them loved the king not at all, and certain of them loved him. And the latter wished to proceed, but the others did not permit it'. Does the dissent within the army account for the king's decision to remain at Inverness, and point to the fact that it was too dangerous for him to move personally into Ross? In the MacWilliam challenges of the next generation, Walter Bower observed that Guthred had invaded Scotland from Ireland, 'as part of a plot (as is commonly said) [hatched by] the thanes of Ross'. Here Bower borrows the phrase 'thanes of Ross' from *Gesta Annalia*, and it should probably be read as 'local lords' and not in its technical sense of managers of royal estates, since only one thanage in this sense has been identified in Ross.[124]

Fortunately, there is better and even more compelling evidence of the nature of MacWilliam support than the vague medieval conspiracy theories voiced by chroniclers. There is, for instance, a charter from the reign of William I, probably belonging to the period between 1187 and 1189, that grants lands in Perthshire to Gilbert, earl of Strathearn (1171–1223). This states that these lands had previously been held by Gillecolm, the king's marshal, who forfeited them because he had 'feloniously surrendered my castle of Heryn [Auldearn] and then went over to my mortal enemies in the manner of a wicked traitor and stood with them against me to do as much harm as he could'.[125] Given both the chronological and geographical framework – Heryn is probably Auldearn – this episode almost certainly belongs to Donald MacWilliam's challenge in the 1180s, and its vituperative language, stressing the gravity of Gillecolm's

123 *Gesta Regis Henrici* i, 277–8; ii, 7–9.
124 *Scotichronicon*, iv, notes on 632; A. Grant, 'Thanes and Thanages, from the Eleventh to Fourteenth Centuries', in *Medieval Scotland*, 39–79; see 47, 72 for the only known thanage in Ross at Dingwall.
125 *Acts of William I*, no 258: 'qui in felonia reddidit castellum meum de Heryn et postea sicut iniquus et proditur iuit ad inimicos meos mortales et cum eis stetit contra me ad forisfaciendum pro posse suo'.

iniquity, speaks volumes. This document thus lends credibility to Howden's statements to the effect that the MacWilliams enjoyed the support of some among the Scottish élite, and also helps to illuminate the divisions that were said to have existed within the leaders of the royal army in 1187. Not only this, but it is noteworthy that the lands forfeited by Gillecolm lay within the heartland of the Scottish kingdom, suggesting that support for the king's rivals was not confined solely to the outer, Atlantic, zones. But for the survival of this document, all knowledge of Gillecolm and his likely role in the events of the 1180s would have been lost; how many like him remain unknown as a result of the paucity of the source materials?

On the other hand, the same document also nicely illustrates the unwavering support that the king received from at least one member of the native nobility: Earl Gilbert of Strathearn. Cynthia Neville, who has made the subject of the earls of Strathearn very much her own, has shown Gilbert to have been more active at court than his predecessors, and to have played an important role in the governance of Scotland during his tenure as justiciar of Scotia.[126] Although speculative, it is tempting to connect the grant of Gillecolm's lands to Earl Gilbert with the latter's support for the king's cause, and it may even be taken to indicate that the earl had played an active role (otherwise unrecorded) in the suppression of the MacWilliam insurrection of the 1180s. His support may not have ended there, either. A decade later, the presence of Gilbert at several royal burghs in the north with the king in 1196 and 1197 strongly suggests that he was involved in the campaigns against Earl Harald Maddadsson of Orkney/Caithness in those years.[127] In both contexts it is worthwhile noting that one of the responsibilities of the earl in twelfth- and thirteenth-century Scotland was summoning and leading the host of his region, and this makes it likely that Gilbert was one of the king's commanders against several implacable foes. Whether or not this was the case, however, there can be no doubt of Gilbert's role as an active supporter of the king, and this in turn provides a potent reminder that any polarisation of twelfth- and thirteenth-century Scotland into Normanophile monarchs and gaelicised rivals is vastly over-simplistic.

Further evidence that the opponents of the Scottish kings enjoyed local support comes from an inventory of Scottish documents, which states that there once existed a roll containing 'recognitions and old charters of the time of King William and King Alexander his son [concerning] those to whom the said kings formerly gave their peace, and those who stood with MacWilliam'.[128] Frustratingly, this roll was lost in England after 1296, together with other Scottish

---

126 Neville, 'Celtic Enclave', especially 75–7.
127 *Acts of William I*, nos. 388, 391, 392, 393, 394, 395. I am grateful to Dr. Cynthia Neville for discussion of these points.
128 *APS* i, 114.

muniments which Edward I sent south to London in the aftermath of his conquest of Scotland.[129] Although this document would fill in many gaps surrounding the MacWilliam uprisings, even this bare description of it corroborates, at least in part, the statements of the chroniclers, and suggests that support for the MacWilliams and others was more widespread than we might otherwise imagine.

Notwithstanding the loss of these tantalising records, it seems likely that one of those who stood with MacWilliam was Harald Maddadson, the powerful and expansionist earl of Orkney and Caithness, whose exploits already have figured in the narrative as an antagonist of the Scottish kings in the late twelfth and early thirteenth centuries. Although Earl Harald had his own axe to grind with the Scottish monarchs, his activities against them cannot be dissociated entirely from the resistance offered by other rivals. There is, as we have seen, good circumstantial evidence linking him with the insurrections of the MacHeths. Earl Harald was related by marriage to Malcolm: sometime after 1168 he put away his first wife, the daughter of Earl Duncan of Fife, and married instead the daughter of Malcolm MacHeth.[130] Since medieval marriages were contracted not for love but rather for political reasons, this act probably represents a conscious association on Harald's part with the faction represented by Mac-Heth, and it may well have been a motivating factor in his disturbances in the north in the 1190s. *Gesta Annalia*, for instance, related that king Harald had been until this time 'a good and trusty man – but at that time, goaded on by his wife . . . he had risen against [the king]'.[131] This contention is strengthened considerably by the fact that a condition of the peace treaty between Earl Harald and King William in 1197 was that the earl should dismiss MacHeth's daughter as his wife – something that Harald refused to consider.[132] It is thus possible that Maddadsson's invasion of Moray in 1196 originated in this marriage alliance, and that the powerful Orkney earl was staking a claim to the earldom of Ross. It must also surely be significant that when Earl Harald submitted to King William in 1196, Harald 'swore to the king that he would bring to him all his enemies . . .' The earl later reneged on his oath, explaining that 'I have allowed them [the king's enemies] to go away, knowing that if I had given them up to you they would not escape your hands . . .'[133] It is difficult to imagine that the enemies referred to here are anyone other than the MacHeths or the MacWilliams, and it may not be coincidence that Earl Harald's challenges in the 1190s coincide with an apparent lull in MacHeth and

129 See Webster, *Scotland from the eleventh century to 1603*, 122–25, and Thomson, *Public Records of Scotland*, Ch. 1.
130 *Chronica* iv, 12.
131 *Chron Fordun* i, 274–75; ii, 270.
132 *Chronica* iv, 12.
133 Howden, *Chronica* iv, 10–12; trans. *SAEC*, 316–7.

MacWilliam opposition in the same period. Whatever the case may have been, the role of the earl of Orkney and Caithness in northern affairs in this period cannot be denied, just as it cannot be denied that his position in Caithness would have been strengthened by attacks that undermined the power and authority of the Scottish kings. It must be almost certain, then, that Harald Maddadsson provided covert assistance for several northern uprisings, and that he may have been one of those anonymous but 'powerful men' who are said to have supported the MacHeth and MacWillliam causes.

Connections between the earls of Orkney/Caithness and the MacHeths and MacWilliams may have endured beyond the death of Earl Harald in 1206. When Guthred MacWilliam landed in Ross in 1211, he was said to have had the support of some of the leading men of the region – a point which is rendered at least plausible by the reference to the lost roll of MacWilliam supporters. In this context it is interesting to note that the *Orkneyinga Saga*, which lists Earl Harald's children by his two marriages, asserts that one of his sons by his first marriage, Heinrek, 'ruled over Ross in Scotland' after Harald's death.[134] Although otherwise uncorroborated, it is tempting to suppose that Heinrek might have been one of those nobles of Ross who supported Guthred in 1211/12. So much is speculation, but if true this would extend the connection between the earls of Orkney/Caithness and the MacHeths and MacWilliams further into the thirteenth century than is usually allowed.

There is, then, some evidence to suggest that support for the rivals of the Scottish kings was more widespread than has been believed, particularly during the period of most intensive challenges in the 1180s and 1190s. Did this translate into a sense of insecurity on the part of the descendants of Malcolm III and Margaret? In an assize of 1197, King William required all the prelates, earls, barons, and thanes of the kingdom to swear an oath to the effect that

> they will not receive or maintain thieves, man-slayers, murderers nor robbers, but wherever they can find them, among their own men or among another's, with all their power they will bring them to a (or the) justice . . . that to their utmost endeavours they will be helpers to the king to seek out misdoers . . .[135]

Although indebted to an English text of 1195 for much of its wording, this assize is generally regarded as authentic, though its relationship to the nearly chronic challenges of the 1180s and 1190s has yet to be worked out.[136] It may be that the timing of the assize is more than coincidence, and that the evident concern with stability and bringing malefactors to justice may in fact be directly related to a

---

134 *OS*, Ch. 105, 112.
135 *Annals of Malcolm and William*, 311; trans., discussed, in Duncan, *Scotland*, 201–2.
136 Duncan, *Scotland*, 201–2; see also Walker, *Legal History of Scotland* i, 305.

degree of turmoil stemming from over a decade of continual challenges. In 1197 the Scottish king was locked in the midst of struggle with Earl Harald of Orkney/Caithness, and only ten years earlier Adam son of Donald was taken and his warband slain at Coupar Angus abbey. It would no doubt be going beyond the bounds of the evidence to suggest a direct causal relationship between the crescendo reached by challenges to the Scottish kings in this period and the assize of 1197. Nevertheless, the suspicion must remain that behind the nameless thieves, murderers, and robbers of the assize lurk individuals like the MacHeths and MacWilliams and their supporters. It is also interesting to note that, only a few years later, in 1200, Pope Innocent III replied to a query from King William regarding the sanctuary of churches. The pope observed that freemen should not be dragged violently from churches and put to death, regardless of the nature of their crimes; the correspondence calls to mind the events at Coupar Angus in 1186, although given the fourteen-year interval, it hardly seems likely that the letter can be directly related to this episode. [137]

'Encountering together the same hazards of war'

Robin Frame has remarked that those who ruled on the margins of the Scottish kingdom 'could often find allies and patrons in Ireland or Norway'.[138] This is certainly true, and external connections are very much in evidence with the enemies of the Scottish kings. The army with which Somerled invaded the Scottish kingdom in 1164 is nicely symbolic of the extent of his insular and mainland kingdom, and illustrates the extensive connections upon which some of the opponents of the Scottish kings could call in their struggles. The *Carmen* states of Somerled's army that it was composed of 'Norsemen and Argyllsmen', while the *Annals of Ulster*, recording Somerled's demise, record that 'along with him, slaughter was made of the men of Argyle and of Kintyre, and of the men of the Hebrides, and the Foreigners of Dublin'. This last reference is, of course, to the Scandinavians of Dublin – the Ostmen – who had been established there since the middle of the ninth century and whose large fleets and plundering activities were legendary.[139] In 1164 Somerled's link to Ireland was at least a decade old, since in 1154 he seems to have formed an alliance with the Irish up-and-comer Muirchertach Mac Lochlainn against their mutual enemy Godfrey, the Manx king. We are told that, for a naval engagement in 1154, Muirchertach commanded a fleet that included ships from Kintyre and the 'shores of

---

137 *Annals of Malcolm and William*, 329.
138 Frame, *Political Development*, 103.
139 See, e.g., S. Duffy, *Ireland in the Middle Ages* (Dublin, 1997), 30–1, 36–8, and *idem*, 'Irishmen and Islesmen in the Kingdoms of Dublin and Man', *Ériu* xliii (1992), 93–133; K.L. Maund, *Ireland, Wales and England in the eleventh century* (Woodbridge, 1991), and the review of this last by S. Duffy, 'Ostmen, Irish and Welsh in the Eleventh Century', *Pertitia* ix (1995), 378–96.

Scotland', probably a reference to the Hebrides and Argyll, Somerled's territory.[140] Appropriately enough, when the Scandinavians launched a major sea-attack on Dublin in 1171, in the aftermath of its capture by the English, Islesmen are said to have assisted them.[141] It was in the context of this engagement that Gerald of Wales made the telling remark that 'it is a sure defence and a source of sweet companionship to have about one the comforting presence of those who enjoy encountering together the same hazards of war',[142] a sentiment with which many of the enemies of the Scottish kings would no doubt have agreed.

Like Somerled, the Galloway dynasty also possessed links to Ireland, which were especially prominent in the events of the 1230s. Keith Stringer has shown that Alan of Galloway was deeply involved in Ireland and the Irish Sea world, and that he strove to establish a power base there for Thomas, his illegitimate son. This included the marriage, in 1226, of Thomas to a daughter of the Manx king Ragnvald, an alliance that was forged with the 'clear intention that Thomas should succeed his father-in-law as king of Man'.[143] The Irish Sea connection paid dividends in 1234/35, when Matthew Paris describes how 'many noble and bold men from the different regions of the western provinces, namely Galloway, and the island which is called Man, and the region of Ireland' came together to back him, along with Hugh de Lacy, the earl of Ulster and father-in-law of Alan.[144] The Irish levies figured prominently in the account of events given in the Melrose chronicle, and it is clear that Thomas used Ireland as a base of operations. Thomas's supporter Gilrod is said to have 'arrived with a fleet from Ireland', and upon landing in Galloway he broke up the ships so that the levies would be unable to return to Ireland.[145] The *Chronicle of Melrose* also records the fate of these warriors after the surrender of Gilrod and Thomas:

> After this, the Irishmen, stealthily departing the country, took their way near the city of Glasgow. Learning this, the citizens went out in a body; and they cut off the heads of as many as they found, and caused them to give up the ghost. But they kept two of the older men, and had them torn asunder by horses, at Edinburgh.[146]

Although the close proximity of both Argyll and Galloway to the Irish Sea ensured a steady supply of Irish and Scandinavian warriors for the rulers of

---

140 *Annals of the Kingdom of Ireland by the Four Masters*, ed. J. O'Donovan (Dublin, 1851), ii, 1110–12 (1154); *ES* ii, 226–27.
141 Gerald of Wales, *Expugnatio*, 77–79.
142 Gerald of Wales, *Expugnatio*, 79 .
143 Stringer, 'Periphery and Core', 96.
144 *Chron Majora*, iii, 364–6;. *SAEC*, 341.
145 *Chron Melrose*, 84 (1235);. *ES* ii, 496–97.
146 *Chron Melrose*, 84–5 (1235); *ES* ii, 497.

these regions, they were not alone among the enemies of the Scottish kings in possessing links to Ireland. In fact, support from Gaelic Ireland is a prominent and important theme of the MacWilliam uprisings, probably beginning with that of Donald MacWilliam in 1181. Roger of Howden says that Donald 'landed in Scotland', and although the language is vague, this might imply that he had actually arrived from somewhere outside the kingdom, quite likely Ireland. Whether or not this is the case, Guthred is explicitly said to have 'come to those parts [i.e. Ross] from Ireland', while the 1215 uprising led by Donald Bàn involved an unnamed Irish prince and presumably Irish and possibly Hebridean forces as well. These references are reinforced by an English chronicle, which stated that Guthred employed both Scottish and Irish levies.[147] There can be little doubt that one of those in Ulster who aided and abetted the MacWilliams was Aedh O Neill of Tir Eoghain (d. 1230), the most powerful leader in the north in the early thirteenth century. Over the course of his career he chalked up an impressive string of victories over the Anglo-Normans, including a victory over John de Courcy in 1199 and the burning of Carlingford in 1213, and although he did on occasion cooperate with the likes of de Courcy and Hugh de Lacy, his support of the MacWilliams made him as much an enemy of the Scottish kings as of the English.[148] It is thus clear, as Seán Duffy has pointed out, that 'there were always men in Ireland willing to throw their muscle about in Scotland and in the islands ... The underdog, the pretender, and the malcontent in Scotland all found Irish support'.[149]

It was the Hebrides, the islands off Scotland's western shores, that provided the link, via the Great Glen, between northern Scotland and Gaelic Ireland, and there is good evidence that this region, too, provided support for the likes of the MacWilliams: not only is at least one Hebridean chieftain on record as playing a role in the insurrections of the 1220s, but it also seems quite likely that mercenary troops from this region, the infamous *galloclaig* or galloglass (the word means literally 'foreign warrior'), were present in the armies of the king's enemies. The *Chronicle of Lanercost*, describing the MacWilliam uprising of the late 1220s, states that 'one Roderic' was also involved. This 'Roderic' is usually identified with Ruairi, the son of Ranald, the son of Somerled, and was the eponymous ancestor of the MacRuairis. His apparent involvement in this insurrection suggests that the MacWilliams enjoyed the support of some of the Hebridean chieftains, but also raises the strong possibility that these chieftains brought with them contingents of fierce galloglass warriors. Certainly within a

---

147 Walter of Coventry ii, 206; *SAEC*, 330 n. 6.
148 On Aedh, see: R. Frame, *Colonial Ireland 1169–1369* (Dublin, 1981), 27–30; M. Dolley, *Anglo-Norman Ireland c.1100–1318* (Dublin, 1972), 99–100, 108, 112, 114–15, 118, 123–24.
149 S. Duffy, 'The Bruce Brothers and the Irish Sea World', *Cambridge Medieval Celtic Studies* xxi (1991), 63.

few decades the MacSorleys were the major suppliers of galloglass to the Irish kings: when Aed O Conchobair of Connacht married a daughter of Dugald MacRuairi in 1259, he brought home with him 'eight score oglaoch (young warriors)' together with Alan MacRuairi, who has been regarded as a galloglass captain. Since Dugald and Alan were the sons of Ruairi, it is not improbable that the MacWilliams were already employing galloglass mercenaries as early as the 1220s, and it is perhaps relevant that the MacRuairis had a well-deserved reputation as predators and buccaneers down to the end of the thirteenth century and into the early years of the fourteenth.[150] The connection between the north of Scotland, the Hebrides, and Gaelic Ireland certainly demonstrates how 'ambitious leaders could maximize their strength by drawing warriors from one part of the closely-knit Gaelic-Norse world to fight in another'.[151]

No doubt one of the attractions that joining campaigns against the Scottish kings held for these warriors was the prospect of plunder. Bower relates that in 1211/12 Guthred '[drove] off booty from the lord king's land'. Gillescop did the same thing around Inverness in the late 1220s.[152] In 1264 Dugald MacRuairi is said to have defeated a Scottish army in Caithness, and to have taken the 'great treasure' that the army was carrying.[153] Plundering was also a favourite activity of the Hebridean chieftains of the thirteenth century. Ruairi, the son of Ranald the son of Somerled – probably the same Ruairi who aided and abetted the MacWilliams in their insurrections of the early thirteenth century – plundered Derry in Ireland together with Thomas the son of Roland in 1212. A praise-poem written for Angus Mor of Islay in the later thirteenth century says: 'You've circled Ireland, scarce the shore where you've not taken cattle'.[154] Jordan Fantosme, describing the Scots invasion of northern England in 1173/74, highlights other goods that could be acquired by soldiers on campaign: 'The king of Scotland's men took off an enormous quantity of booty . . . they have their heart's desire, they have any number of animals, oxen, horses, fine cows, ewes, lambs, clothes, money, brooches and rings'.[155] It has been suggested that 'the ancient and time honoured tradition of plundering to obtain booty seems to have been alive and well and playing an important role in the economy of the western seaboard as late as the thirteenth century'.[156] It would also appear that plundering had a role to play in the uprisings against the Scottish kings as well. No doubt the booty and treasures acquired by leaders like Guthred and

---

150 See McDonald, *Kingdom of the Isles*, 189–91; Barrow, *Robert Bruce*, 290, describes the MacRuairis as buccaneers.
151 Stringer, 'Periphery and Core', 87.
152 *Scotichronicon* iv, 464–5; v, 143.
153 *ES* ii, 648–49.
154 'Poem to Aenghus Mór Mac Domhnaill', in Clancy, *Triumph Tree*, 288–91 at 290.
155 Fantosme, Ch. 120.
156 McDonald, *Kingdom of the Isles*, 151.

Outlaws of Medieval Scotland

Gillescop were distributed to their warbands, thereby ensuring their continued loyalty and support, and perhaps at least partially explaining some of the tenacity of opposition to the Scottish kings. Further, Professor Davies has suggested that, in contemporary Wales, plundering and devastating the lands of an opponent signalled the intent of political and dynastic rivals to mount a challenge: this may have some application in the present context as well, since it is interesting that the MacWilliams, dynastic rivals par excellence of the Canmore kings, are often described as plundering royal lands.[157]

'He Mightily Overthrew the King's Enemies': Ending the Threat

Considering the connections to Gaelic Ireland possessed by their enemies, it is hardly surprising that one strategy pursued by the Scottish kings was to shut down this potentially deadly pipeline. In this endeavour, English support was crucial. We have already seen how King John of England provided mercenaries to aid the Scottish king in quashing the insurrection of Guthred in 1212, and it is no coincidence that the same year saw an Anglo-Scottish treaty. Also in 1212, Alan of Galloway received extensive lands in Ulster from King John of England.[158] Although King John's motive was no doubt to improve the Anglo-Norman position in north-eastern Ireland in the wake of Hugh de Lacy's expulsion in 1210, the grant also had implications for King William, and Keith Stringer has argued that 'Alan's involvement with Ulster ought never-theless to be assessed from other strategic perspectives and, in particular, that of the Scottish government's insecurity in the far north and west . . .'[159] It is likely that this grant of land to Alan enjoyed the approval of the Scottish king, since if Alan successfully took control of these lands, then he would be in an excellent position to reduce the threat from the MacWilliams or, at the very least, cut off or reduce their lines of communication with Ireland, and it may be that several enigmatic entries in the Irish Annals need to be read with this in mind. In 1212, for instance, Thomas, Alan's brother, 'came to Derry of Columcille with seventy-six ships; and the place was to a great extent destroyed by them; and Inishowen was completely destroyed by them, and by the Cenél-Conaill'. Two years later, in 1214, Thomas again plundered Derry, and constructed a castle at Coleraine[160] (it was demolished a decade later by Aedh O Neill in alliance with Hugh de Lacy).[161] Although, on the face of it, these events look like plundering raids on a scale all too familiar on the western seaboard, it is

157 Davies, *Age of Conquest*, 67–8.
158 See R. Greeves, 'The Galloway Lands in Ulster', *TDGNHAS*, 3rd ser. xxxvi (1957–58), 115–22; see also Stringer, 'Periphery and Core', 85–86.
159 Stringer, 'Periphery and Core', 85.
160 *AU* (Hennessy), ii, 252 (1212), 256 (1214); *ES* ii, 393, 395.
161 A.J. Otway-Ruthven, *A History of Medieval Ireland* (London and New York, 1968; repr. New York, 1980), 92.

possible that they are, in fact, related to the events in the north of Scotland in the early thirteenth century, and Keith Stringer has made a convincing argument that they look like 'determined efforts to strike out bases of MacWilliam support' in the aftermath of Guthred's uprising.[162] Their success may be adjudged from the fact that the subsequent MacWilliam uprisings appear much less menacing than those of the 1180s or of 1211/12: that of 1215, for example, was apparently quashed single-handedly by Ferchar Maccintsa-cairt without the mobilisation of a royal army.

Simultaneously, in the first half of the thirteenth century, the pattern of land grants in Scotland provides further evidence that the Scottish kings were actively endeavouring to choke off the MacWilliam lifeline to Ireland and their hold in the remoter parts of Moray and Ross from other directions as well. The settlement and consolidation of the north of Scotland is a phenomenon of the late twelfth century and the early part of the thirteenth. Although some settlement of Flemings is attested in the reigns of David I and Malcolm IV, it was not until the reign of William I that the advance of royal authority in these remote regions gathered momentum; indeed, the pacification of the north has been regarded as the 'major domestic concern' of William's reign.[163] Beginning as early as about 1180, when King William installed his brother, Earl David of Huntingdon (d.1219), in the compact and strategic lordship of Garioch, a whole series of strategically placed, marcher-style lordships was created in the far north and placed in the hands of loyal supporters of the king.[164] At around the same time as Earl David was made lord of Garioch, the earl of Strathearn was given Kinveachie in Inverness-shire (c. 1178–85);[165] a little later, the earls of Fife acquired Stratha'an (Strathavon, Banffshire) from the bishop of Moray; and in 1212 the Comyn family acquired the earldom of Buchan (a large area in north-eastern Scotland) when William Comyn married Marjorie, the heiress of the earl; as earl of Buchan he was well placed to counter threats from the MacWilliams.[166] But the process did not stop there. By the 1220s a whole spate of new lordships was being carved out around Inverness. By about 1226 not only had Thomas Durward been made sheriff of Inverness, but his son Alan had been established as lord of Urquhart on the shore of Loch Ness, while James the son of Morgrund, the earl of Mar, was given Abernethy and John Bisset was made lord of the Aird and granted lands west of Inverness in addition to 'Redcastle' at Eddirdour in southern Ross.[167]

Without doubt, though, the two most important lordships to be created

162 Stringer, 'Periphery and Core', 88.
163 Stringer, *Earl David*, 30.
164 Stringer, *Earl David*, especially Ch. 3; *Acts of William I*, no. 205.
165 *Acts of William I*, no. 206.
166 A. Young, *Robert the Bruce's Rivals: The Comyns 1212–1314* (East Linton, 1997), 22.
167 Grant, 'Province of Ross', 124.

against the backdrop of MacWilliam risings in the far north were those of Badenoch and Ross. The lordship of Badenoch was given to Walter Comyn, almost certainly after the MacWilliam uprising of 1228/30. These territories, in the remotest part of Moray, represented a difficult area for the Crown to control; in conjunction with Comyn interests in Buchan and other scattered estates around the north, they made the Comyns '*key* royal agents in the north to counter the threat of the MacWilliam clan to the Scottish throne and at the same time to consolidate royal authority in the north of Scotland'.[168] Finally, sometime before 1226, Ferchar Maccintsacairt was created earl of Ross. He had already established himself as a supporter of the Canmore kings in 1215, when he crushed a MacWilliam uprising; he would do so again when he saved a royal army in Galloway in 1235. His appointment as earl of Ross is especially significant because it placed a loyal supporter of the Scottish king in charge of a vast bloc of northern territory that included Easter Ross, while his prestige and influence stretched all the way to the western seaboard (North Argyll or Wester Ross were acquired by Ferchar's descendants in the later thirteenth century). Thus, a region that had formerly been a turbulent marchland was consolidated: under Ferchar, Ross ceased to represent the effective limit of royal authority and became at last an integral part of the kingdom.[169] His appointment as earl of Ross, as well as the establishment of the Comyn lordship of Badenoch and the placement of other loyal supporters in compact, marcher-style lordships, severed the MacWilliam umbilical cord to Ireland and drove the final nail into the coffin of the northern uprisings. It is surely no coincidence that by 1230 the MacWilliams had played their final moment upon the stage of Scottish history.

The establishment of Ferchar as earl of Ross is significant for another reason also: it shows how, by the thirteenth century, even native dignitaries in the far north were being integrated and assimilated into the new socio-political order established by the Scottish kings from the time of David I. Ferchar's knighting at the hands of the king as a reward for his suppression of the 1215 MacWilliam uprising elevated him into an elite social group, while his creation as earl of Ross boosted him into the uppermost rank of the Scottish nobility – indeed, Ferchar's is one of the greatest success stories among the Scottish nobility of the entire middle ages. Once men like Ferchar began to support the Scottish Crown instead of opposing it, however, the days of the MacWilliams and other opponents of the Scottish kings were surely numbered.

With the consolidation of Ross underway by the 1220s and exemplified by the creation of Ferchar as earl of Ross, the northward thrust of Scottish royal authority continued into Sutherland. This process is associated with the de

---

168 Young, *Comyns*, 28; see also Barrow, 'Badenoch and Strathspey', 1–16.
169 McDonald, 'Ferchar Macintsaccairt', forthcoming.

Moravia family. The Flemish-sounding Freskin was given Duffus circa 1130, no doubt as part of the consolidation of Moray in the wake of the defeat of Angus and Malcolm at Stracathro.[170] After the defeat of Donald MacWilliam in 1187, Freskin's descendants were probably in the forefront of the Scottish advance into Cromarty, but, as Barbara Crawford put it, 'The family's ambitions were to become only too clear in the period after Earl Harald's death, when they succeeded in establishing themselves in Sutherland . . .'[171] By the early thirteenth century (probably between 1212 and 1214) Hugh son of William possessed lands in Sutherland; some of these in Creich and Skelbo were granted to his relative Gilbert de Moravia, the future (1223–1245) bishop of Caithness who was then archdeacon of Moray.[172] Not too long after that Hugh's son, William, was styled *dominus de Sutherlandia* before 1222. By the 1230s he appeared as earl of Sutherland.[173] By then his relative Gilbert was bishop of Caithness, and it has already been noted that in this role he was also an active agent of royal authority, perhaps even building or strengthening castles in the area under his control. Indeed, by the 1230s the influence of the Scottish king was being felt in Caithness, too: after the death of Earl John in 1231, the earldom of Caithness seems to have been held in turn by Malcolm Earl of Atholl and then Walter Comyn between 1232 and 1235 before reverting to Earl Magnus, a member of the Angus family which took over the title to the earldoms of Orkney and Caithness.[174] By the mid-thirteenth century, Caithness was on its way toward becoming an integral part of the Scottish kingdom.[175]

The king's enemies and their armies were better equipped and more mettlesome than they have sometimes been considered in the past; certainly, in any case, the kings of Scots took them seriously enough. This being the case, it remains to consider why they were, without exception, defeated. It is true, of course, that the Scottish kings were not always successful in bringing their opponents to heel in a single campaigning season: Malcolm troubled David I for a decade after 1124; Wimund was able to force a settlement in the 1140s; Donald MacWilliam remained on the rampage in the north for six years after 1181, probably having taken over much of Moray and Ross; and it took two seasons to liquidate his son Guthred in 1211–12. Ultimately, however, each of these individuals *was* defeated. No doubt there were circumstances specific to

170 Barrow, *Acts of William I*, no. 116; see also the same author's 'Beginnings of military feudalism', 282–83.
171 Crawford, 'Earldom of Caithness', 31.
172 Barrow, *Acts of William I*, no. 258.
173 *Sutherland Book*, 7, 12; see also Crawford, 'Earldom of Caithness', 30–36.
174 Crawford, 'Earldom of Caithness', 34.
175 Ibid., 37.

each royal victory. We will never know whether it was bad luck, bad organisation, or bad leadership that led to the defeat of Somerled at Renfrew in 1164 or Donald MacWilliam at Mam Garvia in 1187; similarly, we will never know what it was that prompted their own men to betray Wimund and Guthred MacWilliam. But there are unquestionably several important and interrelated factors that led to the demise of these men and the ultimate victory of the Scottish monarchs from Stracathro to Mam Garvia and beyond.

Simply put, the struggle between the Scottish kings and their enemies in the twelfth and thirteenth centuries was a contest of David and Goliath proportions, and it was one that the opponents of the kings, cast in the role of underdogs, could not hope to win. The Scottish kings enjoyed too many advantages denied their rivals, so that the contest between these kings and their opponents closely resembles another epic struggle of the same period – namely, that between the English medieval state and its Celtic neighbours. Militarily, there can be little doubt that the armies fielded by the Scottish kings were superior to those of their foes, even if, as I have argued, the armies of their rivals may have been better equipped and larger than is sometimes thought. Above all, the Scottish armies no doubt possessed superior armour and firepower, and their nucleus of heavily armoured knights – however small compared to the English host – must have proved advantageous, if not decisive. Professor Barrow's judgement that the Scottish army was 'doubtless useful to deal with rebellion in the remote and ungovernable parts of the kingdom' therefore has much to commend it.[176] In similar fashion, the kings of Scots also enjoyed the capability to construct and stock castles on a scale that greatly exceeded that of their rivals. William I was a prodigious castle builder in Ross, for instance, and even when Guthred MacWilliam succeeded in reducing a royal stronghold in the region in 1212, he nevertheless preferred to raze it rather than attempt to hold it against the king. The superiority of the Scottish kings over their foes on the periphery is highlighted by the distribution and number of mottes that are known to have existed in the twelfth and thirteenth centuries: they cluster heavily in areas where royal control was weak, like the southwest and the north, insulating these potentially troublesome regions from the heartland of the kingdom.[177]

Underlying these military considerations is what Robin Frame has identified as one of the greatest advantages possessed by the Scottish kings over their dynastic rivals – the control of a firm territorial base.[178] While the enemies of

176 Barrow, 'Beginnings of military feudalism', 286.
177 This is not to suggest that castles were either unknown or unappreciated by those who held power in the peripheral territories of the kingdom and who frequently found themselves at odds with the Scottish kings – the lords of Galloway, the rulers of Argyll and the Isles, and the earls of Orkney/Caithness all constructed strongholds of one form or another in the course of the twelfth and thirteenth centuries.
178 Frame, *Political Development*, 105.

the Scottish kings were forced to operate from the rugged Atlantic zones of north Britain, the Scottish kings were based in a well-governed, stable and wealthy heartland that encompassed the eastern lowlands around Angus, Fife and Lothian and the important centres of St Andrews, Edinburgh, Perth, and Stirling.[179] It must be significant that this royal heartland only seldom forms the backdrop to insurrection (as in 1116 or 1160); more often than not, the key scenes in the twelfth- and thirteenth-century drama of opposition and insurrection were played out in what one chronicler described as the 'remotest territories of Scotland' but which might be more accurately regarded as the heartlands of the king's rivals themselves. Thus, while the likes of Somerled, Malcolm MacHeth and Donald MacWilliam were (with only a few notable exceptions) unsuccessful at penetrating into the heartland of the Scottish kingdom, the Canmore kings showed themselves ready and able to strike deep into the territories of their foes. With each Scottish victory and the inevitable consolidation that followed on its heels, the king's enemies were thrust further back into the periphery, reducing their capacity to strike, and rendering the MacWilliam/MacHeth insurrection of 1215, for instance, so futile that it could be quashed by a local dignitary without the mobilisation of a royal army.

Another significant aspect of the Scottish heartland was its alignment. 'Above all,' says Professor Barrow, 'Scotland was a North Sea country, looking eastward and southward to the other countries which faced the same sea and used it increasingly as the highway for their trade.'[180] This orientation proved to be a key component in the eventual success of the Canmore kings. Not only were they receptive to the foreign influence that flowed freely north from England and the Continent, they were also able to turn that foreign influence to their own advantage. It is no coincidence that in 1134 David had been able to call upon northern English barons to assist him in his ongoing struggle with Malcolm MacHeth, and if the boasts attributed to Robert de Brus before the battle of the Standard in 1138 are any indication, the mere thought of this military might was enough to set potential foes quaking in their boots. It is difficult to avoid the conclusion that, whatever other advantages foreign colonists might have offered, and however peaceful the Anglo-Norman penetration of Scotland may appear, the potential of the incomers to play the role of enforcers and strongmen for the Canmore dynasty should not be underestimated. As Alexander Grant observed, 'they [Scotland's Anglo-Normans] upheld the power of the native Scottish kings, against the latter's Celtic opponents'.[181]

179 See Frame, *Political Development*, 39–44; Webster, *Medieval Scotland*, Ch. 3; Barrow, *Acts of Malcolm IV*, Ch. 2, and *idem, Acts of William I*, Ch. 2; see also the maps in *Atlas of Scottish History to 1707*, ed. P.B. McNeill and H.L. MacQueen (Edinburgh, 1996), 159–162.
180 Barrow, *Robert Bruce*, 9; *Atlas*, 238, 262.
181 Grant, 'Scotland's 'Celtic Fringe', 118–9.

Finally, and perhaps most significantly, there is the question of what might be called economies of scale – that is, the relative economic resources available to the Scottish kings and their adversaries, resources that ultimately dictated how large an army could be mobilised, how long it could stay in the field, or how many and what kind of castles could be constructed. Not only did the Scottish kings possess a larger and firmer territorial base than their enemies, but that base was much more economically developed as well. The heartland of the Scottish kingdom was, hardly surprisingly, the most economically advantaged part of it as well, 'where', Bruce Webster remarks, 'farming land was good, where lay many of the new burghs founded by twelfth-century kings and where merchants could trade across the North Sea and bring in tolls to the crown'.[182] One of the most striking aspects of twelfth- and thirteenth-century Scottish urban and economic history is the disparity between east and west: the burghs tended to be concentrated on the eastern side of the country (reflecting its eastern orientation in this period), and of the forty or so urban centres known to have been in existence by about 1214, over thirty lay in the eastern half of the country.[183] It is hardly a coincidence that the largest and wealthiest burghs clustered within or close to the heartland of the kingdom, including Aberdeen, Perth, Dundee, Montrose, St Andrews, Stirling, Edinburgh, Haddington, Roxburgh and Berwick. With their markets, fairs and tolls these burghs fired the engines of the economy; they were closely associated with coinage, too – itself an innovation of the twelfth century – and many of the mints of Scotland were located at the chief burghs, especially Berwick, Roxburgh, Edinburgh, Stirling and Perth.[184] In contrast, the marginal Atlantic zones of the kingdom were home to not one urban centre in the period under consideration. Most of those burghs that did come into existence on the west coast, in the southwest and in the north grew up as a consequence of Scottish expansion into those regions. Such, for instance, was the case of Moray, where the burghs that eventually developed there, such as Inverness, Elgin, Forres and Auldearn/ Nairn, did so on the initiative of the Scottish kings as part of their colonisation and conquest of that troublesome northern region after the defeat of Angus and Malcolm in 1130; Dumbarton on the Clyde should probably be regarded as having a similar origin since it first appears in the wake of a royal campaign to Argyll and the Isles in 1222. None of these burghs, moreover, could compete in size or wealth with their east-coast counterparts. In stark contrast to the economy of the Scottish heartland, then, the lands of Fergus, Somerled, the MacHeths and MacWilliams lagged behind: it is not without significance that Guthred MacWilliam, for instance, is said to have driven off booty from the

---

182 Webster, *Medieval Scotland*, 35.
183 Barrow, *Kingship and Unity*, 87; *Atlas*, 196–97.
184 Barrow, *Kingship and Unity*, 97.

land of the king and to have accumulated treasure in the course of his 1211–12 challenge, and it thus seems clear that plunder and the acquisition of moveable wealth played a prominent role in these regions as late as the thirteenth century.[185] If, from one perspective, the economy of the Celtic regions of Britain in the twelfth century closely resembled that of eighth-century England, 'a dispersed settlement pattern of farms and hamlets, not many coins, very few towns',[186] then how much more applicable is that same model to the dichotomy between the economies of the centre and periphery of the Scottish kingdom in the twelfth and thirteenth centuries? As John Gillingham put it in the context of the struggles of the English state against its Celtic neighbours, this was 'an unequal struggle between an industrially advanced power and a pastoral economy'.[187] And even if Scotland lagged behind England in terms of economic development, the core of the kingdom was well equipped, in economic terms, to withstand challenges from the relatively under-developed marginal regions.

Viewed from the broader perspective of the British Isles as a whole in the era between about 1100 and 1300, the remote peripheral regions of Scotland that sheltered and supported the enemies of the Canmore kings appear in much the same relationship to Scotland that the Scottish kingdom itself stood to its southern neighbour. Thanks to the work of scholars like John Gillingham and Rees Davies, among others, we are much better informed about some of the advantages enjoyed by the English medieval state in its imperialistic advance into the Celtic regions of Britain.[188] But the Scottish kings enjoyed precisely the same types of advantages over their own adversaries as the English enjoyed over the Scots, Welsh, and Irish: the Scottish kingdom was well equipped to deal with the threat of a Somerled or a Donald MacWilliam in military, territorial, economic, and social terms. This is only fitting since, just as the English medieval state was the most aggressively imperialistic power in the British Isles between about 1100 and 1300, so too were the Scots kings pursuing a vigorous policy of internal colonialism and territorial and dynastic aggrandisement during this same time, making them the imperialistic power in north Britain.[189]

---

185 For discussion of the economy of the western seaboard in this period, see McDonald, *Kingdom of the Isles*, 149–56 and the more detailed study by Benjamin T. Hudson, 'The changing economy of the Irish Sea province', in *Britain and Ireland 900–1300*, 39–66.

186 Gillingham, 'Beginnings of English Imperialism', 12.

187 Gillingham, 'Conquering the Barbarians: War and Chivalry in Twelfth-Century Britain and Ireland', in *The English in the Twelfth Century*, 49.

188 See the collected essays of J. Gillingham in *The English in the Twelfth Century*, as well as Davies, *Domination and Conquest, The First English Empire*, and 'The English State and the 'Celtic' Peoples 1100–1400', *Journal of Historical Sociology* vi (1993), 1–14.

189 There is much of value on the subject of internal colonialism in Hechter, *Internal Colonialism, passim*.

Yet this territorial and dynastic aggrandisement of the kings of Scots descended from Malcolm III and Margaret was accomplished at a price. Among the casualties were other royalties on the periphery of the expanding Scottish kingdom, as well as cast-off segments of the royal kindred who found themselves excluded from the royal office and forced to compete for it by force of arms. As losers in the historical process through which the medieval Scottish kingdom was 'dragged . . . from political infancy . . . into a vigorous and effective manhood',[190] these figures have been relegated to the sidelines of Scotland's history, their stories submerged beneath the tide of historical writing generated by the success of the Canmore dynasty; history is, after all, notoriously unkind to those without indigenous traditions of historical writing. Yet the ultimate success of the Scottish kings descended from Malcolm III and Margaret was not, perhaps, preordained. Despite their advantages, a different turn of events on one of several twelfth- or thirteenth-century battlefields might well have yielded a substantially different development of the medieval kingdom. Even as late as 1187, when William the Lion squared off against Donald MacWilliam and the descendants of Malcolm III and Margaret had occupied the kingship for ninety years without interruption, the army sent to annihilate Donald was divided among itself and some of the leaders argued that they ought to throw in their lot with MacWilliam. The ultimate triumph of the Canmore dynasty should not, however, blind us to the fact that this was often achieved by blunt force and military might, and that it was in some measure through mercilessly crushing rivals and liquidating adversaries that these kings maintained their grip on royal office. The view from the periphery was no doubt very different from that at the centre of the kingdom, however, and from the perspective of an Angus of Moray, Fergus of Galloway, Somerled of Argyll, or Donald MacWilliam, the territorial and dynastic aggrandisement of the descendants of Malcolm III and Margaret must indeed have appeared as something tantamount to a chronicle of carnage.

190 A.A.M. Duncan, 'The Heirs of Canmore', in *The Sunday Mail Story of Scotland* (Glasgow, 1988), i/4, 100.

KINGS, CHRONICLERS AND BARBARIANS:
A VIEW FROM THE CENTRE

This book has attempted to restore a degree of balance to the subject of the challenges faced by the Scottish kings of the twelfth and thirteenth centuries, in part through rejecting the dominant paradigm of these challenges as revolts or rebellions orchestrated by trouble-making warlords who were mere thorns in the sides of progressive kings of Scots. It has been argued that the challenges arose in reaction to profound changes taking place within the royal kindred as well as the territorial aggrandisement of the kings of Scots in the peripheral regions of north Britain. Historians have been quick to applaud the kings of Scots descended from Malcolm III and Margaret for their role in consolidating their dynasty and expanding the territorial base of their kingdom, yet there has been little recognition that, in doing so, they effectively squeezed out both other branches of the royal kindred as well as other royalties on the margins of their expanding kingdom. The leaders of the many challenges faced by the Scottish kings of the period were therefore casualties of the processes by which the Scottish kingdom expanded and developed between about 1100 and 1300.

'The almost complete absence of chronicle evidence . . . may leave the impression that Scotland was freer from friction and violence than was in fact the case.'[1] This observation by Professor Robin Frame highlights one of the central tenets of this study: namely, that the sources fail us through their sparse and incomplete nature. If more source material had survived, the story of challenges to the Scottish kings might be much more complete, and might, accordingly, form a more prominent strand in Scottish history of the period 1058 - 1266. There can be little doubt, however, that a great deal of material has unfortunately vanished, as evidenced by the lost membrane listing those who stood with the MacWilliams against William and Alexander. The survival of even one such document, or some fragment of it, by filling in some of the gaps that now exist, could conceivably alter significantly our understanding of the subject.

Yet if the sources fail us in this usual way, they do so in another manner as well, because they are distorted and display a strong bias in favour of the Scottish kings at the expense of their opponents. It is not just the roles in which the enemies of the kings are cast in these sources, as rebels, traitors, outlaws and brigands who destroyed the peace and stability of the kingdom. Indeed, this characterisation is hardly surprising, given that most of the historical sources at

---

1 'Conquest and Settlement', 57.

our disposal were composed either within the heartland of the Scottish kingdom or by writers whose sympathies lay, for one reason or another, with the dynasty of kings descended from Malcolm III and Margaret, while the challenges themselves were mounted by leaders associated with the peripheral regions. Nor is it merely that, where the rivals of the kings of Scots are concerned, the sources are laconic and matter-of-fact, if not downright cryptic at times. In fact, it almost appears as though, in some sources closely connected to the centre of the kingdom, there is something more sinister taking place. It is therefore appropriate to return to the sources in an attempt to answer one final question: how were the rivals of the Scottish kings viewed by those at the centre of the Scottish kingdom?

Professor John Gillingham has demonstrated how, in the course of the twelfth century, an imperialistic English culture developed which manifested itself in expressions of superiority on the part of the English toward the Celtic inhabitants of the British Isles. This meant that the peoples of Wales, Ireland and Scotland increasingly came to be regarded as 'barbarians' by their English neighbours. Such views became commonplace by the middle of the twelfth century, and, as Gillingham has argued, functioned as an ideology of conquest for the expansive English state within the British Isles.[2] Yet considering that the Scottish kings descended from Malcolm III and Margaret adopted the same role within northern Britain as an aggressive, imperialistic power, it may be instructive to determine whether a similar process of cultural élitism also took place in the kingdom of the Scots. In other words, did the Scottish kings and court chroniclers come to regard some, or all, of their rivals as 'barbarians'? At first glance such a view does not appear to have much to recommend it: after all, although ethnic identities were recognised and acknowledged within the twelfth-century kingdom, it is widely held that such cultural stereotypes did not appear until the later fourteenth century, when divisions between 'highlands' and 'lowlands' are generally seen as solidifying, crystallising around linguistic divisions between Gaelic speakers and English speakers.[3] There is, however, some evidence to suggest that the foundations for this division were laid earlier than is commonly thought.

To begin with, the Scottish kings and the nobility of eastern Scotland were

---

2 'Beginnings of English Imperialism,' *passim*; see also *idem*, 'Foundations of a disunited kingdom', in *Uniting the Kingdom? The making of British History*, ed. A. Grant and K.J. Stringer (London and New York, 1995), 48–64.

3 See A. Grant, *Independence and Nationhood: Scotland 1306–1469* (London, 1984), Ch 8; also Barrow, 'The Highlands in the lifetime of Robert the Bruce', in *Kingdom of the Scots*, 362–3. The growth of a literary tradition denigrating the rivals of the Scottish kings as barbarians is particularly interesting because it occurred at the time – the later twelfth century – when the use of ethnic designations was actually declining in Scottish royal acts: see *Acts of William I*, 77.

closely linked to the Anglo-French culture that had produced the stereotype of the Celt as barbarian in the first place. Indeed, the early Canmore kings posed some interesting dilemmas for English chroniclers who generally regarded the Scots as barbarians. David I, for example, could be described as 'a king not barbarous of a barbarous nation' (rex non barbarus barbarae gentis), while another writer, in an oft-quoted passage, remarked how he had 'from boyhood been polished by familiar intercourse with the English, and rubbed off all the barbarian gaucherie of Scottish manners'.[4] David might, in other words, have been a barbaric Scot, but his close affiliations with Anglo-Normans had served to civilise him. Given the close connection between Scottish kings like David I and the English culture that originated such stereotypes, as well as the territorial aggrandisement of those kings, it may be possible to detect in the twelfth century a process whereby the Scottish kings and court came to regard their opponents, and especially the peoples on the margins of the Scottish kingdom, as barbarians. This is particularly noticeable where the Gallovidians and inhabitants of Argyll and the Isles are concerned.

Walter Daniel, in his life of the English Cistercian abbot and intellectual Ailred of Rievaulx (c. 1170), remarked of Galloway that 'It is a wild country where the inhabitants are like beasts, and is altogether barbarous'.[5] The infamous stereotype of the Gallovidians as barbarians arose in the 1140s, propagated by northern English writers in response to the savagery with which the Scottish army, and especially its Gallovidian contingents, behaved during the invasion of England in 1138. Richard of Hexham (to cite one example of many) described the treatment of war captives by the Gallovidians: 'And then these bestial men, who regard as nothing adultery and incest and the other crimes, after they were weary of abusing these most hapless creatures often in the manner of brute beasts, either made them their slaves or sold them to other barbarians for cows'.[6] But while such vituperative language is fairly common among English chroniclers (as might be expected), it is also to be found in sources with a Scottish provenance, some of which may reflect attitudes current within court circles. Unquestionably the best example of this is a curious text known as the *Roman de Fergus*, an Arthurian romance set in Scotland and composed in the early thirteenth century. The hero, Fergus, who is modelled on the historical Fergus of Galloway, is portrayed as a simpleton and a buffoon, unfamiliar with the civilised behaviour of King Arthur's court. His clothes are rustic, his accoutrements ugly: 'It is plain to his host that he is a simpleton', says

---

4 William of Newburgh, *Historia Rerum Anglicarum*, in *Chron Stephen*, i, 72; William of Malmesbury, ed. Mynors *et al*, i, 727 [Bk. v, 400]

5 *Vita Aelredi*, 45: 'Est autem terra illa fera et homines bestiales et barbarum omne quod gignit'.

6 Richard of Hexham, in *Chron Stephen*, iii, 156. See Brooke, *Wild Men and Holy Places*, 95–9 on the origins and evolution of the stereotype.

the author; elsewhere, as Fergus seeks accommodation at Carlisle, 'with his lance erect he goes up and down the streets like an idiot'.[7] D.D.R. Owen has made a convincing argument that the author of the *Roman*, known only as Guillaume le Clerc, was in fact William Malveisin (d. 1238), a clerk who was prominent in royal service as chancellor for William the Lion and who became bishop of Glasgow in 1199 and of St Andrews in 1202.[8] Although the *Roman* is regarded, at least in part, as a parody of chivalric romance, the views expressed in the text no doubt '[echo] a widespread prejudice against the unruly Gallovidians',[9] and it is difficult to believe that such attitudes were not shared by the court, particularly given Malveisin's status as a courtier. Certainly prejudices against the inhabitants of Galloway were remarkably long-lived: even as late as the second half of the fourteenth century, Archibald Douglas (Archibald 'the Grim', d. 1400), who acquired the Lordship of Galloway in 1358, adopted a motif of two 'wild men' of Galloway to support the Douglas arms, an interesting visual representation of a literary theme that was by then some two centuries old.[10]

The Gallovidians were not unique among the inhabitants of Scotland in being characterised as barbarians. Ailred of Rievaulx, in his famous eulogy for David I, hailed David as a conqueror, remarking upon how he 'had subdued to himself so many barbarous tribes [barbaras naciones] . . . with little effort had triumphed over the men of Moray and of the Isles'.[11] Clearly for Ailred, then, the inhabitants of Moray and the Isles, like the Gallovidians, were also barbarians.[12] Significantly, however, Ailred, like William Malveisin, possessed especially strong connections to the Scottish kings. He had, in fact, been raised at David's court and may have spent as many as ten years there before joining the Cistercian order in about 1134. Even after entering Rievaulx abbey Ailred maintained his links to Scotland, and he returned for several subsequent visitations to Scottish daughter-houses of Rievaulx. Ailred was also a lifelong friend of David's son, Earl Henry.[13] Ailred's prejudices against the Scots have often, and correctly, been viewed within the broader framework of the northern

7 Guillaume le Clerc, *Fergus of Galloway: Knight of King Arthur*, trans., with introduction and notes, by D.D.R. Owen (London, 1991), 15, 19.
8 See *Fergus of Galloway*, Appendix B, 162–9, and *William the Lion*, Ch. 6, *passim*; on Malveisin's career, see also *Acts of William I*, 30–1, and *passim*.
9 Owen, *William the Lion*, 131.
10 M. Brown, *The Black Douglases: War and Lordship in Late Medieval Scotland 1300–1455* (East Linton, 1998), 63–4 and plate 6.
11 *SAEC*, 230 n.1; Bower, *Scotichronicon* iii, 154–5.
12 See J.P.B. Bulloch, 'The Mind of Aelred: Race and Class', *Scottish Church History Society Records* xiii (1959), 64–72, and especially 71–2.
13 See *Vita Aelredi* xxxix-xli, 2, and also F.M. Powicke, 'The Dispensator of King David I', *SHR* xxiii (1926), 34–41, and Bulloch, 'Mind of Aelred', 64–6, 69–70.

English historiographical traditions of his age, and were no doubt informed by those same traditions. Yet, considering his strong links with kings of Scots and the cultural affiliations that he shared with those rulers, the possibility remains that Ailred's outlook toward the inhabitants of the remoter regions of Scotland echoes, in some degree, that of the contemporary Scottish court. Whether that is the case or not, similar views on the Argyllsmen are evident in the *Carmen de Morte Sumerledi*, which described Somerled's invasion of the Scottish mainland in 1164 and his eventual demise. The author, a clerk of Glasgow known as William, vilified Somerled as 'hate-filled' and 'foul with treachery, the cruellest of foes', while his Argyllsmen were portrayed as barbarians: 'the gentle, menaced by barbarous hands [manus barbara], were overwhelmed'.[14] Interestingly, Somerled also made an appearance in the *Roman de Fergus* as Soumillet, the peasant father of the hero, Fergus. Though he resided in a 'dwelling splendidly situated on a great rock, encircled by clay and wattle walls', and was married to a woman of noble status, his behaviour was nevertheless boorish, and he could only provide his son with rusty armour and weapons when Fergus decided to set off and join King Arthur's court.[15] It is surely ironic – and the irony can hardly have been lost on the audience – that the mighty Somerled of Argyll, described in Irish annals as 'king of the Hebrides and Kintyre', should be reduced in the *Roman* to the status of an ignorant and unsophisticated peasant. The treatment of Somerled at the hands of writers in the heartland of the Scottish kingdom raises the intriguing possibility that, as one of the most formidable foes of the Scottish kings in the twelfth and thirteenth centuries, he was subjected to a smear campaign designed to discredit him and possibly his kindred within a generation or two after his death.

Oddly, it is more difficult to discern a similar degree of vilification directed against the reputation of those most implacable foes of the Canmore kings, the MacWilliams, although it has also to be admitted that the Scottish sources are particularly laconic where they are concerned – a fact in itself which may be significant. Nevertheless, it is possible to detect an attitude of hostility toward them, even if it does not match the venom reserved for the Gallovidians and the Argyllsmen. It seems clear, for instance, that writers of the next generation sought to portray the progenitor of the MacWilliams, Duncan II, as illegitimate, no doubt in an attempt to solidify the position of the sons of Malcolm III and Margaret. Beyond this, however, the writings of the English chronicler Roger of Howden, our most important source for Donald MacWilliam, also reveal something of the attitudes of the Scottish kings and court toward their rivals. It has been observed elsewhere in this book that Howden was hardly sympa-

14 'Carmen de Morte Sumerledi', in Symeon of Durham, *Symeonis Monachi Opera Omnia* ii, 386–7; trans. Clancy, *Triumph Tree*, 212.
15 *Fergus of Galloway*, 6–9.

thetic to MacWilliam; he concluded his narration of Donald MacWilliam's demise with the pointed remark that 'because of the evils he had wrought neither grief nor lamentation, neither even any sorrow was caused by his death'. But what is particularly significant about this is that not only was the English chronicler relying upon a Scottish informant for information on the MacWilliams, but that Howden himself was well acquainted with court circles, having acted as an envoy to the Scottish king on several occasions in the 1170s, 1180s, and 1190s.[16] Howden's account of Donald MacWilliam, and especially the vitriolic comments that the chronicler reserved for MacWilliam, almost certainly preserve for us something of the attitude of the Scottish king and court; in undertaking an examination of Howden's attitudes towards the Celtic neighbours of the English, Gillingham has observed that 'Only the Scottish court's western and northern enemies continued to evoke the hostile tone with which he [Roger of Howden] had once written about Scots in general'.[17]

Perhaps most significant of all where the attitudes of the Scottish kings and court to their MacWilliam foes is concerned is the simple scarcity of Scottish material on the topic. Scottish texts and documents have very little to say about the MacWilliams, so that the historian is forced to rely on English chronicles and annals for most of what is known about them. Indeed, were it not for English sources (as well as Bower's fifteenth-century *Scotichronicon*), next to nothing would be known of the activities of Guthred MacWilliam in 1211–12. The Melrose chronicler, for example, remarked merely that 'the king of Scotland left behind him the lifeless corpses of many men, when he pursued the son of MacWilliam, Guthred'.[18] The profound silence of the Scottish sources about the MacWilliams may not be a mere coincidence after all, but rather a concerted effort to wipe these determined foes of the Scottish kings from the pages of history altogether. If so, it must be conceded that it very nearly succeeded.

To date, few scholars have entertained the notion that the cultural stereotyping applied by the English to their Celtic neighbours from the middle of the twelfth century may have percolated into Scotland, where harmony, concord, partnership and cooperation are considered the dominant paradigms for ethnic relations. Nevertheless, considering that much of the contempt directed towards the likes of Fergus and Somerled originated in sources that were closely connected, in one way or another, with the Scottish kings and court, it is difficult to avoid the conclusion that a deliberate policy of denigration and

---

16 Gillingham, 'Travels of Roger of Howden', 156–161.

17 'Travels of Roger of Howden', 162.

18 *Chron Melrose*, 56 (1211); *ES* ii, 389. The Holyrood chronicle breaks off in 1187/89 with subsequent entries relating to the events of 1266 and the death of Alexander III.

vilification of the inhabitants of Galloway and Argyll and their rulers evolved, while it is certainly possible to detect something of the attitudes prevalent at court toward other foes like the MacWilliams. As one scholar, writing of the attitudes of Ailred of Rievaulx and his contemporary Scottish ecclesiastics, has summed it up, 'for the older Celtic inhabitants [of Scotland] they had all the dislike and contempt of a conquering race . . .'[19] The analogy is apt: since violence and crude force played a larger role in the consolidation of the Canmore dynasty and the developing Scottish kingdom than is usually credited, it may well be that treating their enemies with contempt and characterising them as barbarians provided an ideology of conquest for the Canmore kings over dynastic and political rivals. Whether this is so or not, the views expressed by Scottish writers with connections to the court about the enemies of the kings provide a valuable barometer of the degree of insecurity on the part of the Scottish kings in the mid- to late twelfth century. For the line of Malcolm III and Margaret it may not have been enough simply to vanquish their rivals; it may also have been necessary to discredit, denigrate, and vilify many of them as barbarians in the process.

19 Bulloch, 'Mind of Aelred', 72; see also, more recently, H. Leyser, 'Cultural Affinities', in *The Twelfth and Thirteenth Centuries*, 174–6.

BATTLEFIELD SCOTLAND:
Scottish Royal Armies on Campaign in Scotland

Date and Location	Versus	Main Authority/ies
1078 Moray (?)	Máelsnechtai	ASC
1116 'Stockfurd' in Ross	Men of Moray	Wyntoun/ Bower
1124 'two wars,' (?) (*)	Malcolm	Orderic
1130 Stracathro/Moray	Angus and Malcolm	Orderic/ Irish Annals
1134 unknown location(s)	Malcolm	Ailred
1140s Cumbria	Wimund	Newburgh
1153–60 western seaboard, Galloway (*)	Somerled/ sons of Malcolm	Holyrood
1160–61 Galloway	Fergus	Holyrood/Melrose
1163 Moray (?)	Men of Moray	Gesta Annalia (GA)
1164 Clyde/Renfrew (+)	Somerled	Carmen/ Irish Annals
1175–85 Galloway	Gilbert/ Roland	Howden
1179 Ross	Donald MacWilliam (?)	Melrose/GA
1187 Moray; Ross (Mam Garvia)	Donald MacWilliam	Howden/Holyrood/ Melrose
1196 Moray; Caithness (Thurso)	Harald Maddadsson	Howden/Orkneyinga Saga (OS)
1197 Moray; Caithness	Harald Maddadsson	Howden/OS
1201/02 Caithness	Harald Maddadsson	Howden/OS
1211/12 Ross	Guthred MacWilliam	Bower
1221 Inverness	Donald MacNeil	APS
1221/22 Argyll, Isles	MacSorleys	GA
1222 Caithness	John, earl of Orkney	Melrose/OS
1228 Moray(?); Inverness	Gillescop MacWilliam	Bower
1230 (?) (*)	MacWilliams (?)	Lanercost Chronicle
1235 Galloway; Glenluce, Tongland	Thomas of Galloway	Melrose/Paris
1249 Argyll; Kerrera	Ewen of Argyll	Hakon's Saga/Paris
1262 Skye	none specified	Hakon's Saga
1263 Largs	Norwegians/ Hebrideans	Hakon's Saga
1264 Caithness	Dugald MacRuairi	Hakon's Saga

Notes: (?) denotes uncertainty about the locality or individual involved. (*): there is no firm evidence for royal armies campaigning during the course of these insurrections, although this seems at least probable. (+): on the available evidence it does not appear that a royal army was involved in the defeat of Somerled in 1164.

THE FATES OF THE SCOTTISH KINGS' RIVALS

Deaths in Battle
1057 Macbeth
1058 Lulach
1130 Angus of Moray
1164 Somerled of Argyll
1187 Donald MacWilliam
1215 Donald Bàn MacWilliam and Kenneth MacHeth

Executions
1186 nephew of Adam son of Donald
1212 Guthred MacWilliam
1230 infant MacWilliam

Mutilations
c. 1148 Wimund
1174 Uhtred son of Fergus
1201/02 Thorfinn son of Harald Maddadsson

Imprisonments
1134–57 Malcolm 'MacHeth'
1156–? Donald MacHeth
1196–1202 Thorfinn son of Harald Maddadsson
1235–96 Thomas son of Alan of Galloway

Forced Monastic Retirements
c. 1078 Máelsnechtai (?)
c. 1148 Wimund
1161 Fergus of Galloway

Burnings Alive
1186 Adam son of Donald's warband

Other
1154 Arthur slain in judicial combat
1186 Adam son of Donald seized at Coupar Angus
1229 Gillescop MacWilliam[1]

---

1 Whether Gillescop died in battle, was betrayed, or executed is not clear from the source.

BIBLIOGRAPHY

PRIMARY SOURCES

The Acts of Malcolm IV, King of Scots, 1153–1165, ed. G. W. S. Barrow (Regesta Regum Scottorum Volume I. Edinburgh, 1960).

The Acts of Robert I, King of Scots, 1306–1329, ed. A.A.M. Duncan (Regesta Regum Scottorum Volume V. Edinburgh, 1988).

The Acts of the Parliaments of Scotland, ed. T. Thomson and C. Innes (Edinburgh, 1814–75).

The Acts of William I, King of Scots, 1165–1214, ed. G. W. S. Barrow (Regesta Regum Scottorum Volume II. Edinburgh, 1971).

The Anglo-Saxon Chronicle, ed. and trans. M. Swanton (London, 1996).

Anglo-Scottish Relations 1174–1328: Some Selected Documents, ed. E. L. G. Stones (2nd ed. Oxford, 1970).

Annals of Dunstable in *Annales Monastici,* ed. H.R. Luard (Rolls Series, London, 1864–69).

The Annals of Inisfallen (MS. Rawlinson B.503), ed. S. MacAirt (Dublin, 1951, repr. 1977).

Annals of Loch Cé, ed. and trans W. M Hennessy (Rolls Series, London, 1871).

Annals of the Kingdom of Ireland by the Four Masters, ed. J. O'Donovan (Dublin, 1851).

Annals of the Reigns of Malcolm and William, Kings of Scotland AD 1153–1214, ed. Sir A.C. Lawrie (Glasgow, 1910).

Annales Sancti Edmundi, in Memorials of St Edmund's Abbey, ed. T. Arnold (Rolls Series, London, 1890–96).

Annals of Tigernach, ed. W. Stokes, in *Revue Celtique,* xvi-xviii (1895–7).

The Annals of Ulster, ed. and trans W.M Hennessy and B. McCarthy (Dublin, 1887–1901).

The Annals of Ulster (to AD 1131), ed. S. MacAirt and G. MacNiocaill (Dublin, 1983).

BARBOUR, J., *The Bruce,* trans. A.A.M. Duncan (Edinburgh, 1997).

The Black Book of Carmarthen, trans. M. Pennar (Lampeter, 1989).

Book of the Dean of Lismore: English and Gaelic Selections, ed. W. F. Skene (Edinburgh, 1862).

BOWER, W., *Scotichronicon,* gen. ed. D. E. R. Watt (Aberdeen, 1987–97).

Brut Y Tywysogyon or The Chronicle of the Princes. Red Book of Hergest Version, ed. T. Jones (Cardiff, 1955).

Calendar of Documents Relating to Scotland Preserved in Her Majesty's Public Record Office, London, ed. J. Bain *et al* (Edinburgh, 1881–1986).

CAMBRENSIS, GIRALDUS [GERALD OF WALES], *Expugnatio Hibernica: The Conquest of Ireland,* ed. and trans. A.B. Scott and F.X. Martin (Dublin, 1978).

——, *The Journey Through Wales/ The Description of Wales,* trans. L. Thorpe (London, 1978).

'Carmen de Morte Sumerledi,' in Symeon of Durham, *Symeonis Monachi Opera Omnia*, ed. T. Arnold (Rolls Series London, 1882–85).

Charters, Bulls, and Other Documents Relating to the Abbey of Inchaffray, ed. W. A. Lindsay *et al* (Edinburgh, 1908).

The Charters of David I: The Written Acts of David I King of Scots 1124–53 and his son Henry Earl of Northumberland 1139–52, ed. G.W.S Barrow (Woodbridge, 1999).

Chronica Pontificum Ecclesiae Eboracensis in *The Historians of the Church of York*.

Chronicle of the Kings of Mann, trans. G. Broderick (Edinburgh, 1973).

Chronicle of Man and the Sudreys, ed. P. A. Munch and Rev. Dr Goss (Douglas, 1874).

The Chronicle of Melrose from the Cottonian Manuscript, Faustina B. IX in the British Museum. A Complete and Full Size Facsimile in Collotype, with an Introduction by A. O. Anderson and M. O. Anderson and an index by W. C. Dickinson (London, 1936).

Chronicles of the Picts and Scots, ed. W. F. Skene (Edinburgh, 1867).

Chronicles of the Reigns of Stephen, Henry II and Richard I, ed. R. Howlett (Rolls Series, London, 1884–9).

Chronicon de Lanercost, ed. J. Stevenson (Edinburgh, 1839).

Cronica Regum Mannie & Insularum. Chronicles of the Kings of Man and the Isles BL Cotton Julius Avii, transcribed, translated with an introduction by G. Broderick (Douglas, 1991).

DANIELIS, W., *Vita Aelredi Abbatis Rievall'*, ed. and trans. F. Powicke (London, 1950).

DICETO, RALPH DE, *The Historical Works of Master Ralph de Diceto, dean of London*, ed. W. Stubbs (Rolls Series, London, 1876).

Early Scottish Charters prior to A.D. 1153, ed. Sir A.C. Lawrie (Glasgow, 1905).

Early Sources of Scottish History, A.D. 500–1286, ed. A.O. Anderson (London, 1922; repr. Stamford, 1990).

The Ecclesiastical History of Orderic Vitalis, ed. and trans. M. Chibnall (Oxford, 1968–80).

FANTOSME, J., *Jordan Fantosme's Chronicle*, ed. with introduction, translation and notes by R.C. Johnston (Oxford, 1981).

FORDUN, JOHN OF, *Johannis de Fordun Chronica Gentis Scotorum*, ed. W.F. Skene (Edinburgh, 1871–2).

The four ancient books of Wales, containing the Cymric poems attributed to the bards of the sixth century, ed. W. F. Skene (Edinburgh, 1868).

The Gaelic Notes in the Book of Deer, ed. and trans. K. Jackson (Cambridge, 1972).

GUILLAUME LE CLERC, *Fergus of Galloway: Knight of King Arthur*, trans., with intro and notes by D.D.R. Owen (London, 1991).

HEXHAM, RICHARD OF, *De Gestis Regis Stephani*, in *Chronicles of the Reigns of Stephen, Henry II, and Richard I*.

Highland Papers, ed. J.R.N. Macphail (Edinburgh, 1914–34).

Historians of the Church of York and Its Archbishops, ed. J. Raine (Rolls Series, London, 1879–94).

The Historical Collections of Walter of Coventry ed. W. Stubbs (London, 1872–1873).

Historical Manuscripts Commission: Tenth Report, Appendix, Part IV. The Manuscripts of the Earl of Westmorland, Captain Stewart, Lord Stafford, Lord Muncaster, and Others (London, 1885).

HOWDEN, R., *Gesta Regis Henrici Secundi Benedicti Abbatis*, ed. W. Stubbs (Rolls Series, London, 1867).

——, *Chronica Magistri Rogeri de Houedene*, ed. T. Arnold (Rolls Series, London, 1868–71).

Icelandic Sagas and other historical documents relating to the settlements and descents of the Northmen on the British Isles, ed. G. Vigfusson and G.W. Dasent (Rolls Series, London, 1887–94; repr. 1964).

Liber S. Marie de Melros *(Edinburgh, 1837).*

MALMESBURY, WILLIAM OF, *Gesta Regum Anglorum. The History of the English Kings*, ed. and trans. R.A.B. Mynors, R.M. Thomson and M. Winterbottom (Oxford, 1998).

A Mediaeval Prince of Wales: The Life of Gruffudd ap Cynan, ed. and trans. D. Simon Evans (Lampeter, 1990).

MONMOUTH, GEOFFREY OF, *History of the Kings of Britain*, trans. L. Thorpe (Harmondsworth, 1966).

Morkinskinna: The Earliest Icelandic Chronicle of the Norwegian Kings (1030–1157), trans. T.M. Anderson and K.E. Gade (Ithaca and London, 2000).

NEWBURGH, WILLIAM OF, Historia Rerum Anglicarum, in *Chronicles of the Reigns of Stephen, Henry II, and Richard I.*

——, *The History of William of Newburgh*, in *The Church Historians of England* iv/1 trans. J. Stevenson (London, 1856).

——, *The History of English Affairs*, trans. P.G. Walsh and M.J. Kennedy (Warminster, 1988).

Orkneyinga Saga. The History of the Earls of Orkney, trans H. Pálsson and P. Edwards (Harmondsworth, 1978).

Orkneyinga Saga, trans. J.A. Hjaltalin and G. Gordie, ed. with notes and an intro. by J. Anderson (Edinburgh, 1873; repr. 1973).

PARIS, M., *Chronica Majora*, ed. H.R Luard (Rolls Series, London, 1872–83).

'The Prophecy of Berchan', ed. A.O. Anderson in *Zeitschrift fur Celtische Philologie* xviii (1930).

The Prophecy of Berchán: Irish and Scottish High-Kings of the Early Middle Ages, ed. and trans. B.T. Hudson (Westport, Conn., and London, 1996).

Regiam Majestatem and Quoniam Attachiamenta, ed. Lord Cooper (Edinburgh, 1947).

Register of the Priory of St. Bees, ed. J. Wilson (Durham and London, 1915).

Registrum Magni Sigilli Regum Scotorum, ed. J.M Thomson *et al* (Edinburgh, *1882– 1912).*

Registrum Monasterii de Passelet, ed. C. Innes (Edinburgh, 1832).

RIEVAULX, AILRED OF, *Relatio De Standardo*, in *Chronicles of the Reigns of Stephen, Henry II, and Richard I.*

The Saga of the Icelanders in *Sturlunga Saga*, trans. J.H. McGrew, intro. R.G. Thomas (New York, 1970–74).

Scottish Annals from English Chroniclers, A.D. 500–1286, trans. A. O. Anderson (London, 1908).

A Scottish Chronicle known as the Chronicle of Holyrood, ed. and trans. M. O. Anderson (Edinburgh, 1938).

Scottish Historical Documents, trans. G. Donaldson (Edinburgh, 1970; repr. Glasgow, n.d.).

SCOTUS, M., *Mariani Scotti Chronicon,* ed. G. Waitz, *in Monumenta Germaniae Historica, Scriptores V* (Hannover, 1844).

TORIGNI, ROBERT OF, *Chronica Roberti de Torigneio,* in *Chronicles of the Reigns of Stephen, Henry II, and Richard I.*

The Triumph Tree: Scotland's Earliest Poetry AD 550–1350 ed. and trans. T.O. Clancy (Edinburgh, 1998).

WORCESTER, JOHN OF, in FLORENCE of WORCESTER, *Chronicon ex chronicis,* ed. B. Thorpe (London, 1848–49).

WYNTOUN, A., *Orygynale Cronykle of Scotland,* ed. D. Laing (Edinburgh, 1872).

SECONDARY SOURCES

AITCHISON, N., *MacBeth: Man and Myth* (Stroud, 1999).

ANDERSON, A.O., 'Wimund, Bishop and Pretender,' *SHR* vii (1910).

APPLEBY, J. C., and DALTON, P. (eds.), *Government, Religion and Society in Northern England 1100–1700* (Stroud, 1997).

ASHLEY, A., 'Odo, Elect of Whithern, 1235', *TDGNHAS* 3rd ser xxxvii (1958–59).

BALDWIN, J. (ed.), *Caithness: A Cultural Crossroads* (Edinburgh, 1982).

—— (ed.), *Firthlands of Ross and Sutherland* (Edinburgh, 1986).

BANNERMAN, J., 'MacDuff of Fife', in Grant and Stringer, *Medieval Scotland.*

BARBER, R., *The Knight and Chivalry* (Woodbridge, 1970).

BARLOW, F., *William Rufus* (London, 1983).

BARRELL, A. D. M., *Medieval Scotland* (Cambridge, 2000).

BARROW, G. W. S., *Feudal Britain* (London, 1956).

——, *The Kingdom of the Scots* (London, 1973).

——, 'The beginnings of military feudalism,' in *Kingdom of the Scots.*

——, 'The royal house and the religious orders,' in *Kingdom of the Scots.*

——, 'The earliest Stewarts and their lands,' in *Kingdom of the Scots.*

——, 'The Highlands in the lifetime of Robert the Bruce,' in *Kingdom of the Scots.*

—— (ed.), *The Scottish Tradition,* (Edinburgh, 1974).

——, 'Macbeth and Other Mormaers of Moray' in MacLean, *The Book Of Inverness and District.*

——, 'The pattern of lordship and feudal settlement in Cumbria,' *JMH* i (1975).

——, 'Some Problems in Twelfth-and Thirteenth-Century Scottish History – A Genealogical Approach', *Scottish Genealogist* xxv (1978).

——, *The Anglo-Norman Era in Scottish History* (Oxford, 1980).

——, *Kingship and Unity: Scotland 1000–1306* (London, 1981, repr. Edinburgh, 1989).

——, 'The Sources for the History of the Highlands in the Middle Ages', in MacLean, *The Middle Ages in the Highlands.*

——, *David I of Scotland (1124–1153): The Balance of new and old* (Reading, 1985), repr. in *Scotland and Its Neighbours..*

——, *Robert Bruce and the Community of the Realm of Scotland,* 3rd ed. (Edinburgh, 1988).

——, 'Badenoch and Strathspey, 1130–1312. 1: Secular and Political,' *Northern Scotland* viii (1988).

——, 'The Army of Alexander III's Scotland', in Reid, *Scotland in the Reign of Alexander III.*

——, *Scotland and Its Neighbours in the Middle Ages* (London and Rio Grande, 1992).

——, 'The Reign of William the Lion,' in *Scotland and Its Neighbours.*

BARRETT, J. *et al,* 'What Was the Viking Age and When did it Happen? A View From Orkney,' *Norwegian Archaeological Review* xxxiii (2000).

BARRY, T. B., FRAME, R., and SIMMS, K. (eds.), *Colony and Frontier: Essays Presented to J.F.Lydon* (London and Rio Grande, 1995).

BARTLETT, R., *Trial by Fire and Water: The Medieval Judicial Ordeal* (Oxford, 1986).

——, *The Making of Europe: Conquest, Colonization and Cultural Change, 950–1350* (London and Princeton, 1993).

——, *England Under the Norman and Angevin Kings 1075–1225* (Oxford, 2000).

BARTLETT, T., and JEFFERY, K., *A Military History of Ireland* (Cambridge, 1996).

BATES, D., 'Kingship, government and political life to c. 1160', in Harvey, *The Twelfth and Thirteenth Centuries.*

BATEY, C., JESCH, J., and MORRIS, C. (eds)., *The Viking Age in Orkney, Caithness and the North Atlantic* (Edinburgh, 1995).

BELLAMY, J., *Crime and Public Order in England in the Later Middle Ages* (London and Toronto, 1973).

BLACK, G.F., *The Surnames of Scotland. Their Origin, Meaning and History* (New York, 1946).

BOARDMAN, S. and ROSS, A. (eds.), *The exercise of power in Medieval Scotland, 1200–1500* (Dublin, forthcoming).

BOWEN, E. G., *Saints, Seaways and Settlements* (Cardiff, 1969).

——, *Britain and the Western Seaways* (London, 1972).

BRADBURY, J., *The Medieval Siege* (Woodbridge, 1992).

——,'Battles in England and Normandy, 1066–1154', in Strickland, *Anglo-Norman Warfare.*

BRADY, C., *Worsted in the Game: Losers in Irish History* (Dublin 1989)

BREMNER, R. L., *The Norsemen in Alban* (Glasgow, 1923).

BROOKE, D., 'Fergus of Galloway: Miscellaneous Notes for a Revised Portrait,' *TDGNHAS* 3rd ser. lxvi [Hoddom Volume 2] (1991).

——, *Fergus the King* (The Medieval Lords of Galloway 1. Whithorn, 1991).

——, *Wild Men and Holy Places: St Ninian, Whithorn, and the Medieval Realm of Galloway* (Edinburgh, 1994).

BROTHERSTONE, T., and DITCHBURN, D. (eds.), *Freedom and Authority. Historical and Historiographical Essays Presented to Grant G. Simpson* (East Linton, 2000).

BROUN, D., *The Charters of Gaelic Scotland and Ireland in the Early and Central Middle Ages* (Quiggin Pamphlets on the Sources of Mediaeval Gaelic History 2. Cambridge, 1995).

—— , 'A New Look at *Gesta Annalia* Attributed to John of Fordun', in Crawford, *Church, Chronicle and Learning in Medieval and Early Renaissance Scotland.*

BROWN, E. A. R., 'The Tyranny of a Construct: Feudalism and the Historians of Medieval Europe', *American Historical Review* lxxix (1974).

BROWN, M., *The Black Douglases. War and Lordship in Late Medieval Scotland 1300–1455* (East Linton, 1998).

BUCHANAN, G., *History of Scotland*, trans. J. Aikman (Glasgow, 1827).

BULLOCH, J.P.B., 'The Mind of Aelred: Race and Class,' *Scottish Church History Society Records* xiii (1959).

BYOCK, J., *Viking Age Iceland* (London, 2001).

CANT, R.G., 'The Medieval Church in the North: Contrasting Influences in the Dioceses of Ross and Caithness,' in Baldwin, *Firthlands of Ross and Sutherland.*

CASSON, T.E., 'Wymund,' *Transactions of the Cumberland and Westmorland Antiquarian and Archaeological Society*, new series, xxxix (1939).

CHARLES-EDWARDS, T. M., *Early Irish and Welsh Kinship* (Oxford, 1993).

CHIBNALL, M., *The World of Orderic Vitalis* (Oxford, 1984).

CHURCH, S. D. (ed.), *King John: New Interpretations* (Woodbridge, 1999).

CLANCY, T. O., 'A Gaelic polemic quatrain from the reign of Alexander I', *Scottish Gaelic Studies* xx (2000).

CORNER, D., '*The Gesta Regis Henrici Secundi* and *Chronica* of Roger, Parson of Howden', *Bulletin of the Institute for Historical Research* lvi (1983).

COSGROVE, A. (ed.), *New History of Ireland Volume II: Medieval Ireland 1169–1534* (Oxford, 1987).

COSS, P., *The Knight in Medieval England 1000–1400* (Stroud, 1993).

COUTTS, J., *The Anglo-Norman Peaceful Invasion of Scotland 1057–1200. Origin of Great Scottish Families* (Edinburgh, 1922).

COWAN, E. J., 'Caithness in the Sagas', in Baldwin, *Caithness: A Cultural Crossroads.*

——, 'Norwegian Sunset-Scottish Dawn: Hakon IV and Alexander III', in Reid, *Scotland in the Reign of Alexander III.*

——, 'The Historical MacBeth',in Sellar, *Moray: Province and People.*

——, 'The Invention of Celtic Scotland' in Cowan and McDonald, *Alba.*

——, and McDONALD, R. A. (eds.), *Alba: Celtic Scotland in the Middle Ages* (East Linton, 2000).

COWAN, I. B. and EASSON, D. E. (eds.), *Medieval Religious Houses Scotland* 2nd ed. (London, 1976).

CRAWFORD, B., 'Peter's Pence in Scotland' in Barrow, *The Scottish Tradition.*

——, 'The Earldom of Caithness and the Kingdom of Scotland, 1150–1266', in Stringer, *Essays on the Nobility of Medieval Scotland.*

——, *Scandinavian Scotland* (Leicester, 1987).

——,(ed.), St *Magnus Cathedral and Orkney's Twelfth-Century Renaissance* Aberdeen, 1988).

——, *Earl & Mormaer: Norse-Pictish relationships in Northern Scotland* (Rosemarkie, 1995).

——, 'Norse Earls and Scottish Bishops in Caithness: A Clash of Cultures', in Batey, Jesch, and Morris, *The Viking Age in Orkney, Caithness and the North Atlantic.*

——,(ed.), *Church, Chronicle and Learning in Medieval and Early Renaissance Scotland* (Edinburgh, 1999).

CROUCH, D., *The Image of Aristocracy in Britain 1000–1300* (London and New York, 1992).

CUNLIFFE, B., *Facing the Ocean: The Atlantic and Its Peoples* (Oxford, 2001).

DALTON, P., *Conquest, Anarchy and Lordship: Yorkshire 1066–1154* (Cambridge, 1994).

DAVIES, R. R., *The Age of Conquest: Wales 1063–1415* (Oxford, 1987).

——(ed.), *The British Isles, 1100–1500: Comparisons, Contrasts and Connections* (Edinburgh, 1988).

——, *Domination and Conquest: The experience of Ireland, Scotland and Wales 1100–1300* (Cambridge, 1990).

——, 'The English State and the 'Celtic' Peoples 1100–1400,' *Journal of Historical Sociology* vi (1993).

——, *The First English Empire: Power and Identities in the British Isles 1093–1343* (Oxford, 2000).

DICKINSON, W. C., *Scotland from the Earliest Times to 1603* 3rd ed., revised and edited by A.A.M. Duncan (Oxford, 1977).

DOLLEY, M., *Anglo-Norman Ireland c.1000–1318* (Dublin, 1972).

DONALDSON, G., *Scottish Kings* (London, 1967, repr. New York, 1992).

——, *A Northern Commonwealth: Scotland and Norway* (Edinburgh, 1990).

DOUBLEDAY, H. A. (ed.), *Victoria History of the County of Cumberland* (London, 1901, repr. 1968).

DUFFY, S., 'The Bruce Brothers and the Irish Sea World', *Cambridge Medieval Celtic Studies* xxi (1991).

——, 'Irishmen and Islesmen in the Kingdoms of Dublin and Man', *Eriu* xliii (1992).

——, 'The First Ulster Plantation: John de Courcy and the Men of Cumbria', in Barry, Frame and Simms, *Colony and Frontier: Essays Presented to J.F. Lydon.*

——, 'Ostmen, Irish and Welsh in the Eleventh Century', *Pertita* ix (1995).

——, *Ireland in the Middle Ages* (Dublin, 1997).

——, 'Ireland and Scotland 1014–1169: contacts and caveats,' in *Seanchas. Studies in Early and Medieval Irish Archaeology, History and Literature in Honour of Francis J. Byrne.*

DUNCAN, A. A. M., 'The Earliest Scottish Charters', *SHR* xxxvii (1958).

——, *Scotland: The Making of the Kingdom* (Edinburgh, 1975).

——, 'The Heirs of Canmore,' *Sunday Mail Story of Scotland* i/4 (Glasgow 1988).

——, 'Roger of Howden and Scotland 1187–1201,' in Crawford, *Church, Chronicle and Learning in Medieval and Early Renaissance Scotland.*

——, 'John King of England and the Kings of Scots', in Church, *King John: New Interpretations.*

——, 'Sources and uses of the Chronicle of Melrose, 1165–1297', in Taylor, *Kings, clerics and chroniclers in Scotland..*

——, *The Kingship of the Scots, 842–1292: Succession and Independence* (Edinburgh, 2002).

——, and BROWN, A. L., 'Argyll and the Isles in the earlier Middle Ages', *PSAS* xc (1956–57).

ELLSWORTH, R., and ELLIS, P. B., *The Book of Deer* (London, 1994).

FLANAGAN, M. T., 'Irish and Anglo-Norman warfare in twelfth-century Ireland', in Bartlett and Jeffery, *A Military History of Ireland.*

FOOTE. P., 'Observations on *Orkneyinga Saga*' in Crawford, *St Magnus Cathedral and Orkney's Twelfth-Century Renaissance.*

FORSYTHE, K. (ed.), *Studies in the Book of Deer* (Dublin, forthcoming).

FRAME, R., *Colonial Ireland 1169–1369* (Dublin, 1981).

——, *The Political Development of the British Isles, 1000–1400* (Oxford, 1990).

——, 'Conquest and Settlement', in Harvey, *The Twelfth and Thirteenth Centuries.*

FRANCE, J., *Western Warfare in the Age of the Crusades 1000–1300* (Ithaca, 1999).

FRASER, W. *The Sutherland Book* (Edinburgh, 1892).

GIFFARD, J., *Dumfries and Galloway: The Buildings of Scotland* (London 1996).

GILLINGHAM, J., 'The Beginnings of English Imperialism', *Journal of Historical Sociology* v (1992).

——, 'Foundations of a disunited kingdom,' in Grant and Stringer, *Uniting the Kingdom?*

——, 'The Travels of Roger of Howden and his views of the Irish, Scots, and Welsh,' *Anglo-Norman Studies* xx (1997).

——, 'Killing and mutilating political enemies in the British Isles from the late twelfth to the early fourteenth century: a comparative study', in Smith, *Britain and Ireland.*

——, *The English in the Twelfth Century. Imperialism, National Identity, and Political Values* (Woodbridge, 2000).

——, '1066 and the Introduction of Chivalry into England,' in Gillingham, *The English in the Twelfth Century.*

——, 'The Introduction of Knight Service into England,' in Gillingham, *The English in the Twelfth Century.*

GRANSDEN, A., *Historical Writing in England, c.550 to c.1307* (London, 1974).

GRANT, A., *Independence and Nationhood: Scotland 1306–1469* (London, 1984).

——, 'Scotland's "Celtic Fringe" in the Late Middle Ages: The MacDonald Lords of the Isles and the Kingdom of Scotland', in Davies, *British Isles.*

——, 'Thanes and Thanages, from the Eleventh to Fourteenth Centuries', in Grant and Stringer, *Medieval Scotland.*

——, 'To the Medieval Foundations', *SHR* lxxiii [Special Issue: Whither Scottish History? Proceedings of the 1993 Strathclyde Conference] (1994).

——, 'The Province of Ross and the Kingdom of Alba', in *Alba.*

——, and STRINGER, K. J. (eds.), *Medieval Scotland: Crown, Lordship and Community. Essays Presented to G. W. S. Barrow* (Edinburgh, 1993).

——, and STRINGER, K.J. (eds.), *Uniting the Kingdom? The making of British History* (London and New York, 1995).

GRANT, I. F., and CHEAPE, H., *Periods in Highland History* (London, 1987).

GRAY, J., *Sutherland and Caithness in Saga-Time* (Edinburgh, 1922).

GREEN, J., 'David I and Henry I,' *SHR* lxxv (1996).

GREEVES, R., 'The Galloway Lands in Ulster', *TDGNHAS* 3rd ser. xxxvi (1957–58).

GREGORY, D., *History of the Western Highlands and Isles of Scotland* (2nd ed. Edinburgh, 1881, repr. 1975).

GRIMBLE, I., *Highland Man* (Inverness, 1980).

HALSALL, G. (ed.), *Violence and Society in the Early Medieval West* (Woodbridge, 1998).

HARVEY, B. (ed.), *The Twelfth and Thirteenth Centuries 1066–c.1280* (Oxford, 2001).

HECHTER, M., *Internal Colonialism. The Celtic Fringe in British National Development 1536–1966* (London, 1975).

HILL, P., *Whithorn & St. Ninian: The Excavation of a Monastic Town, 1984–1991* (Stroud, 1997).

HOOPER, N., 'Edgar the Aetheling: Anglo-Saxon Prince, rebel and crusader', *Anglo-Saxon England* xiv (1985).

HOPE-TAYLOR, B., 'Excavations at Mote of Urr. Interim Report, 1951 season', *TDGNHAS* 3rd ser., xxix (1950–51).

HUDSON, B. T., 'Historical Literature of Early Scotland', *Studies in Scottish Literature* xxvi (1991).

——, *Kings of Celtic Scotland* (Westport, Conn., and London, 1994).

——, 'The changing economy of the Irish Sea province', in Smith, *Britain and Ireland.*

HUGHES, K., *Early Christian Ireland: Introduction to the Sources* (Ithaca and New York, 1972).

JOHANNESSON, J., *Islendinga Saga: A History of the Old Icelandic Commonwealth* (Winnipeg, 1974).

KAPELLE, W. E. *The Norman Conquest of the North: The Region and Its Transformation 1000–1135* (London, 1979).

KEEN, M., *The Outlaws of Medieval Legend* (London and New York, revised ed. 1977, repr. New York 1989).

KIRBY, D. P., review of A. A. M. Duncan's *Making of the Kingdom*, in *English Historical Review* xci (1976) .

——, 'Moray in the Twelfth Century', in McNeill and Nicholson, *Historical Atlas of Scotland.*

LATHAM, R. E., *Revised Medieval Latin Word-List from British and Irish Sources* (London, 1965).

LEE, S. (ed.), *Dictionary of National Biography* (London, 1885–1900).

LEYSER, H., 'Cultural Affinities,' in Harvey, *The Twelfth and Thirteenth Centuries.*

LYNCH, M., *Scotland: A New History* (London, revised ed. 1992).

—— (ed.), *The Oxford Companion to Scottish History* (Oxford, 2001).

MACDONALD, C., *The History of Argyll* (Glasgow, 1950).

MACKAY, A., *The Book of Mackay* (Edinburgh, 1906).

MACKAY, R.L., *The Clan MacKay* (Wolverhampton, 1977).

MACLEAN, L. (ed.), *The Hub of the Highlands: The Book of Inverness and District* (Inverness, 1975).

—— (ed.), *The Middle Ages in the Highlands* (Inverness, 1981).

MARSDEN, J., *Somerled and the Emergence of Gaelic Scotland* (East Linton, 2000).

MAUND, K., *Ireland, Wales and England in the eleventh century* (Woodbridge, 1991).

——, *The Welsh Kings: The Medieval Rulers of Wales* (Stroud, 2000).

—— (ed.), *Gruffudd ap Cynan: A Collaborative Biography* (Woodbridge, 1996).

MAXWELL, SIR H., *History of Dumfries and Galloway* (Edinburgh and London, 1896).

McDONALD, R. A., 'Monk, Bishop, Impostor, Pretender: The Place of Wimund in Twelfth-Century Scotland', *Transactions of the Gaelic Society of Inverness* lxviii (1992–94).

——, 'Scoto-Norse Kings and the Reformed Religious Orders: Patterns of Monastic Patronage in Twelfth-Century Galloway and Argyll', *Albion* xxvii (1995).

——, 'Matrimonial politics and core-periphery interactions in twelfth- and early thirteenth-century Scotland', *JMH* xxi (1995).

——, 'Images of Hebridean Lordship in the Late Twelfth and Early Thirteenth Centuries: The Seal of Raonall MacSorley', *SHR* lxxiv (1995).

——, *The Kingdom of the Isles: Scotland's Western Seaboard c. 1100–c. 1336* (East Linton, 1997, repr. 1998, 2002).

——, 'Coming in from the margins: the descendants of Somerled and cultural accommodation in the Hebrides, 1164–1317', in Smith, *Britain and Ireland.*

——, "Treachery in the Remotest Territories of Scotland:' Northern Resistance to the Canmore Dynasty 1130–1230', *Canadian Journal of History* xxxiii (1999).

——, 'Rebels Without a Cause? The Relations of Fergus of Galloway and Somerled of Argyll with the Scottish Kings, 1153–1164,' in Cowan and McDonald, *Alba.*

——, (ed.), *History, Literature and Music in Scotland 700–1560* (Toronto, 2002).

——, 'Introduction: Medieval Scotland and the New Millennium', in *History, Literature and Music in Scotland.*

——, 'Old and New in the Far North: Ferchar Macintsaccairt and the early earls of Ross, c. 1200–1274', in Boardman and Ross, *The Exercise of power in Medieval Scotland, 1200–1500..*

McNEILL, P. AND NICHOLSON, R. (eds.), *An Historical Atlas of Scotland c. 400–c. 1600* (St. Andrews, 1975).

McNEILL, P., and MACQUEEN, H. (eds.), *Atlas of Scottish History to 1707* (Edinburgh, 1996).

MEGAW, B., 'The Barony of St Trinian's in the Isle of Man', *TDGNHAS*, 3rd ser. xxvii (1948–49).

MITCHELL, D., *A popular History of the Highlands and Gaelic Scotland from the Earliest Times to the Close of the 'Forty-Five* (Paisley, 1900).

M'KERLIE, P. H., *History of the Lands and their Owners in Galloway* (Edinburgh, 1870–79).

NEVILLE, C., 'A Celtic Enclave in Norman Scotland: Earl Gilbert and the Earldom of Strathearn, 1171–1223', in Brotherstone and Ditchburn, *Freedom and Authority.*

NEWTON, M., *A Handbook of the Scottish Gaelic World* (Dublin, 2000).

Ó CORRAIN, D., 'Irish Regnal Succession: A Reappraisal', *Studia Hibernica* xi (1971).

OMAND, D. (ed.), *The Moray Book* (Edinburgh, 1976).

ORAM, R., 'Fergus, Galloway and the Scots', in Oram and Stell, *Galloway: Land and Lordship.*

——, 'Bruce, Balliol and the Lordship of Galloway: South-West Scotland and the Wars of Independence', *TDGNHAS* 3rd ser lxvii (1992).

——, 'A Family Business? Colonisation and settlement in twelfth- and thirteenth-century Galloway', *SHR* lxxii (1993).

——, 'David I and the Scottish Conquest and Colonisation of Moray', *Northern Scotland* xix (1999).

——, *The Lordship of Galloway* (Edinburgh, 2000).

——, 'Gold into Lead? The State of Early Medieval Scottish History', in Brotherstone and Ditchburn, *Freedom and Authority*.

——, *The Canmores: Kings & Queens of the Scots 1040–1290* (Stroud, 2002).

——, and STELL, G. (eds.), *Galloway: Land and Lordship* (Edinburgh, 1991).

OTWAY-RUTHVEN, A. J., *A History of Medieval Ireland* (London and New York, 1968; repr. New York, 1980).

OWEN, D. D. R., *William the Lion 1143–1214: Kingship and Culture* (East Linton, 1997).

PARTNER, N., *Serious Entertainments: The Writing of History in Twelfth-Century England* (Chicago and London, 1977).

PHYTHIAN-ADAMS, C., *Land of the Cumbrians* (Aldershot, 1996).

POOLE, A. L., *Domesday Book to Magna Carta* (2nd ed., Oxford, 1955; pb. ed. 1993).

POWER, R., 'Scotland and the Norse Sagas', in Simpson, *Scotland and Scandinavia*.

POWICKE, F.M., 'The *Dispensator* of David I,' *SHR* xxiii (1926).

PRESTWICH, M., *Armies and Warfare in the Middle Ages. The English Experience* (New Haven and London, 1996).

PULSIANO, P. (ed.), *Medieval Scandinavia: An Encyclopedia* (New York and London, 1993).

REID, N. H. (ed.), *Scotland in the Reign of Alexander III 1249–1286* (Edinburgh, 1990).

——, 'Alexander III: The Historiography of a Myth', in Reid, *Scotland in the Reign of Alexander III*.

REUTER, T. (ed.), *The Medieval Nobility: Studies in the Ruling Classes of France and Germany from the Sixth to the Twelfth Centuries* (Amsterdam, 1979).

REYNOLDS, S., *Kingdoms and Communities in Western Europe 900–1300* (Oxford, 1984).

——, *Fiefs and Vassals: The Medieval Evidence Reinterpreted* (Oxford, 1994).

RITCHIE, A., *Iona* (London and Edinburgh, 1997).

RITCHIE, R. L. G., *The Normans in Scotland* (Edinburgh, 1954).

ROBERTS, J. L., *Lost Kingdoms: Celtic Scotland and the Middle Ages* (Edinburgh, 1997).

ROBERTSON, E. W., *Scotland Under Her Early Kings: A History of the Kingdom to the Close of the Thirteenth Century* (Edinburgh, 1862).

——, *Historical Essays In Connexion With The Land, Church, & c* (Edinburgh, 1872).

ROESDAHL, E., *The Vikings*, trans. S.M. Margeson and K. Williams, 2nd ed. (London, 1998).

ROYAL COMMISSION ON THE ANCIENT AND HISTORICAL MONUMENTS OF SCOTLAND, *An Inventory of the Ancient and Historical Monuments of Roxburghshire* (Edinburgh 1956).

SCOTT, A.B., 'The Celtic Monastery and Roman Abbey of Fearn', *TGSI* xxviii (1912–14).

SELLAR, W. D. H., 'The Origins and Ancestry of Somerled', *SHR* xlv (1966).

——, 'Highland Family Origins – Pedigree Making and Pedigree Faking', in MacLean, *Middle Ages in the Highlands*.

—— (ed.), *Moray: Province and People* (Edinburgh, 1993).

——, 'Hebridean Sea Kings: The Successors of Somerled', in Cowan and McDonald, *Alba*.

SIGURÐSSON, I., and SKAPTASON, J. (eds.), *Aspects of Arctic and Sub-Artic History* (Reykjavik, 2000).

SIMMS, K., *From Kings to Warlords: The Changing Political Structure of Gaelic Ireland in the Later Middle Ages* (Woodbridge, 1987).

——,'Gaelic warfare in the Middle Ages', in Bartlett and Jeffery, *A Military History of Ireland.*

SIMPSON, G. G. (ed.), *Scotland and Scandinavia 800–1800* (Edinburgh, 1990).

——, and WEBSTER, B., 'Charter Evidence and the Distribution of Mottes in Scotland', in Stringer, *Essays on the Nobility of Medieval Scotland.*

SKENE, W. F., *The Highlanders of Scotland: Their origin, History, and Antiquities; with a Sketch of their Manners and Customs, and an account of the clans into which they were divided, and of the state of society which existed among them* (London, 1837).

——, *Celtic Scotland: A History of Ancient Alban* (Edinburgh, 1876–80; 2nd edition 1886–90).

SMITH, B. (ed.), *Britain and Ireland 900–1300: Insular Responses to Medieval European Change* (Cambridge, 1999).

SMYTH, A. P., *Warlords and Holy Men: Scotland A.D. 80–1000* (London, 1984; repr. Edinburgh, 1989).

—— (ed.), *Seanchas. Studies in Early and Medieval Irish Archaeology, History and Literature in Honour of Francis J. Byrne* (Dublin, 2000).

STELL, G., 'Mottes', in McNeill and Nicholson, *Historical Atlas of Scotland.*

——, *Exploring Scotland's Heritage: Dumfries and Galloway* (Edinburgh, 1986).

STENTON, F. M., *Anglo-Saxon England* (3rd ed., Oxford, 1971; pb. ed. 1989).

STEVENSON, J. H., and WOOD, M., *Scottish Heraldic Seals* (Glasgow, 1910).

STRICKLAND, M., 'Securing the North: Invasion and the Strategy of Defence in Twelfth-Century Anglo-Scottish Warfare', in Strickland, *Anglo-Norman Warfare.*

STRICKLAND, M. (ed.), *Anglo-Norman Warfare. Studies in Late Anglo-Saxon and Anglo-Norman Military Organization and Warfare* (Woodbridge, 1992).

STRINGER, K. J., *Earl David of Huntington 1152–1219: A Study in Anglo-Scottish History* (Edinburgh, 1985).

—— (ed.), *Essays on the Nobility of Medieval Scotland* (Edinburgh, 1985).

——, *The Reign of Stephen: Kingship, Warfare and Government in Twelfth-Century England* (New York and London, 1993).

——, 'Periphery and Core in Thirteenth-Century Scotland: Alan son of Roland, Lord of Galloway and Constable of Scotland', in Grant and Stringer, *Medieval Scotland.*

——, 'State-Building in Twelfth-Century Britain: David I, King of Scots, and Northern England', in Appleby and Dalton, *Government, Religion and Society in Northern England.*

——,'Acts of Lordship; The Records of the Lords of Galloway to 1234', in Brotherstone and Ditchburn, *Freedom and Authority.*

——, 'Reform Monasticism and Celtic Scotland: Galloway c.1140–1240', in Cowan and McDonald, *Alba.*

SUMMERSON, H., *Medieval Carlisle: The City and the Borders from the Late Eleventh Century to the Mid-Sixteenth Century* (Kendal, 1993).

TABRAHAM, C., *Scotland's Castles* (London, 1997).

TAYLOR, S. (ed.), *Kings, clerics and chroniclers in Scotland 500–1297* (Dublin, 2000).

THOMSON, J.M., *The Public Records of Scotland* (Glasgow, 1922).

THOMSON, W. P. L., *History of Orkney* (Edinburgh, 1987).

TOPPING, P., 'Harald Maddadson, Earl of Orkney and Caithness, 1139–1206', *SHR* lxii (1983).

TURVEY, R., *The Welsh Princes 1063–1283* (London and New York, 2002).

—— 'Two Ancient Records of the Bishopric of Caithness . . . With a prefatory note by Cosmo Innes', in *Bannatyne Miscellany* (Edinburgh, 1855).

WALKER, D., *The Normans in Britain* (Oxford, 1995).

WALKER, D.M., *A Legal History of Scotland* (Edinburgh, 1988).

WATT, D. E. R., *Fasti Ecclesiae Scoticanae Medii Aevi ad annum* 1638 (Edinburgh, 1969).

WEBSTER, B., *Scotland from the Eleventh Century to 1603* (Ithaca, New York and London, 1975).

——, *Medieval Scotland: The Making of an Identity* (Basingstoke and London, 1997).

WERNER, K. F., 'Kingdom and principality in twelfth-century France', in Reuter, *The Medieval Nobility.*

WILLIAMS, A., *The English and the Norman Conquest* (Woodbridge, 1995).

WILSON, J., 'Introduction to the Cumberland Domesday, Early Pipe Rolls and Testa de Nevill', in Doubleday, *Victoria History of the County of Cumberland.*

WOOLF, A., 'The 'Moray Question' and the Kingship of Alba in the Tenth and Eleventh Centuries', *SHR* lxxix (2000).

YOUNG, A., *Robert the Bruce's Rivals: The Comyns 1212–1314* (East Linton, 1997).

INDEX

Abbreviations:
ab. = abbot (of); bp. = bishop (of); d. = died; dau. = daughter (of); e. = earl (of); k. = king (of).
Tables and maps are not indexed.